An Imperial War
and the
British Working Class

STUDIES IN SOCIAL HISTORY

edited by
HAROLD PERKIN

Professor of Social History, University of Lancaster

⟡⟡⟡

For a list of books in the series see back endpaper

An Imperial War and the British Working Class

Working-Class Attitudes and Reactions to the Boer War 1899—1902

Richard Price

Assistant Professor of History
Northern Illinois University, Dekalb

LONDON: Routledge & Kegan Paul
TORONTO: University of Toronto Press

First published 1972
by Routledge and Kegan Paul Ltd
and in Canada and in the United States of America by
University of Toronto Press
Toronto and Buffalo
Printed in Great Britain by
Western Printing Services Ltd, Bristol
Copyright © Richard N. Price 1972
RKP ISBN 0 7100 7229 5
UTP ISBN 0 8020 1882 3
UTP Microfiche ISBN 0 8020 0222 6

TO MY MOTHER AND FATHER

Contents

Tables

Figures

Acknowledgments

This book evolved from a D.Phil. thesis submitted in the University of Sussex in 1968. Many people and institutions assisted me in the preparation of the original thesis and the book. To those friends who are not mentioned here by name, yet who were close to me during the period when I was engaged with this problem, I would like to express my gratitude for any assistance they may have given me.

Foremost among those whose counsel must be directly acknowledged is my friend and teacher, Ranajit Guha, who presided over the problem from its earliest stages to its fruition. He saved me from many gross errors; his encouragement, patience and enthusiasm were a perpetual source of strength. I should also like to thank Peter Keating for many hours of relaxed and valuable discussion about nineteenth-century England, and John Springhall for the interesting debates and exchanges relating to the subject of the book. My thanks are also due to Professor Asa Briggs and Dr Eric Hobsbawm for their assistance at various stages of the project, and to Professor J. O. Baylen of Georgia State University who kindly shared with me his knowledge of W. T. Stead. I spent a fascinating afternoon with the late Dr G. P. Gooch whose reminiscences about the Liberal Party during this period were of great interest and help. Last, but hardly least, I thank my wife, Barbara, for her invaluable companionship, understanding and assistance.

I would like to express my thanks to those libraries that made available to me their valuable manuscript collections. These include the British Library of Political and Economic Science (for the Broadhurst, Courtney and Solly Collections), the British Museum (for the Burns, Campbell-Bannerman, Gladstone, Lafone and Spender Papers), the Guildhall Library (for the CIV Collection), Islington Public Library (for the minutes of the North London Socialist Club), Leeds City Library (for various papers relating to the Liberal Party in that city), the

Brotherton Library of the University of Leeds (for the Mattison Collection), Sheffield Central Library (for the H. J. Wilson Papers), and the Public Records Office, London (for the Imperial Yeomanry files, various Home Office papers, the Buller Papers and Colonial Office Files). Special thanks must go to Viscount Harcourt of Stanton Harcourt, Oxfordshire, who very kindly gave me permission to look through the papers of his grandfather; also to Mr Julius Jacobs who allowed me to examine the London Trades Council minutes in his possession; and to Mr W. J. Evans, Warden of the Working Men's College, with whom I spent an enjoyable evening, for allowing me to rummage in the Muniment Room.

This book could not have been written without the never-failing help and assistance of the staff of the British Museum Reading Room and of the Newspaper Library at Colindale where I consulted all of the newspapers cited. To these people special acknowledgment is due.

I should also like to express my thanks to Northern Illinois University and the American Philosophical Society, for research grants which enabled this work to be completed.

Abbreviations

CIV	City Imperial Volunteers
ILP	Independent Labour Party
NDL	National Democratic League
SACC	South African Conciliation Committee
SDF	Social Democratic Federation
SIU	Social Institutes Union

Introduction

T H E *fin de siècle* of Victorian Britain was a time for self-doubt. There was an increasing fear that the 'place in the sun' that had so long been hers was being shadowed by the rising powers of Germany and the United States of America. Doubts arouse about her economic strength, her military prowess, even the viability of the two-party system.[1] The South African War of 1899–1902 served for a time as the focus for all the fears that many Britons had about their country's future. The patriotism it engendered was exaggerated by the early military failures to resolve the problem of the troublesome Boers. Even the absurdity of Baden-Powell's position at Mafeking was turned around into a heroic touchstone of British ingenuity and virility. The war and its impact on the domestic scene was an appropriate climax to the race for African colonies. It provided the finest excuse for England to throw aside traditional reserve and loudly prove that her people were still the finest race on earth. It was accompanied by an orgy of patriotism, the like of which had never been seen before; men really did flock to the colours to show their involvement in the dreams of Empire.

Historians have long recognized that the South African War was unique in scale and significance. It was a 'little war' which involved the whole nation. It was the purest example of an 'imperialist' war. Not only did it revive the moral issue of the right of small, weak nations to independence, it also provided the clearest case for an economic interpretation of imperialism. These facets of the question have been examined almost to the point of extinction. The Jameson Raid and Chamberlain's complicity, the influence of the Rand gold-owners, the determination of Milner to drag a sometimes reluctant Chamberlain and Cabinet into armed conflict, the significance of the war in the

---

[1] See E. Halévy, *Imperialism and the Rise of Labour* (2nd ed., London, 1951). Certain politicians, like Rosebery, hankered after a government of National Efficiency.

1

wider context of the scramble for Africa, have all been authoritatively and exhaustively researched.[2] Similarly, the problems that the war created for the struggling, fratricidal Liberal Party have received some, lesser, attention.[3] There remains one very important gap, that of the working-class reaction to this imperialistic episode.

In the past historians have been content to accept the interpretation of contemporary Conservatives and Liberals that the war illustrated a working-class attachment to imperialism. Indeed, the belief in working-class imperial sentiment rests almost entirely upon supposed working-class behaviour during the Boer War. It is, therefore, appropriate to examine this conventional wisdom in some detail, testing the episodes upon which the assumptions of contemporary observers were based.

The problem and its treatment, however, have wider implications than merely filling a gap in nineteenth-century history. It is hoped that this study will help to make fashionable slightly different approaches to the study of working-class history. Previous analyses of this particular question illustrate this need. The one outstanding reason why they have all failed to deal with the problem satisfactorily has been because they treated working-class history as if it were merely a reflection of Labour Movement history. Thus, Tsiang in his book, *Labor and Empire*, published in 1923, concentrated solely upon the attitudes of Labour members of parliament to questions of colonial policy that arose in the House. More recently an article by Frank Bealey published only in France took his source material entirely from socialist-society, Trade Union or Trades Council records.[4] It is time that historians began to look at working-class history not as an expression of the rise and development of a Labour Movement but as an expression of an indigenous subculture within the wider framework of Victorian Britain. E. P. Thompson has done this admirably for the early part of the century and studies of social unrest have shown historians new methods that should be used.[5] But most historians of the British working classes have yet to realize that what they are dealing

[2] For example the work of Ethel Drus, Jeffrey Butler, Bernard Porter.
[3] See G. B. Pyrah, *Imperial Policy and South Africa 1902–1910* (Oxford, 1955).
[4] F. Bealey, 'Les Travaillistes et la Guerre des Boers', *Le Mouvement Social* (October–December, 1963).
[5] Thus, G. Rudé and E. Hobsbawm, *Captain Swing* (New York, 1969).

with is a 'society' in the truest expression of the word and concept, a 'society' with its own value system, its own *mores*, its own culture.

In part, the question boils down to one of methodology. To approach working-class history through different media automatically focuses the failings of the conventional approach. The availability of Labour Movement and socialist-society source material has been one important factor in determining the methodology of working-class history. Another factor has been the sympathy most middle-class Labour historians have felt for the ideals of that movement; a bourgeois sympathy, often very 'Victorian' in its expression, which was and is incapable of extending to and understanding working-class society. It is to a different series of methodologies that the future writing of working-class history must look. This is not to claim that this work presents any radically new or enlightening methodology, but it is hoped that the way in which this particular problem has been analysed will encourage other historians to become more adventurous.

Much of the reason for the equation of working-class history with Labour history has been the readily available source material of Labour institutions. It is clearly true that the institutional approach to the history of the inarticulate is very important and the choice of different institutions is in itself a new approach. Of course, the problems that it creates are very great. As a social observer in the early part of the present century noted: 'No future historical novelist will be able to reconstruct from contemporary documents the inner life of Pentonville or Camberwell.'[6] The institution grants us little more than a bird's-eye view. But the fact remains that it is usually the only source which enables us to determine generalizations about working-class attitudes and reactions. What traditional working-class historiography has ignored is the existence of many working-class institutions which can be of great value to the historian of the proletariat. One such example, well suited to the purposes of this study, is the working men's club. This is an institution that, at its best, can represent a collective expression of the social, cultural, political and educational facets of working-class society, but it is an institution which has been totally ignored by Labour historians. Yet this historian has found it

---

[6] [C. F. G. Masterman], *From the Abyss* (London, 1902), p. 26.

3

crucial in helping to build a composite picture of working-class attitudes to imperialism.

The limitations of the institutional approach are fairly obvious. Starting out with the naïve hope that he could find out what individual working men really thought about imperialism and the war, it fairly soon became clear that given the nature of the subject and the source material, this was impossible. It is fruitless to look for a systematized and distinct framework of ideology or thought into which working-class attitudes to problems like imperialism can be placed. The formally educated are trained to view events according to a contextual and ideological frame of reference, and historians are no exception to this. To look for a recognizably consistent political and cultural value system through which the working classes could view the Boer War and imperialism is to look for something which did not exist. This is not to imply that working men did not have an opinion: they always did. What it does mean is that what appear to educated minds to be two seemingly contradictory opinions can be held at the same or different times about one event.[7] This phenomenon, recognized and studied by anthropologists, has not yet been examined by historians or sociologists within the context of an industrial working class. It will be illustrated very clearly in relation to working-class attitudes to the soldiery of the war and to the Mafeking Night saturnalia.

None of this is intended to imply that working men possessed some kind of lower mentality. It merely emphasizes that middle-class historians have to accept that the working class does not use the same frames of reference that the more formally educated would and that, consequently, these frames of reference are irrelevant to the study of working-class history. Again, this will be illustrated by the study of the failure of Radical rhetoric to find a receptive audience among the working classes at this time. Often, a working man's perception of social and political phenomena is more acute than that of the sophisticated middle-class observer. It is certainly just as valid.

[7] The frequent apparent ambivalence of working-class attitudes has seldom been noted; neither, to the best of my knowledge, has it received any investigation. For an example see Robin Blackburn, 'A Brief Guide to Bourgeois Ideology', pp. 200–1, in *Student Power* (London, 1969). For an anthropological study of this question in Burma see E. R. Leach, *The Political Systems of Highland Burma* (London, 1956).

This work illustrates the difference. Thus, it will be shown that the question that has dominated this problem heretofore, and the question which presupposes an intellectual frame of reference, i.e. did working men oppose or support the war, is in the final analysis invalid and pointless. The middle-class Radicals who opposed the Boer War did so within the very clear framework of moralistic 'Gladstonianism'. They expected working men to react the same way and were disappointed when this failed to happen. Men like Leonard Courtney, H. J. Wilson, John Morley and others looked at the issue of the war from the historical perspective of a supposed Liberal tradition of foreign policy and from the moral perspective of the loss of certain values that they believed should guide Britain's relations with the rest of the world. Their attitude was clearly understandable within the context of their known and recognizable political values. Working men had no such value framework: they could only develop one if personally involved. Hopefully, the meaning and implications of this will become clear as a result of this study.

The lack of a preconceived view of events that are remote from working-class life is one reason why looking for attitudes and reactions through institutional evidence is difficult. It is well known that working men were not and are not in the habit of committing their thoughts to paper. Thus, there is very little manuscript material to which one can turn and find what the working class thought about particular events and episodes. Even the minuscule amount of first-hand source material that does exist is not much use.[8] Thus, it becomes necessary to look at 'indirect' evidence to build up a composite picture, and this is why certain domestic episodes that involved the war have been examined in some detail.

Henry Pelling has recently pointed out how the case for working-class jingoism rests almost entirely upon working-class reaction during the South African conflict to the Khaki Election, the anti-war campaign and the call for army volunteers.[9] No one, however, has felt the need to examine these phenomena; it has

---

[8] E.g. the Mattison Papers contain nothing that could be used in this respect and Mattison was a 'thinking working man' active in the peace movement.
[9] Henry Pelling, *Popular Politics and Late Victorian Society* (London, 1968), p. 87.

been accepted that the Conservative electoral victory in 1900 meant, in part, a working-class support of their policy in South Africa. No attention has been paid to working-class constituencies to see if this was true, if it was false or if it was irrelevant to the working-class voters. The violence that accompanied anti-war meetings and that was related to Mafeking Night, has automatically been laid at the feet of the working-class mob. The enthusiastic and emotion-charged volunteering for the war is commonly held to be indicative of a pure and selfless patriotism by working-class recruits.

In examining these phenomena the basic question has been, how did the working class react to each situation? These three episodes, however, require different techniques and methods of study. The analysis of the General Election of 1900 is a combination of statistical method and qualitative evidence that will fail to satisfy fully the dedicated quantifier. There can be little doubt of the need for in-depth statistical study of late-nineteenth-century British elections on the same scale as that done by some American researchers.[10] Yet much of the difficulty lies in the source material itself. Thus, no really accurate correlation can be made between the census data and electoral results, for the reason that the census districts did not coincide, in most cases, with the constituency boundaries. Thus the social composition of a constituency such as East Northants can only be approximated. It is primarily this consideration that has dictated the compromise followed here of trying to detect a statistical trend in certain constituencies and combining this with the candidate's political programme.

The treatment of the jingo crowd will illustrate how little we know about crowd behaviour and how little help historians are receiving from sociologists and social psychologists. Indeed, at the present time it would seem that the only people interested in crowds are governments and historians. Nevertheless, there are many misconceptions about the jingo crowd that hopefully will be cleared away. Just as Rudé has shown the crowd of the French Revolution to have been a rational political force, so the crowd of this period was not a 'mob' but a deliberate and sometimes organized weapon of repressive jingoism.

Volunteering for service in South Africa was the ultimate

[10] E.g. Paul Kleppner, *The Cross of Culture* (New York, 1970).

6

imperial sacrifice. It could, as was commonly thought at the time, imply a preparedness to lay down one's life for the cause of Empire. Fortunately, investigation in this area is not bedevilled by the same kind of pitfalls that accompany a study of the 1900 election and the jingo crowd. Owing to the sudden, unexpected strain of a 'little war' that could not be handled by the professional army alone, new units of Volunteers were created solely for service on the veldt. The Imperial Yeomanry was the most important of these. Some strange prescience, unusual in the preservation of army records, has ensured that all the Attestation Forms of that particular unit exist. These forms list a variety of useful information, the age, place of birth, place of recruitment and occupation of the Volunteer, and have been used primarily to make an occupational analysis of the unit.

There is, however, a methodological problem connected with this that needs to be explained: what criterion are we to use to decide who was working class and who was not. It is a difficulty which conventional working-class historiography, because of its concentration on the institutionalized Labour Movement, does not face. In the penultimate chapter of this study, however, the occupational analysis of the Imperial Yeomanry raises the question in its clearest form. Prior to this analysis it is permissible and almost necessary to discuss the issue in wider terms.

The essence of the problem is that there is no established criterion which can be applied to a profession or trade to determine whether that occupation should be characterized as a working-class activity. Such yardsticks as wage rates can be used by economic historians but are unsatisfactory for use here because of the great number of occupations and because such criteria ignore the vital element of status-consciousness. This difficulty can be illustrated by Eric Hobsbawm's classic statement on the Labour Aristocracy where the upper stratum of the working class is taken to be virtually synonymous with the lower-middle class.[11] The result is that such occupations as clerks or teachers become identified with the working classes in a way that would have been unacceptable to both sides. This problem is not new. The whereabouts of the line separating the

[11] E. J. Hobsbawm, *Labouring Men: Studies in the History of Labour* (London, 1964), pp. 273–5. This, of course, does nothing to alter Hobsbawm's main contention that the upper-working class were co-opted.

working class from the middle class was confusing to many contemporary observers.

Leone Levi illustrates this uncertainty as to who was working class and who was not. In the 1867 edition of his *Wages and Earnings* he asserted that, although it was difficult to fix the exact meaning of certain terms and to classify them correctly, 'there was no difficulty in apprehending the general designation of working men'.[12] His criterion was to include all who 'either as workers for others or as workers for themselves, are employed in manual labour, be it productive of wealth or not'. He pointed out that only when the term 'lower' class was used, in contradistinction to the term 'working', as an indication of the social position of a portion of people, would it include 'many general dealers and the lower description of tradesmen'.[13] In the 1885 edition the problem still remained but there was a slight change of emphasis in that his criterion was composed of the following elements: 'The nature of the work in which they are employed, the mode in which they are paid, and *the social position they occupy*' (italics added). He admitted that 'the distinction between the lower-middle and labouring classes is often very slender';[14] but he recognized that there was a distinction.

The characteristic members of the lower-middle class were the clerk, the teacher and the poor clergyman.[15] This is apparent from the work of Rowntree and Booth who recognized that wages and earnings were comparatively unimportant in the concept of class; that it was social status and status-consciousness that were the operative factors.[16] This was especially true at the level of the lower-middle class, many of whom had originated in the working class and who were environmentally close enough to desire to be distinguished from them.[17] Thus, whilst it is true that to be a clerk was often to earn less than an artisan or, at the most, to be on the same financial level, the

---

[12] Leone Levi, *Wages and Earnings of the Working Classes* (1st ed., London, 1867), p. xxiii.
[13] *Ibid.*, p. 6.   [14] *Ibid.* (2nd ed., 1885), p. 2.
[15] *Ibid.*, p. 51.
[16] D. Lockwood, *The Black Coated Worker* (London, 1958), pp. 13–14.
[17] Even this was not necessarily true. Booth calculated that his Class G, which corresponded to the lower-middle classes, contributed a mere 4 per cent to the population of the East End compared with 5 per cent of the servant-keeping class and 42 per cent of the artisan class.

social prestige of 'clerking' was 'looked upon as an advance'.[18] The evidence for this social distinction is overwhelming. Booth noted that a junior clerk may earn far less than a van-boy but he was influenced by the hope of future success 'and certainly by the social feeling which places the clerk's work above manual employment'.[19] He also noted how the clerk and the artisan were on entirely different social and economic planes:[20]

From top to bottom clerks associate with clerks and artisans with artisans—but comparatively seldom with each other. A clerk lives an entirely different life . . . has different aims and different ideas, different possibilities and different limitations. A clerk differs from an artisan in the claims each make on society no less than the claim society makes on them.

This was not just a feature of the end of the century. Thomas Wright, himself a working man, wrote in 1873 that the working classes[21]

may be taken as broadly meaning the artisan and manual labouring classes, excluding even the clerks and shopmen who, though no better paid, and in other respects less advantageously situated than the artisan, are yet ranked apart from and above the latter class, on the ground that they follow 'genteel occupations'.

Modern Marxist theory emphasizes how the working class has become larger rather than smaller as more and more people sell their labour power and are divorced from the control of production. Thus, the managerial class and many of the professions are in reality workers. Historically, therefore, the clerk was quite clearly a worker. But the historian must also deal with how people saw themselves, and although the facts illustrate that the clerk was as exploited and as underpaid as the labourer, the bestowal of 'status' sufficiently blinded, or compensated, him to accept this. The social pretensions of the clerk of our period, the reality *for him* of his separation from the working class, is nowhere better illustrated than in the character of Pooter in *The Diary of a Nobody*. He was shocked to find that his ironmonger

---

[18] B. Seebohm Rowntree, *Poverty. A Study of Town Life* (London, 1902), p. 72; Charles Booth, *Life and Labour of the People in London* (2nd ed., London, 1902–3), 2nd Series, III, p. 277.
[19] Booth, *op. cit.*, p. 275.   [20] *Ibid.*, p. 278.
[21] T. Wright, *Our New Masters* (London, 1873), p. 4.

had been invited to the Lord Mayor's reception and that he was on friendly terms with the Sheriff: 'To think that a man who mends our scraper should know a member of our aristocracy.'[22] There can be little doubt that if 'economically they were sometimes on the margin, socially they were definitely a part of the middle class'.[23]

The same kind of considerations apply to the working men. It is possible for us to see skilled workmen as virtually lower-middle class but they certainly regarded themselves as members of the working class. Status-consciousness, it is true, separated the labourer from the artisan, but contempt for 'pen-pushing' interposed possibly a wider gulf between the artisan and the clerk. The essence of working men's class-consciousness was a pride in being a member of the working class. This was the whole point behind the success of the working men's colleges and clubs. Indeed, those 'labour aristocrats' who did leave their reminiscences for posterity give no indication that they regarded themselves as anything but working men.

The clerk is a fairly easy example with which to illustrate this distinction. He is also an important one for this study as will become apparent, for he played such a large role in volunteering for service in South Africa. But there are many other similar occupations which present the same kind of problems and for which no comparable evidence exists. In the absence of detailed work on such professions as commercial travellers, salesmen, shopkeepers, there is no doubt that the criterion of 'manual labour' is the best for distinguishing working-class occupations.

This study is intended to determine the working-class attitudes and reaction to imperialism through the prism of the Boer War. The actual course of the struggle, the diplomacy preceding the conflict, the impact of the contest on theories of imperialism, will all be ignored. The war itself is only the case-study through which we can examine attitudes and reactions. As such it is invaluable. For the South African War synthesized all the prevailing emotions and arguments about imperial expansion. At no other time was there so perfect a confluence of the differing factors that characterized late-nineteenth-century imperialism and jingoism. During no other imperial war was there an elec-

[22] George and W. Grossmith, *The Diary of a Nobody* (London, 1965), p. 22.
[23] Lockwood, *op. cit.*, p. 35.

10

tion, a call for volunteers, jingo rowdyism, attempts to create mass anti-imperial agitation, all happening at the same moment in time. Neither, for any other occasion, has there remained such an abundance of relevant and usable source material.

It is obvious that in a study of this kind no continuity—evolutionary or chronological—can be maintained. Diverse and different problems have all contributed to create this essentially 'static' analysis of the working-class attitudes and reactions to imperialism. But although each chapter is, to a certain extent, complete in its own right, each one will also be seen to fit into the broader composite picture. Furthermore, each chapter often helps to illuminate problems that are evident in other parts of the work. Thus, by bringing together the different features of each individual area of concentration, valid conclusions can be drawn.

I

The Failure
of Radicalism

A T its simplest level the argument for working-class support of imperialism finds evidence in the lack of mass opposition to the Boer War. It is assumed, as it was assumed by contemporaries, that the failure of the working class to respond to the immorality of the war illustrated its surrender to the prevailing enthusiasm for the Empire. Superficially, this is a convincing argument. The moral issues raised by the war were obvious and clear cut. Like most other imperialist ventures, it was justified on the dubious grounds of moral responsibility and strategic necessity. But the nature of the conflict made it easier to deny apologists' assertions that the Boers were a savage, uncivilized race.[1] Thus, to accept the war, one had to accept the assumption that British racial superiority bestowed the right to rule white men as well as black. The anti-imperialists' rejection of this was followed, however, by an equally invalid assumption of their own. They believed that all that was needed to generate an

---

[1] The Boers were portrayed as uncivilized in the popular literature that justified the war. They were accused of being dirty, corrupt, immoral and shifty. There were many unflattering references to their physiognomy. It was believed that they were at a lower stage of evolution. For examples see G. Leveson Scarth, *South Africa: Past and Present* (Bath, 1899), pp. 18–23; Henry Cust, 'The Dutch in South Africa', *North American Review*, February 1900, pp. 200–11; Knox Little, *South Africa* (London, 1900); Douglas Blackburn, *Prinsloo of Prinsloosdorp* (London, n.d. 1900?); A. Conan Doyle, *The Great Boer War* (London, 1900); Bertram Mitford, *Aletta. A Tale of the Boer Invasion* (London, 1900) for an attempt to present a more balanced picture; a love story about an English gentleman and a Boer girl whose family is one of the 'better' class of Boers who 'do not go to bed in their clothes; who do wash, and whose persons and dwelling houses are distinguished by the ordinary conditions of cleanliness and civilisation'.

effective opposition to the war was to expose its immorality to the public just as Gladstone had exposed Disraeli's foreign policy of the late 1870s. The shadow of the Midlothian continually lurked over the Radical analysis.

There was, of course, a very real difference in the 'spirit of the times' between the late 1870s and 1900 that was too often ignored by the anti-imperialists. But more importantly, there were significant political and structural differences in the forces of Radicalism that predicated the effectiveness of anti-imperialism in 1900. There was, for example, no sustained and effective press campaign against the war which could rival that of the *Northern Echo*; there was no unified 'moral conscience' to mobilize; there was no one of sufficient political stature to enthuse local Liberals with the righteousness of opposition.[2]

The extent of a potential mass opposition to the war is difficult to gauge. From the early days of the dispute in June until the beginning of November there were about 200 resolutions sent to the Colonial Office which were hostile to British policy.[3] The vast majority of these came from non-conformist bodies such as the National Council of Evangelical Free Churches which sent a characteristic resolution recognizing Uitlander grievances but urging patience on the government.[4] As war drew closer the resolutions became more urgent. Thus, the United Methodist Free Church's Quarterly Meeting resolved on 9 October 1899 that 'This meeting views with grave alarm . . . the probability of this country entering into a war with the South African Republic' and urged that the 'matters at issue . . . should be settled by force of reason and not by arms'.[5] Such resolutions represented the 'Nonconformist conscience' that was to figure large in the Stop-the-War Committee but which, it must be recognized, was not in the mainstream of Nonconformist opinion. Of all the churches only the Baptist presented a united front against the war.

[2] The importance of a recognized leader to inspire enthusiasm is often underrated. This was the significance of Gladstone in 1877–80. The pro-Boers had no leaders. See Augustine Birrell, *Things Past Redress* (London, 1937), pp. 175–6 where he notes 'Our Pro-Boers, though they contained among their number some good speakers and very many enthusiastic followers, felt . . . that they were never really led. "Oh! for an hour of honest John Bright," . . . This was the cry of the Pro-Boers.'

[3] Public Records Office, C.O. 417/277 and 278. There were about 600 resolutions in all.   [4] C.O. 417/277 f. 797–8.   [5] C.O. 417/278 f. 151.

The most powerful Methodist leader, Hugh Price Hughes, was lavish in his praise of imperialism: 'The British can no more leave Africa, with honour, to the Dutch . . . than we could leave Egypt to the Dervishes.'[6] W. T. Stead complained to James Bryce of the 'evil influence' that Hughes's support of the war had among Nonconformists.[7] Even the Quakers were tainted with imperial fervour. John Bellows, the Gloucestershire publisher, wrote a pamphlet entitled *The Truth about the Transvaal War and the Truth about War* which drew a sophisticated distinction between the justice of war in the abstract and the justice of a particular war. He claimed that he could find no blame attached to the government for the cause of the South African War and, *ipso facto*, asserted the irrelevancy of opposition.

Thus, while there was a definite current of Nonconformist opinion opposed to the prospect of war and later to the war itself, and while there was usually a Nonconformist minister on local peace committees, the fact remains that in 1899 the 'Nonconformist conscience', which had been an essential ingredient of the 1877–9 agitation, failed to speak with a clear, strong and united voice on the issue of imperialism versus anti-imperialism.

Working men's organizations were even less certain. Very few seemed to be sufficiently interested in the crisis to express a collective opinion about it. There were only seven hostile resolutions from Trades Councils, one from a Trade Union branch of the Amalgamated Society of Carpenters and Joiners, and four from clubs that can be identified as working men's clubs. The Trades Councils usually contrasted imperialism with the failures and inadequacies of domestic policy,[8] the clubs tended to show signs of the influence of W. T. Stead's recent arbitration agitation. Thus, Newington Reform Club sent a resolution to the Colonial Office urging that there was nothing in the dispute that could not be settled by arbitration 'as proposed and sanctioned at the Hague Conference'.[9]

Thus, there was no clearly recognizable mass base around which opposition to the war could be organized. More important than this, however, was the inadequacy of the organizations

[6] Quoted in *Life of Hugh Price Hughes by His Daughter* (London, 1904), p. 556.
[7] Stead to Bryce, 30 September 1899, Campbell-Bannerman Papers, Add. MSS. 41211 f. 33.
[8] C.O. 417/277 f. 653–5.   [9] *Ibid.*, f. 610.

which hoped, or could be expected, to create the impetus for a successful agitation. The nature and methods of the anti-war committees, the paralytic dissension within the Liberal Party, explain the impotence of opposition to the war far more satisfactorily than imperial patriotism. In quantitative terms there were many Liberals who would have eagerly responded to a crusade against Chamberlainite imperialism. But a crusade must derive from structurally healthy, and politically relevant, organizations which can channel this enthusiasm and translate the issues into understandable terms for the mass of the apolitical electorate. It is within this context that the explanation for the failure of Radicalism during these years must be sought.

The first of the protest committees to prepare for the coming war was appropriately an organization revived from the 1877–80 agitation: the Transvaal Committee. It was created in July 1899 by the executive committee of the Liberal Forwards, a group of advanced Liberal MPs which included C. P. Scott, H. J. Wilson and Thomas Burt, with the object of rousing 'public opinion to prevent a war' with the Transvaal.[10] It held a few public meetings during the summer, but once war broke out it directed the major part of its activities to addressing meetings in working men's clubs. In Manchester, on 5 September, Scott formed the second of the pre-war committees, the Manchester Transvaal Peace Committee, which began with a burst of activity issuing sixteen pamphlets in two weeks and culminating in a mass meeting on 15 September where John Morley and Leonard Courtney spoke. And, as with the London committee, it devoted itself to ensuring a fair peace once war had broken out.[11]

But neither of these committees retained any lasting impact upon the anti-war movement and with the formation of the South African Conciliation Committee (SACC) their work was virtually finished. Both seem to have continued to exist but the SACC assumed their role of nation-wide agitation. The South African Conciliation Committee was formed on 1 November 1899, but was not publicly launched until January 1900.[12]

[10] Transvaal Committee, *Report of Six Months Work* (London, 1900).
[11] *The Times*, 19 November 1899, p. 7.
[12] G. P. Gooch, *Life of Lord Courtney* (London, 1920), p. 393.

Characterized by its rationality and moderation, SACC propaganda mainly took the form of pamphlet literature devoted to contradicting the many myths about the Boers and the war created by the jingo press.[13] Its few public meetings mirrored this seriousness of purpose. They were usually addressed by a prominent antiwar Liberal, such as James Bryce or Robert Reid who delivered an academic speech about the harmful effects of some aspect of government policy.[14] This was at once its great strength and its great weakness. Taking the form of a political discussion circle it did not suffer from jingo rowdyism; it meant, however, that its appeal was limited to the intellectual middle classes. And this, in turn, was a reflection of those who were its leading spirits.

The two men who formed the committee were both Liberal Unionists.[15] Its Chairman, Frederic Mackarness, was opposed to the 'greedy and ruthless imperialism' which had exploited the Uitlanders and ignored the Dutch.[16] Leonard Courtney, its President and MP for Liskeard, was still in many respects a Gladstonian Liberal. He had originally broken with Gladstone over Ireland,[17] but failed to move in sympathy with the party

[13] Thus, one pamphlet contradicted the false views of the Boers disseminated by 'ill-informed and sometimes unscrupulous writers' and contained favourable opinions of the Boers written by 'distinguished Englishmen': *The War in South Africa—Sketches of Boers by distinguished Englishmen*, SACC Pamphlet No. 3 (1899). Another pamphlet (No. 13) tried to destroy the myth of an Afrikaaner conspiracy. Another (No. 12), showed how Boer rearmament was a response to their fear of attack after the Jameson Raid. This concern with destroying jingo myths was probably the most important aspect of its work. Courtney certainly so regarded it: see letter to *The Times*, 17 January 1900, p. 10.

[14] I have discovered only six meetings held in London that were reported by *The Times*. That addressed by Bryce was reported in *The Times*, 6 April 1900, p. 11; that addressed by Reid in *The Times*, 9 November 1901, p. 12.

[15] There was a group of Conservative and Liberal Unionist MPs who strongly disapproved of the way the crisis had been handled, and who were opposed to the war. This group included Sir Edward Clarke, MP for Plymouth, Arthur Elliott, MP for Durham, J. M. Maclean, member for Cardiff. It was probably a larger group than these few men; P. M. Thornton recalled in his autobiography how 'there were cabals going on amongst those sitting upon the Unionist benches . . . I was asked at Lord's Cricket Ground to sign a round robin adverse to any war with the Boers'. See *Some Things We Have Remembered* (London, 1912), p. 270. Those who did have doubts either kept silent, like Elliott, or lost their nominations, like Clarke and Maclean. See Sir Edward Clarke, *Story of My Life* (London, 1918), pp. 343–61; J. M. Maclean, *Memories of Westminster and India* (London, 1902), pp. 122–40.

[16] G. P. Gooch, *Frederic Mackarness, A Brief Memoir* (London, 1922), p. 10.

[17] See Leonard Courtney, *Cornish Granite: Selections from Courtney's Writings* (London, 1925), p. xi.

16

as it drew nearer to Conservatism and imperialism.[18] He had always been a critic of imperial expansion,[19] and so during the South African Crisis it was inevitable that he should attack the government's provocative policies.[20]

Immediate reasons why Courtney opposed the war were reasons echoed by many pro-Boer Liberals; they found a kind of spiritual home in the South African Conciliation Committee. They were based on the twin pillars of legality and morality. In the first place, as he wrote to Morley, there was no claim to suzerainty beyond a check on foreign treaties. In the second place, 'our moral claim . . . is so far satisfied by what has been conceded that to fight for more is an atrocious crime'.[21] He concluded that 'unjustifiable war is a crime and an unjustifiable war with the South African Republic would be a war . . . producing in South Africa racial animosities the end of which cannot be foreseen'.[22]

But his objection to Chamberlain's desire to 'reduce the Transvaal to a British province',[23] was not based solely upon the ethical considerations of this particular issue. It was essentially a result of his whole attitude to Empire which he believed should be characterized by a sense of duty rather than a sense of acquisition. He desired an 'imperialism of service in the discharge of . . . education and developing the capacities and the powers of . . . vast populations, in leading them to undertake the functions of self-government'.[24] To destroy the ideal of self-government was, he believed, to strike at the very foundations of the Empire.[25]

[18] Gooch, *Life of Lord Courtney*, pp. 310, 336. Thus, throughout the 1894 session he supported the Liberal government on everything but Home Rule; in 1898 on the Sudan question, he voted with Labouchere against the advance to Dongola.

[19] In 1877 he had protested against the annexation of the Transvaal and although given a minor post in the 1880 government had refused to support it in the lobbies until that annexation had been repudiated. Over the Egyptian question he had had grave doubts about the suppression of Egyptian nationalism. See James Anthony Froude, *Oceana* (3rd ed., London, 1886), p. 53; Gooch, *op. cit.*, pp. 153, 174.

[20] He welcomed Chamberlain's offer of a seven-year franchise, condemned as menacing the despatch of troops, and protested against an insistence on the use of the word 'suzerainty'. Gooch, *op. cit.*, pp. 356–66.

[21] Courtney to Morley, 1 September, Courtney Papers, Vol. 7 f. 16.

[22] Proposed Manifesto, *ibid.*, Vol. 16 f. 7.

[23] Courtney to Morley, *loc. cit.*   [24] Courtney, *Cornish Granite, op. cit.*, p. 48.

[25] This was very evident in a letter he wrote to Rosebery in 1901 commenting on the latter's appeal for the country to be put on a more 'efficient' basis with

It was because of his belief in a 'constructive' imperial policy that he was unwilling to follow many opponents of the war in admitting that the best solution that could be hoped for was a quick end to the war and the incorporation of the Republics into the Empire. Under his influence the SACC passed resolutions opposing annexation as a solution and protesting against the government's policy of unconditional surrender.[26]

But by the beginning of 1901, there were those within the Conciliation Committee who felt that it had outlived its usefulness.[27] There was a rising tide of sentiment that wearied of the war, and the acquisition of the *Daily News* by Lloyd George and R. C. Lehman had provided a national forum for anti-war opinion. The media was no longer dominated by the jingo press.[28] And it was certainly true that the practical influence of the South African Conciliation Committee was very small. It was not a mass organization and it had no desire to become one. It was entirely middle class in membership[29] and by November 1900 could boast 1,700 members and thirty-three provincial branches. Of these members one-half were in Liverpool which possessed a very strong and active branch, distributing 100,000 pamphlets in 1900.[30]

Liverpool illustrated the nature of the provincial anti-war campaign. Although the town was politically a Tory stronghold, the older generation of Liberals remained actively loyal to the

---

regard to education, trade and military preparedness. Courtney objected to the emphasis on force, command and mastery: 'It is a call to arms with no suggestion of worship and of the services of labour of which that temple should be the home!' To Courtney, the real problem of Empire was that there were 300 million subjects 'the government of which lies . . . at the foot of the Parliament of Britain'. Empire should be utilized for the good of all these subjects and should facilitate them to 'rise and become members of the great international society of men'. In order to do this, Britain's relationship with them could not rest on force: 'We must make it our duty to strengthen and intensify feelings of reciprocal attachment between the governing communities and the governed.' Courtney Papers, Vol. 8 f. 71.

[26] *The Times*, 26 May 1900, p. 16; 1 March 1901, p. 11.

[27] F. C. Selous resigned as Vice-Chairman in February 1901 because he believed that to protest against annexation was futile, the government had determined upon it, the Liberal Party offered no resistance and there was nothing that the SACC could do. Letter to Courtney, 21 February 1901, Courtney Papers, Vol. 8 f. 20.

[28] The most prominent of the anti-war newspapers included *Morning Leader*, *Manchester Guardian*, *The Speaker*, *Edinburgh Evening News*.

[29] Thus, in March 1900, there were 640 full members of which 125 held some ecclesiastical post. SACC List of Members, 1900.

[30] Joseph Edwards (ed.), *The Reformer's Yearbook* (Wallasey, 1900), p. 54.

old Gladstonian principles and it was the 600-strong Senior Reform Club that provided the core of SACC membership. These men—among them William Bowring, R. A. Armstrong, R. D. Holt and Sir John Brunner—were non-conformists and their pro-Boer views were propagated from the pulpits of Hope Street Chapel, where Armstrong was minister, and Pembroke Place Baptist Church, whose minister was Charles Aked. Pembroke Place was interesting because the church was traditionally 'Liberal in theological outlook, democratic in origin and proletarian in social composition, and fiercely radical in political outlook'.[31] Aked was a brilliant orator, a vigorous Socialist and a virulent anti-imperialist. He denounced the war as a 'crime against humanity, a capitalist war worked up by a kept press, initiated by treachery and lying'. He always preached to a packed church, and on 5 January 1902, when he preached his most famous sermon 'The Cowardly War', there were 2,000 people unable to gain admission.[32]

But there were few such orators among the Conciliationists; it was alien to the reasonable and persuasive methods of the SACC and it is significant that Aked was also a member of the Stop-the-War Committee. The attempt to argue rationally during a war is seldom successful and the SACC belonged to an eminently rational tradition. Further, it had no leader of national importance. Courtney had never had, nor had he sought, mass popularity. He was no orator, was losing his health and was handicapped by his blindness. The men who formed the backbone of the South African Conciliation Committee, such as H. J. Wilson, J. E. Ellis, member of parliament for Rushcliffe; F. A. Channing, the member for East Northants; and C. P. Scott, the member for Leigh, were all important backbenchers. But they were leaderless. Their leader had been Gladstone.

The second major anti-war organization, the Stop-the-War Committee, was very different from the sane, rational Conciliation Committee. Essentially a 'crank' organization, it was described by G. P. Gooch, who was involved in the peace agitation, as 'worse than useless' as an anti-war organization.[33]

---

[31] I. Sellers, 'The Pro-Boer Movement in Liverpool', *Transactions of the Unitarian Historical Society* (October, 1960), pp. 75–81.

[32] *Ibid.*, p. 81.

[33] George Peabody Gooch, *Under Six Reigns* (London, 1958), p. 75.

19

The personalities it attracted by its extremist rhetoric were men like Auberon Herbert who tried to organize a 'Peace Army' which would adopt 'an aggressive attitude towards militarism'.[34] Most of all, however, it was the result of the dynamism and eccentricity of W. T. Stead.

The life and character of William Thomas Stead almost defy description and understanding. A strong supporter of Gladstone, he idolized Cecil Rhodes—and until 1901 was an executor of his will.[35] His protégés included Milner, E. T. Cook and Edmund Garrett, all of whom worked with him on the *Pall Mall Gazette* where they had received their imperialist apprenticeships. His 'crusades' included the Bulgarian agitation, the white-slave traffic, the 'Bitter Cry of Outcast London', the despatch of Gordon to Khartoum, a campaign for a stronger navy, Imperial Federation—which *Review of Reviews* was designed to propagate —and International Arbitration and Peace. He was an enthusiast for whatever scheme occupied his mind at a particular moment. A man of many missions, his great talent was his ability to communicate his urgency through the medium of his racy, sensationalist journalism.

The fact that there was a seeming contradiction between his advocacy of the cause of Empire, his adulation of Rhodes as the man most fitted to unify the English-speaking races,[36] and his violent tirades against the war as 'Hell let Loose', as a 'crime against civilization and Christianity',[37] led many people to believe him a hypocrite.[38] For Stead, however, it was Rhodes and Milner who had betrayed their trust. The point about the Empire for him, as for Courtney—and here one can see again the Gladstonianism that provides a thread of continuity for many who opposed the war—was that it was a sacred trust which

---

[34] *War Against War in South Africa*, 15 December 1899, p. 132.

[35] William Thomas Stead (ed.), *The Last Will and Testament of Cecil Rhodes* (London, 1902), p. 111.

[36] After first meeting Rhodes Stead wrote: 'I have never met a man, who upon broad Imperial matters was so entirely of my way of thinking.' *Ibid.*, p. 81.

[37] W. T. Stead, *The Candidates of Cain: A Catechism for the Constituencies* (London, 1900), p. 2.

[38] J. Saxon Mills caught the truth about Stead when he wrote that Stead's uncompromising pro-Boerism was 'characteristic of his tangential mobilities, and simply meant that a passion stronger than his Liberal Imperialism had hold of him at the time—in this case the fierce militancy of his Peace Crusade'. J. Saxon Mills, *Sir Edward Cook* (London, 1921), p. 57.

should be used for the good of the governed. Britain must 'govern for the sake of the governed' and 'train the governed to govern themselves'.[39] The fact that Britain was undoubtedly 'the superior and more civilized power',[40] was precisely the reason why the war was unjust.[41]

Following a visit to the Tsar of Russia in 1898, where he was supposed to have been instrumental in the calling of the Hague Conference, he formed the 'Crusade of Peace'. Its object was to propagate arbitration as a means of resolving disputes between nations, and in the early part of 1899 an extensive agitation was carried on.[42] It is important to note, however, that his efforts were met with suspicion on the part of the established organs of the peace movement, suspicions which derived from his previous support of the Big Navy craze and which would obviously hamper any effective and unified anti-war agitation in which Stead played a major role.[43]

The outbreak of the South African War was, to Stead, a confirmation of the necessity of arbitration as a substitute for war and he tried to reactivate the 'Crusade for Peace', which had been wound up in June, as an anti-war group. The journal of the Crusade, *War against War*, became *War against War in South Africa* and Stead began to issue lengthy pamphlets which illustrated the baseness of the government's policy.[44] He appealed to the supporters of the Crusade to organize themselves as 'Friends of Peace' into an effective protest movement; and in January he was instrumental in calling a conference of the

---

[39] Frederic Whyte, *Life of W. T. Stead* (London, 1925), I, p. 112.

[40] *Ibid.*, II, p. 169.   [41] W. T. Stead, *loc. cit.*

[42] *Concord*, March 1899, p. 49.

[43] Thus, an editorial in *Concord* January 1899: 'Mr Stead is generally remembered as the infuriated partisan of the Russian aristocracy and the journalistic leader of the Big Navy craze. . . . The narrow fear that the permanent machinery of the Peace Movement may be weakened by this large and sensational appeal will be easily pardoned by those who know how hard a struggle the existing organisations have and how much more work they could do if they were more adequately endowed.' This attitude did soften as the year went on but Stead was regarded as, at best, a Johnny-come-lately. See *Concord*, March 1899, *loc. cit.*

[44] E.g. *Shall I Slay My Brother Boer?* which was described as an 'appeal to the conscience of Britain' and to which a counter pamphlet replied *Shall I Kick My Brother Stead?*—a question it answered with a strong affirmative. There was also in October 1899 a pamphlet by Stead reviewing the maze of negotiations which preceded the war and indicting the government's handling of the negotiations: *Are We in the Right?*

'Friends of Peace' which created the Stop-the-War Committee. [45]

Stead held only a minor office on the committee which was chaired by the much-respected Nonconformist, Dr J. Clifford, but the mandate and declarations of the committee so accurately represented Stead's attitude to the conflict that it is hard to believe that he was not the driving force behind it. [46] It declared the war a scandal to Christendom; it mirrored Stead's belief that the root of the problem was the burghers' justified suspicion of Chamberlain's role in the Jameson Raid; it reflected Stead's current obsession with arbitration as a means of ending the conflict; and it anticipated the need to fight the war wherever possible, including an appeal to the constituencies whenever by-elections should occur. [47]

The Stop-the-War Committee was a far greater object of hatred and jingo sentiment than the SACC; but it was also more active. It probably had more branches than any other peace committee, throughout 1900 three and a half million pamphlets were distributed at meetings held all over the country, and when *War against War in South Africa* ceased publication, *New Age* took its place. And on the eve of the General Election Stead issued a manifesto eulogizing the Boers as 'superior to us' and urging electors not to vote for candidates with the 'blood of righteous Abel in their hands'. [48]

The essence of the Stop-the-War Committee appeal was a religious one. Stead had always seen God's work in an Anglo-Saxon imperialism governed by 'common sense and the Ten Commandments', and he now came to see it in arbitration. [49] It

[45] See *War Against War in South Africa*, 17 November 1899, p. 71, for his appeal to the supporters of his arbitration crusade. See edition of 29 December 1899, p. 167, for the planning of the Conference.

[46] Thus, S. G. Hobson in *Pilgrim to the Left* (London, 1938) wrote of how when the decision to form the committee had been taken Stead 'collected every bit of scrip and security he possessed' and dumped it before the group adding 'there, it's all I've got'.

[47] See Stop-the-War Committee, *Report and Statement of Accounts* (London, 1901), pp. 3–4. The last proposal was definitely Stead's; in November 1899 he had published an appeal for a Stop-the-War fund of £10,000, the object of which was to contest every by-election on a Stop-the-War platform. See W. T. Stead, *Blastus, The King's Chamberlain* (London, 1896), for his belief of Chamberlain's role in the Jameson conspiracy.

[48] Stead, *The Candidates of Cain*, p. 74.

[49] In 1877 he had written in his diary that 'I am an imperialist within the limits of sanity and the Ten Commandments' quoted in J. W. Robertson Scott, *The Life*

was this religious appeal which formed the basis of the alliance represented by the committee between the 'Nonconformist conscience' and Stead's wing of the peace movement. Silas Hocking, one of the founder members, expressed the sentiments of those who were attracted to the committee:[50]

There are a few people . . . who . . . are asking among themselves what has become of the non-conformist conscience, and what means the inexplicable silence of the leaders of the Free Churches? . . . Is Christ to be crucified afresh, and His Gospel to be sacrificed on the altar of national prestige and pride? Men are asking everywhere, is Christianity dead?

Stead's comment on Black Week was similar: 'We could, we thought, slay our brother with our own right hand without any need to invoke God's blessing on the enterprise', and, 'we have not even assimilated so much Christianity as will make us anxious to . . . [settle] a dispute peacefully before rushing out at our brothers' throats with murderous intent'.[51]

The resolutions of the committee abound with references to the anti-Christian policies of the government. In May 1900 the government's rebuttal of Boer peace-feelers was censured: 'Such an appeal should have met with an immediate and sympathetic response from the government of any professedly Christian people.'[52] Stead's writings abound with Biblical quotations and allusions,[53] but the message was always the same: 'For the wicked shall be turned into Hell and all nations that forget God.'[54]

This emphasis on Christian duty was one obvious difference between the Stop-the-War Committee and the Conciliationists. Although they both sprang from the same generic tradition of protest, they were of differing species. The SACC was eminently

---

and Death of a Newspaper (London, 1952), p. 109. He used exactly the same phrase in *The Candidates of Cain.*

For the religious basis of his belief in arbitration see *War Against War in South Africa,* 22 December 1899, p. 152.

[50] *Ibid.,* p. 150. [51] *Ibid.,* p. 152.

[52] Stop-the-War Committee, *op. cit.,* p. 7.

[53] E.g. *ibid.,* p. 13. 'Never before have we waged unrelenting war upon women and children. . . . This professedly Christian nation is now proceeding in a policy of murder, wholesale and retail, which renders our religion a hollow farce and exposes us to the contempt and execration even of the heathen world.'

[54] Stead, *Are We in the Right?,* p. 71.

rational and reasonable. It realized and faced practical politics. It did not expect to end the war, it hoped rather to influence the settlement.[55] Conciliation of the two opponents through public education was its object. The Stop-the-War Committee had no programme except to stop the war through public agitation and ensure a restitution of the independence of the Republics.[56] It represented the more extreme of the pro-Boer movements.

This extremism was also illustrated in other ways. In the provinces it would seem that the formation of a Stop-the-War Committee was dependent upon the strength of the local branch of the Social Democratic Federation (SDF). *Justice* in its columns gave precedence to its work over that of the SACC. In Battersea, the local committee was formed by SDFers[57] and as a result John Burns would have nothing to do with it. In Aberdeen, where the SDF was very firmly entrenched, the impetus for the formation of the local committee came from its members.[58] This was in marked contrast to the local SACC groups which were usually founded by solid middle-class Liberals. We have already noted Liverpool Conciliation Committee. In Sheffield, it was the family of H. J. Wilson which took the initiative in gathering together a group of middle- and working-class (Trades Council members especially) sympathizers; in Scarborough, it was the creation of the powerful, though unpopular, Rowntree family; in Newcastle, Spence Watson was the main influence in the formation of a Conciliation Committee.

Material does not exist to test thoroughly this hypothesis; there was at least one Stop-the-War Committee, that of Gateshead, that affiliated both to the London Stop-the-War Committee and the South African Conciliation Committee, but this almost contradictory position appears to have been unique.[59]

---

[55] Thus, one of the objects of the Bradford Conciliation Committee was 'to create a state of public opinion in which the rights of the Boers as well as the rights of England will have full and generous consideration'. *War Against War in South Africa*, 12 January 1900, p. 201.

[56] The object of the committee was to 'Stop the War now because it is wrong, to redress our sins of conspiracy, bad faith and slaughter, to expose and punish the criminals, to make peace and compensate the victims'.

[57] S. C. Cronwright-Schreiner, *The Land of Free Speech* (London, 1906), pp. 280–3.

[58] The SDF took the initiative in forming the committee, see *Daily Free Press*, 3 May 1900. Also, Cronwright-Schreiner, *op. cit.*, p. 326.

[59] *Ibid.*, p. 140.

The organizations were not completely separate; there was a considerable amount of cross-membership. But, in spite of this, differences of policy and of personality existed which prevented the formation of a united front of protest and thus lessened its effectiveness.

Initially, it would appear that Stead had hoped that the anti-war protest could be encompassed within his Stop-the-War campaign.[60] But when the SACC was formed Stead reacted sourly. He felt obliged to point out that[61]

the raison d'être of the Conciliation Committee is that there are many persons who, while convinced that the war is unjust, are not logical enough, or not bold enough, to say definitely that it ought to be stopped. For such persons the Conciliation Committee is created.

And he openly condemned those who accepted the inevitability of a British victory and annexation.[62] Stead's attitude contained a very strong element of intolerance; he could not understand why those who accepted the premise that the war was immoral, would not accept the logical conclusion that it should and could be stopped with a reversion to the *status quo ante*. It is, therefore, hardly surprising that there was never a concerted effort between the two main anti-war organizations. Stead did make several attempts to enlist Courtney's help, but each time he was coldly rebuffed.[63]

There were, then, two separate organizations each opposed to the war for broadly the same reasons but disagreeing as to what sort of action was desirable or practicable under the circumstances. The Stop-the-War Committee was completely Utopian in what it tried to accomplish and could only appeal to men like Stead or Hocking: men of uncompromising and limited political vision. These were the very worst sort of persons to run a mass agitation. Its main support came from the Socialists and the

[60] Thus, he wrote in *War Against War in South Africa*, 17 November 1899, p. 71, that: 'There is no attempt at this moment to form a new organisation. . . . All that we wish to do is to bring together all Friends of Peace whether already enrolled as members of any existing organisation or not. We want to enrol them for the specific purpose of combating the present war. . . . Those who join it will not be committed to any ideas either as to Peace or arbitration. The only common ground that we should need to occupy is the wickedness of the present war.'

[61] *Ibid.*, 19 January 1900, p. 212.   [62] *Ibid.*, 26 January 1900, p. 220.

[63] Stead to Courtney, 8 January 1901, 27 March, 25, 27 June, Courtney Papers, Vol. 8, ff. 1, 39, 66, 68.

extreme Nonconformists; its programme, a radical mixture of evangelicalism and arbitration, had no appeal to a mass audience.[64] The Conciliationists appealed to the sophisticated middle-class Liberal who was inspired by the political principles that he believed Gladstone had represented. Its urbane, drawing-room character was ill suited to mobilizing a potential anti-war support among the mass of the population. Thus, neither of these organizations possessed the necessary qualifications to arouse and conduct a mass agitation. Furthermore, neither had a leader, or personality, who was widely known and respected and who could adequately carry the message to the people.

If neither of the protest committees was equipped to organize anti-war sentiment, there remained the logical vehicle of Radicalism—the Liberal Party. Unfortunately, the Liberal Party, too, was unable to play any real role in militant opposition to the war. Indeed, for much of the period, it was unable to agree upon any consistent policy with which to assault the government's policy on the war. The reasons for this failure were, at root, historical, but the significance of the South African War in bringing to a head the complex series of personality and policy conflicts can hardly be overestimated.

The basic problem was that there were many who felt that the party should move with the times and rid itself of the suspicion of being anti-imperialist. Part of the Liberal's traditional armoury, however, was the probable myth of a Gladstonian tradition of foreign policy which had been based upon correct moral and ethical principles. Whether this was true, or not, is irrelevant. All that mattered was that the anti-imperialists within the party believed it to be true. They fully accepted that there were moral absolutes which should govern foreign policy, that these had been implemented and applied most successfully by Gladstone, and that they were the last defenders of these true principles. Most of these men had served their political apprenticeship under the awesome influences of the Midlothian speeches and the trauma of the second Gladstone government. Thus, when the South African War broke out, they knew where their duty lay. The aggressive, materialistic imperialism of the

[64] The Socialist societies held some meetings of their own, but typically the agitation was non-sectarian; the organizations cut across party loyalties.

previous decade had at last shown its true character. Not only must they oppose the war with all their individual strength, they should also drag the Liberal Party, kicking, screaming, and fissured if need be, back on to the right path.

Imperialism had been an issue seriously dividing the Liberal Party since at least 1892 and its centrifugal tendencies became progressively stronger as the decade proceeded.[65] The problem was complicated because of the involvement of two personalities representing the imperialist and anti-imperialist wings of the party. Neither Rosebery nor Harcourt were capable of inspiring great devotion,[66] but both were symbols of hatred for those in the party who disagreed with them.[67] By early 1899, the hints that a yardstick of anti-imperial orthodoxy should be imposed upon the party, and the intention of the anti-imperial Liberals to take a stand on this issue, were plain for all to see.[68] The Liberal imperialists were equally insistent upon their right to retain their freedom of opinion and expression on the question of imperial expansion. Thus, the lines were clearly drawn for the cathartic experience of the years 1899–1902.

What has not been fully understood, however, is that the split

[65] For the divisiveness of imperialism among the Liberals see Peter Stansky, *Ambitions and Strategies* (Oxford, 1964). On the Uganda, Fashoda and Sudan issues see *ibid.*, pp. 97, 259–60, 293.

[66] 'Even the mild Campbell-Bannerman was capable of deploring Harcourt's sulks and despondency.' *Ibid.*, p. 150. The Liberal imperialists were constantly frustrated by Rosebery's seeming apathy and his willingness to let his agents do his work for him. See Heber L. Hart, *Reminiscences and Reflections* (London, 1939), pp. 221, 229–30.

[67] Thus, a letter H. J. Wilson wrote to his family recounting the events of the meeting of 6 February 1899 to ratify Campbell-Bannerman as leader where he, Bryn Roberts and Sam Evans had hatched a plan to humiliate the Roseberyites: 'The idea was to move an amendment making "C-B" the "Leader of the Party" omitting "in the House of Commons." That would put the Rosebery faction in this position—they must vote for a Lord as leader, and face their constituents on that. Of course we knew what the answer would be, but we meant to laugh at the 30, or so, Liberal Lords and to rub in that Kimberley is leader there.' H. J. Wilson Papers, M.D. 2615. f. 22.

[68] Thus, the jubilation of Harcourt on the division on the Sudan question in February 1899 when thirteen Liberals voted with the government. He wrote to Morley: 'The boasted unity has been conspicuously refuted. . . . You have opened the campaign in a masterly manner.' Quoted in Stansky, *op. cit.*, p. 293. Also, Morley's speech at Brechin in January of that year: 'There is a spread of dangerous doctrine that . . . has in my judgement found its way into our own party', see *The Liberal Magazine for Year 1899* (London, 1899), p. 8. And Spence Watson's claim that 'the differences were already beginning to concern those in the Party who looked forward'. Robert Spence Watson, *The National Liberal Federation* (London, 1907), p. 237.

27

in the Liberal Party during these years was more than just a disagreement 'between those who felt it their duty to drop all criticism of the government . . . and those who felt themselves to be so at variance with the government . . . that they held it their duty to continue criticism'.[69] It was more than just a disagreement about the war. It was a fundamental dispute as to the very nature of Liberalism. Furthermore, the war was merely the issue that provided the starkest and most threatening visibility of this split in the party; a showdown was bound to occur sometime, the Boer War was the excuse. The actual course of the dispute was essentially a result of the desire of the anti-imperialists to force the Liberal Party into its supposedly traditional role of guardian of the nation's moral conscience, and of the lengths to which this faction was prepared to go to accomplish this end. Everything followed from this fact: the latent battle plans of both factions were uncovered for all to see; a unified policy with regard to the war was an inherent impossibility. And so, ultimately, was the anti-imperialist and pro-Boer desire to make the party an organ of Radical protest. It is, therefore, crucial to understand the processes involved in the struggle during these years, for they go far to explaining the failure of Radicalism during this period.

From the beginning of the conflict, pressure was applied on Campbell-Bannerman to speak out along pro-Boer lines against the war. Having been a compromise candidate for the leadership in February 1899, and regarded with equal suspicion by the supporters of both Harcourt and Rosebery, he moved cautiously and assiduously, tried to formulate phrases and sentiments which would quench the anti-imperialist passion for strong words without alienating the Liberal imperialists.[70] This 'centre'

[69] G. B. Pyrah, *Imperial Policy and South Africa 1902–1910* (Oxford, 1955), p. 41.

[70] Thus, in speeches at Ilford and Maidstone in June and October, he expressed doubts about the government's policy but explained that 'we have been forced from patriotic motives to keep silent'. And 'we are not in a position to form an opinion on the policy of the Government'. See 'The Transvaal Question', *Liberal Publication Department Yearbook 1899* (London, 1900), n.p., 'Great Britain and the Transvaal', Liberal Publication Department Leaflet 1805 (1899). By November the tone had got a little stronger; thus, at Birmingham: 'When, however, . . . our acquiescence in and our approval of the policy which underlay our recent transactions with the Transvaal Republic (is sought) then, I say, the demand is neither reasonable nor fair.' 'The Transvaal Question, Imperialism and Social Reform', *Liberal Publication Department Yearbook 1899*.

policy did not, of course satisfy the ardent spirits amongst the anti-imperialists. John Ellis wrote to him on 3 November complaining that[71]

that attitude [cannot] . . . be maintained indefinitely . . . I earnestly hope that the 'big speeches' in November may sound a note of clear warning that the Liberal Party must not be taken to be committed to acquiescence in the policy of the war—and that it is *fundamentally* opposed to those advocates of territorial expansion, Imperial aggression which must result in a disastrous militarism.

James Bryce, who earlier in the autumn had seemed to be supporting Campbell-Bannerman's centre policy, also urged that he take a more aggressive approach to satisfy the indignation of the Liberals in the country about the war.[72]

But the desire of the pro-Boers to launch a full-scale assault on the government's policy and to ignore the Liberal imperialists was nowhere better illustrated than in a letter F. A. Channing wrote to Campbell-Bannerman on 8 November. He began by asserting that the materials were ready to hand for another and more sweeping Midlothian campaign and he continued with sentiments that were at the heart of the pro-Boer case:

I have an entire faith and earnest desire to see the principles of Gladstone and Bright—the only basis on which Liberalism can be worked and live—triumph once again. The great hindrance to accomplishing this lie in the fact that Rosebery, Grey, etc. by their support of the Government on the causes of the war . . . are, in effect destroying the party as a fighting power and ensuring its complete ruin in the next election. . . . The cornerstone of Liberalism is to appeal to the national conscience the recognition [*sic*] that morality means the same for nations as for individuals. That is the touchstone of the vital forces underlaying Liberalism which if withered away bring with their death the death of the Party that won in 1868 in 1880 and in 1892.

He urged Campbell-Bannerman to point out to the Liberal imperialists that 'it is impossible for them to have their way and to recognise that this persistent schism means the destruction of the party'. He recognized that the basic disagreement was on the cause of the war, but it was this that was the vital point for a new Midlothian:[73]

---

[71] Campbell-Bannerman Papers, Add. MSS. 41214, f. 64.
[72] See letters of 5 and 13 October, *ibid.*, ff. 45, 55.
[73] *Ibid.*, Add. MSS. 41213, f. 12.

Of course, I am assuming that there is unequivocal agreement that after the Ultimatum the war could not be stopped and must be carried through to the speediest conclusion. . . . But I do think we ought not to put off for an instant longer the full exposure and criticism of Chamberlain's policy and its frightful results.

In the correspondence that followed, Campbell-Bannerman doubted the practicability of such an approach; Channing, in turn, deplored the 'surrender' of Liberal policy to the principle of 'might makes right' and advocated a campaign against 'the seamy side of jingoism' claiming that it would be a 'clean and intelligible line which would win the Liberal Party the biggest and best deserved victory it has ever won'.[74]

The implicit assumption behind these letters was that the Liberal imperialists were verging on heresy and preventing the party from fulfilling its historic mission. Writing to Campbell-Bannerman at the end of the year he urged a 'carefully worded challenge to the policy of extermination' but added that if Grey and his friends opposed it[75]

[the party] ought to ignore them. I hope this may not be the case. But just as there is a limit beyond which war becomes mere barbarity . . . so there is a limit beyond which Liberalism dies off if it is compelled to acquiesce in what is *morally* detestable and alien to any Liberal voter.

Labouchere was another Radical who faced the prospect of a split with equanimity. Several times he urged Campbell-Bannerman to assert his leadership and to force a showdown by laying down an amendment which would condemn government policy previous to and during the war. He predicted that if the worst came to the worst only half-a-dozen Liberals would break away and pointed out that:[76]

As long as everything is subordinated to keeping on terms with Asquith and Co., the Party is paralysed. You may depend upon it, they are determined not to accept your leadership unless you accept their policy. . . . I do not think you quite realise the strength of your own position in the party. Purposely handled . . . it would follow you like a flock of sheep. . . . Let them taste blood and they will cure Asquith and Co. as . . . traitors to the Party.

[74] *Ibid.*, ff. 22–4.   [75] *Ibid.*, f. 49.
[76] *Ibid.*, 20 October 1901, Add. MSS. 41222, f. 66. See also letters of 7, 8 November 1899, ff. 33–5.

Harcourt and Morley were also unafraid of some kind of showdown with the imperialists in the party. They both resembled a pair of grumbling old ladies who, on the one hand, chafed at their exclusion from positions of leadership and, on the other, were continually congratulating themselves upon their freedom. Neither was particularly disturbed at the prospect of schism, but they were not irresponsible enough to work for it openly. Thus, Harcourt wrote to Morley on 1 October 1899; 'There will be a serious schism which will greatly affect political prospects for which, as you know I care as little as you do.'[77] But Harcourt, although pressed to 'stump the country', chose to work from within in an attempt to push Campbell-Bannerman into a clear anti-war position.[78] His purpose was to achieve some kind of joint action with the leader whereas Morley preferred to remain self-righteously unattached writing the biography of Gladstone, and watching, with malicious pleasure, the party flounder.[79] Thus, neither was primarily concerned about party unity and both were somewhat scornful of what Morley sarcastically called 'C-B's beautiful policy of . . . keeping the party together'.[80]

Harcourt's attitude was illustrated at the end of 1901. In November he wrote to Campbell-Bannerman congratulating him on a fairly strong speech he had made at Plymouth, adding: 'I suppose it elicited a groan from Asquith and a howl from Haldane. So much the better.'[81] Later in the year, just after the National Federation meeting in December, when the Liberals found some common ground in their united protests against the suspension of constitutional government and the imposition of martial law,[82] Harcourt wrote: 'I feel strongly that the declaration of the incapacity of Milner to make peace ought to be a cardinal point . . . from the first in his "helot" despatch he has

---

[77] Harcourt Papers, Box 10. See also Morley to Harcourt, 12 October 1899, 'I confess I am not sanguine of holding the party together.'

[78] See letter to Spencer, 18 August 1900, Harcourt Papers, no box number.

[79] See Harcourt to Morley, 11 October 1899, 'The great thing to aim at is some joint action with C-B.' Morley to Harcourt 13 October 1899, and 28 July 1900 where he writes: 'What is it to you and me whether C-B turns to the right or to the left, or stands shivering and unclad at the cross roads. Why did we leave them, if we are to be sneaked back again by rubbish about unity?' *Ibid.*, Box 10.

[80] Morley to Harcourt, 10 September 1900, *ibid.*

[81] Campbell-Bannerman Papers, Add. MSS. 41219, f. 277.

[82] Spence Watson, *op. cit.*, p. 261.

been the principle obstacle to peace.'[83] This would have meant, as Harcourt well knew,[84] an immediate rupture. Both Haldane and Grey and, to a lesser extent Asquith, were profound admirers of the High Commissioner. Campbell-Bannerman had long been aware that it was impossible to attack Milner although he regarded him as a prime culprit. He had written to his cousin, James Campbell, that 'the real arch-offender is Milner—but we can't get at him'.[85]

Campbell-Bannerman always kept his distance from Harcourt and firmly rebuffed a proposal that Harcourt made to 'enter into joint action and cooperation with you'.[86] It is clear why Campbell-Bannerman was anxious to avoid any entanglements with Harcourt; it would only serve to turn the suspicion of the Roseberyites into hostility. And it would have made the uncertain unity that Campbell-Bannerman was trying to maintain even less stable.

The liability Harcourt would have been was illustrated by his attitude at the end of 1901 when there was the serious possibility of Rosebery returning to official party life. The Chesterfield speech of that winter had been well received. Spender claimed that it performed the 'miracle of uniting the extremist sections of the Liberal Party'.[87] The truth was that there was relief on the one hand that it had not been a declaration of war, and a belief on the part of the imperialists that nothing could now prevent Rosebery's return to the party, if not to the leadership. Nothing had really changed. Campbell-Bannerman had reacted very strongly to Herbert Gladstone against the

[83] 7 December 1901, Campbell-Bannerman Papers, Add. MSS. 41220, f. 2.

[84] A. G. Gardiner, *The Life of Sir William Harcourt* (London, 1923), II, p. 535.

[85] 19 November 1899, Campbell-Bannerman Papers, Add. MSS. 41246, f. 75.

[86] Harcourt to Campbell-Bannerman, 5 December 1900, and Campbell-Bannerman to Harcourt, 7 December 1900, *ibid.*, Add. MSS. 41219, ff. 159, 162. A. G. Gardiner, in his biography of Harcourt has much overestimated the extent to which Campbell-Bannerman depended on Harcourt and the claim that Harcourt was the 'mainstay' of the 'centre policy' is ridiculous. See Gardiner, *op. cit.*, p. 519. The only evidence for these assertions is a letter Harcourt wrote to Spencer in August 1900 on the occasion of the famous 'three-way split' in the party caused by Sir Wilfred Lawson's motion of censure on Chamberlain, where Harcourt wrote: 'The mess that had been made by the folly of Lawson, on the side, the malignity of the Roseberyites on the other was so bad that . . . they made the position of poor C-B intolerable. . . . I therefore plucked up my courage to give him a helping hand.'

[87] J. A. Spender, *Life of Sir Henry Campbell-Bannerman* (London, 1923), II, p. 13.

assumptions of the speech dismissing it as 'mere rechauffé of Mr. Sidney Webb',[88] but he was under strong pressure from moderates like Gladstone who believed that the speech provided the opportunity for reconciliation.[89] He was, therefore, obliged to make an effort and one afternoon, at the end of December, he visited Rosebery in London and talked for a few hours, supposedly to pave the way for the return of Rosebery in some position of authority. Spender claims that he was sincere in his bid for Rosebery's return but this is doubtful. It seems more plausible that he was making a tactical move to safeguard his moderate flank, composed of men like Gladstone. He must have realized that Rosebery would not descend from his 'tabernacle' —he had repeated his conviction not to do so many times. The only thing that would induce him to do so would be a call from the party, and that would have meant the end of Bannerman. He, therefore, had no interest in getting Rosebery back, but he had to take the risk and make the gesture. The very same day, he took care that it should be known that it was not he who was the obstacle to Rosebery's return. He wrote C. P. Scott a letter, marked secret, stating: 'There never had been (with one exception) any unwillingness on our part for his return, this is absolute. The impediment is that he won't. I am ready to cooperate; *but no cooperation is offered.*'[90] Scott was editor of the *Manchester Guardian*; Spender, the editor of the *Westminster Gazette*, also received a similar letter.[91]

Harcourt's attitude to the overture was extremely disparaging. Although he did not believe that 'Rosebery . . . will be entrapped by . . . the blandishments, sycophancies, trembling compromises etc.' he wanted to be doubly sure that Rosebery did not sneak back into a leadership position. Thus, both he and Morley urged Campbell-Bannerman to be intransigent and inflexible, believing that as a result of the Derby meeting he was in a position of some strength.[92] Harcourt wrote two letters to Campbell-Bannerman on 27 and 29 December condemning the Chesterfield policy and another on 30 December in which his

[88] Campbell-Bannerman to Herbert Gladstone, 18 December 1901, Herbert Gladstone Papers, Add. MSS. 45987, f. 212.
[89] Gladstone to Campbell-Bannerman, 17 December 1901, *ibid.*, f. 209.
[90] 26 December 1901, Campbell-Bannerman Papers, Add. MSS. 41236, f. 257.
[91] 1 January 1902, Spender Papers, Add. MSS. 46388, f. 9.
[92] Morley to Harcourt, 25 December 1901, Harcourt Papers, *op. cit.*

attitude to Rosebery and reunification becomes explicit. 'His terms are like those of the Government "unconditional surrender" of the Liberal Party and the Liberal creed.'[93] Harcourt no longer regarded his old adversary a Liberal; the Chesterfield speech had confirmed his worst fears: 'R[osebery] has shaken the dust of the Liberal Party from his shoes and has abjured "Hounsditch." '[94] At the beginning of January he urged Campbell-Bannerman to outflank the Liberal imperialists by emphasizing the similarities between his policy and that of Rosebery: 'To show that as to the war there are more points of agreement in your policy with Rosebery than with those who now purport to be his followers;' and then came the crucial line: 'And, of course, . . . to repudiate the "clean slate" as unworthy of the Liberal Party.' This was not all, however, for he pressed Campbell-Bannerman to point out—what was in fact true—that 'the differences are not really on the war but on the fundamentals of Liberalism . . . and not temporary like the war'.[95]

Throughout the first two weeks of January there was a constant stream of letters from Malwood. The position in the party was critical at this time—it was the week of the Grey ultimatum[96]—and Harcourt's object was to stiffen Campbell-Bannerman against any possible compromise with the Liberal imperialists.[97] It was his letters of 12 January which illuminatingly revealed the nature of the crisis and threatened split as they appeared to Gladstonian Liberals like Harcourt. He wrote in the first letter of the day:[98]

I hope you will very distinctly repudiate the 'clean slate' and 'a new Liberal Party.' We belong to the old Liberal Party. So far from it

---

[93] Campbell-Bannerman Papers, Add. MSS. 41220, ff. 19–22.
[94] 30 December 1901, *ibid.*, f. 24.   [95] *Ibid.*, f. 29.
[96] Grey had threatened to repudiate publicly Campbell-Bannerman's leadership unless he accepted Rosebery's views on martial law, the camps, Milner and peace overtures. Morley believed that this meant 'the split overt'. But Asquith seems to have been very active through Gladstone in patching the thing up. In fact the whole thing was probably a result of Grey misunderstanding Rosebery's position—an easy thing to do. Thus, over Milner and peace overtures, Grey was opposed to the former's recall and was sceptical of the value of the latter; Rosebery had an open mind on both. Campbell-Bannerman was in favour of recalling Milner and of pursuing peace feelers from the Low Countries. See Gardiner, *op. cit.* p. 538; Spender, *op. cit.*, pp. 10, 20; Gladstone Papers, *op. cit.*, f. 218, Add. MSS. 45989, f. 51; Campbell-Bannerman Papers, Add. MSS. 41211, ff. 188, 192.
[97] Harcourt to Campbell-Bannerman, 7 January 1902, *ibid.*, Add. MSS. 41220, f. 45.   [98] *Ibid.*, f. 48.

being true that it does not accommodate itself to the spirit of the age, its 'slate' shows that it has been a constant vehicle of advanced legislation on each question. . . . I know you will make it clear that you fly the old flag and are not prepared to shunt the old traditions and the old creeds. There never was more need for 'Peace, Retrenchment, and Reform.'

He viewed calmly the reaction of the Liberal imperialists to a proposed motion of censure on the government, believing that[99]

the *main body* of the Party would feel obliged to support a vote of censure and that the Liberal Party in the country expects it and will be greatly disappointed if nothing is done . . . the . . . boldest course is probably the best and those who stand out will have to answer for it to the constituencies.

But in spite of this heavy pressure from Harcourt, Campbell-Bannerman waited until the National Liberal Federation meeting in February before coming out strongly against the 'clean slate' suggestion of the Chesterfield speech. He pointed out that if Rosebery's advice was taken, the party would become a 'sort of Liberal Party' and he firmly rejected any intention of abandoning the old tenets of Liberalism.[100] Thus, after two years of avoiding the central issue, Campbell-Bannerman asserted himself and lined up with the anti-imperialist and anti-Rosebery wing of the party. In one sense this was an *ex post facto* assertion: the Liberal League had already been formed and Campbell-Bannerman's speech, made some three months after Chesterfield, was a last resort. In another sense, the danger crisis had passed, the war was almost over, there were new issues to unite the party: Harcourt was soon to be consulting with Fowler and Asquith on the Opposition amendment to the Education Bill.[101]

The fact remains that throughout all these pro-Boer efforts to drive him into an intransigent position, Campbell-Bannerman remained steadfast. He was the man in the middle with the duty of holding the party together. Temperamentally, he belonged with the anti-imperialists over this issue,[102] but he refused to do anything which would drive the imperialists to a breach. His

[99] *Ibid.*, f. 52. [100] Quoted in Spender, *op. cit.*, pp. 27–8.
[101] Harcourt to Campbell-Bannerman, 29 April 1902, Campbell-Bannerman Papers, *op. cit.*, f. 60.
[102] See his letters to Bryce, 10 November 1899, 14 January 1900, *ibid.*, Add. MSS. 41211, ff. 61, 86.

success was due to several factors. He knew that the Liberal imperialists had no real desire to leave the party; they were, therefore, in a far weaker position than the pro-Boers who could propagandize with righteous impunity. The Liberal imperialists were constantly frustrated by Rosebery's consistent lack of resolution and aimlessness. Their one purpose was to get him into the leadership, but they received no help from him in accomplishing this end. This left Campbell-Bannerman comparatively free to travel in a pro-Boer direction, which he did with a marked emphasis throughout 1901. This was especially true because the issues of martial law and the concentration camps were ones that could hardly provide the occasion for a schism. At the same time, however, he resisted pressure from the pro-Boer faction which desired to push him into a policy that would have left the Liberal imperialists little alternative but to depart from the party. His leadership was, after all, the only chance the party had of avoiding fratricidal collapse and this was the ultimate strength of his 'centre' position.

There were times, however, when it seemed that his efforts were to prove fruitless. The most serious crisis for the party and the moment when it really seemed to be falling apart came in the summer of 1901.[103] A visit by Milner to England provided the occasion for the pro-Boers to attack him and for the Liberal imperialists to show their support for the High Commissioner.[104] Coincidental with this was the euphoric reaction of the anti-imperialists to Campbell-Bannerman's fierce attack on the 'methods of barbarism', an attack which seemed to indicate his final public conversion to the anti-war position.[105] The crisis escalated with Asquith's rejoinder to the left-wing attacks and his clear warning that the Liberal imperialists had no intention of recanting their pro-war views or of being driven out of the party.[106] To Asquith's acute embarrassment, a series of dinners

[103] This period was known as the 'war to the knife and fork' because its progress was marked by a series of dinners.

[104] Thus, Morley chose this moment to characterize Milner as 'an imitation Bismarck'. Grey went to meet the High Commissioner at Southampton and spoke at a dinner in his honour. Spender, I, *op. cit.*, pp. 333–4.

[105] Campbell-Bannerman had spent two hours with Emily Hobhouse on 14 June where she had recounted the horrors of the concentration camps and he went on to denounce them in a speech at the National Reform Union.

[106] Asquith, in a speech at Liverpool Street Station, entered into open dispute with Morley, denying that the left wing of the party represented the true Liberalism

was planned by enthusiastic back-bench Liberal imperialists ostensibly to consolidate their strengthened position, but which in reality threatened to turn into an attempted *coup* against Campbell-Bannerman's leadership.[107] For Campbell-Bannerman, with the divisions in the party crystallizing into publicly intransigent positions, there was only one option left open and that was to appeal openly to the party for support against the fratricidal strugglings of the two wings. He called a meeting of all MPs on 9 July and castigated both factions equally:[108]

I am no partisan . . . in these antagonisms: they are confined to a few individuals. . . . They do not know the infinite mischief they do to the Party. . . . I impartially blame all who take part in them.

Thus, both Liberal imperialists and pro-Boers were condemned, and what he said applied as much to Morley and Harcourt as it did to Haldane or Grey.

The antagonisms that Campbell-Bannerman condemned at the Reform Club were, by this time, institutionalized. The sectional organization of the Liberal Party had begun early in 1900, when a conference of pro-Boers had formed the League of Liberals Against Aggression and Militarism.[109] The con-

---

and warned 'we have not changed our views . . . we shall not recant'. This was serious because Asquith was regarded as the man the 'Limps' would really like to catch, he was seen as a compromise candidate for the leadership who would lean towards the imperialist side. But this seems to have been a momentary lapse on his part and he was anxious to assure Campbell-Bannerman of his continued loyalty. Asquith knew he was a strong contender for the leadership but only if he could avoid too strong an identification with factionalism. *Ibid.*, p. 339; also J. A. Spender and C. Asquith, *Life of Lord Oxford and Asquith* (London, 1932), I, p. 340.

[107] Asquith wrote to Gladstone: 'The dinner as you know was no idea of mine, but it was put to me in such a way that I did not feel able to decline. The distinct understanding was that it was to be *in no sense* anti-C-B.' And, in a memorandum on the crisis, Gladstone wrote that the whole episode of the dinners was concocted by Haldane, Ferguson, Douglas, Grey and Trevelyan who believed that the 'iron was hot' to 'bring about a revolution in the party attitude on the war', and that Asquith was misled by these men: 'I am certain Asquith had no disloyal intention against C-B . . . and meant only to maintain his own views.' See Gladstone Papers, *op. cit.*, ff. 49, 51, and Add. MSS. 46105, f. 210.

[108] Spender, *op. cit.*, p. 344.

[109] The League grew out of an informal body of advanced Liberals, the Liberal Forwards, which had been formed in 1895 as a watch-dog committee. Those attending the conference included the most prominent anti-imperialists, both in and out of parliament: Sir Wilfred Lawson, Scott, Channing, W. E. Russell, Lloyd George, R. C. Lehman, W. S. Caine, S. Smith, F. Maddison. See Thomas Shaw, *Letters to Isabel* (London, 1921), pp. 128–9.

ference mainly concerned itself with reaffirming its 'adherence to the uniform Liberal tradition, maintained by Fox, Canning, Lord John Russell, and Mr Gladstone, of supporting and stimulating the importance of small nationalities' and it deliberately placed on record its[110]

deep sense of gratitude towards Sir Henry Campbell-Bannerman, Sir William Harcourt, John Morley, Mr Bryce, Mr Leonard Courtney, and all others who have during the crisis courageously maintained the true principles of Liberalism, and affirms its entire confidence in the leaders of the Liberal Party in the House of Commons.

It also declared its intention of conducting 'a vigorous political propaganda' to reassert the anti-imperial tradition of Liberalism and indicated that it would do this through the local Liberal Associations. And in 1901 the League claimed to have prepared 500 meetings at the local level.[111] Thus, the anti-imperialists gave early notice of their intention to purge Liberalism of the imperialist infection and ensure a return to the old traditions. This, in truth, was an open declaration of factionalism; the fact that it was to fail made it no less serious at the time.

The Liberal imperialists were much less eager to form such organizations. They were more sensitive to charges of sectionalism because of the difficulty of placing imperialism within the context of a Liberal tradition (they could hardly claim Gladstone as a spiritual leader in spite of the historical fact of the 1880-5 ministry) and they were continually at pains to emphasize their desire to work within the party. There can be little doubt that the anti-imperialists won the propaganda battle; it was very easy for them to portray the 'Limps' as factionalists and heretics. The truth, however, is just the reverse. The Liberal League— conceivably the beginning of a new party—was not formed until the crisis had passed and the war virtually over. It was not, however, the first of the Liberal imperialist organizations; it was born from the Imperial Liberal Council, formed in early 1900, in response to the formation of the anti-imperialist League against Aggression and Militarism.[112] None of the founders, Heber

[110] *The Times*, 15 February 1900, p. 4.
[111] *Ibid.*, 19 August 1901, p. 8.
[112] See Heber L. Hart, *op. cit.*, p. 198 and 'The Imperial Liberal Council', *New Liberal Review*, April 1901, pp. 383–90.

Hart, Saxon Mills and E. J. Slater, was an MP and it was not until March 1900 that Robert Perks—the leading back-bench Liberal imperialist—gave his support.[113] The Council had been formed to defend 'sound Imperial principles' from the attacks of the Little Englander group within the parliamentary party.[114] But it stressed that: 'They had no hostility to the great Liberal organisations such as the National Liberal Federation. . . . They were loyal both to the Liberal Party and to the Empire.'[115]

It was also significant that leading Liberal imperialists were very hesitant about supporting the Council. Thus, Haldane, the leading organizer of the Roseberyites,[116] wrote in reply to an invitation to a proposed dinner: 'I am sure that it is wiser that I should not come. . . . It would simply tend to arrest the smoothing over process which is going on on our benches.'[117] Similarly, Rosebery and Grey avoided any formal attachment to the Council although Rosebery probably kept in touch with Hart through Lord Brassey, the President.[118] Indeed, the first public recognition the Council received from a leading Liberal imperialist was the attendance of Grey at one of its functions on 25 March 1901.[119] Likewise, Rosebery did not come out in support of its work until 30 July 1901, when, in a public letter, he expressed appreciation of the League's work in counterbalancing 'other bodies of a different colour'. He also suggested that the name of the Council be changed to the Liberal (Imperial) League and the suggestion was adopted.[120]

But it is important to note that it was only in the crisis atmosphere of the summer of 1901 that the leading Liberal imperialists were prepared to declare formally their attachment to this sectional organization. Grey was elected President on 30 October and Asquith became Vice-President on 15 November. From this point onwards, to the distress of Heber Hart, the Liberal (Imperial) League becomes a creature of the parliamentary Liberal imperialists; and, coincidental with the Grey ultimatum, seemed by December to be abandoning its policy of

[113] Hart, *Reminiscences and Reflections, op. cit.,* p. 200.

[114] *Ibid.,* p. 198.

[115] *Ibid.,* p. 202. This was part of a resolution passed at the first house dinner of the Imperial Liberal Council.

[116] According to Beatrice Webb, *Our Partnership* (London, 1948), p. 198.

[117] Hart, *op. cit.,* p. 205.   [118] *Ibid.*

[119] *Ibid.,* p. 216.   [120] *Ibid.,* p. 218.

working within the party.[121] The Liberal imperialists appeared to be steeling themselves for open schism when, in February 1902, it was announced that the organization was to be re-constituted into the Liberal League and was to become the vehicle for propagating the Chesterfield policy.[122] If the Liberal League was intended to be the beginnings of a new party the intention was soon abandoned; and both Asquith and Rosebery —perhaps restraining Grey—were soon emphasizing the necessity of Liberals working within their own local organiza-tion.[123]

What is clear, however, is that the initial impetus for the creation of a Liberal imperialist pressure group had arisen from the desire to counterbalance those of the anti-imperialists. It was linked with the desire to reinstate Rosebery as leader, but it was obvious that parliamentary imperialists were hesitant about supporting it and only did so in the summer and autumn of 1901 which, as has been shown, was the real crisis period for the party. It is also clear that the Liberal imperialist fears about ostracism were not unreal. The pro-Boers would have shed no tears had Grey, Haldane, Asquith and Perks left the party and it was, in large part, only the good sense of Campbell-Bannerman that prevented this. The 'Limps' had no real desire to split away but were hampered and circumscribed by Rosebery's chronic indecision and by the success with which they were portrayed as

[121] Thus, Grey in an interview with Hart claimed that 'unless they were to be excluded from office indefinitely, some decisive step in repudiation of the existing leadership in the House of Commons or of the non-imperialist members of the party had become imperative'. When the decision was taken to form the Liberal League, Hart read a letter to the Council from Robson, a back-bench Liberal imperialist whose views reflected his own: 'If he (Rosebery) wants to do or be anything . . . it can only be within and through the Liberal Party . . . do not let us encourage the idea of secession which would place the centre of the party . . . in necessary opposition to us and leave them to the guidance of the Little Englanders.' *Ibid.*, pp. 225, 229–30.

[122] *Ibid.*, p. 241.

[123] Thus, Rosebery said it would be a mistake for Liberals to leave their local Liberal Associations, Asquith at St Leonards claimed he would have 'nothing to do with any attempt to destroy or weaken the general organisation of the party'. Sir Robert Perks claimed it to be a unifying force which 'enabled a large number of experienced and talented men who might have left the Liberal Party to maintain their connection with Liberalism'. Probably the opposition of men like Hart and Robson was an important restraining factor. See Spender and Asquith, *op. cit.*, pp. 144–5; Spender, II, *op. cit.*, p. 35; Sir Robert Perks, *Notes for an Autobiography* (London, 1936), p. 143.

sectionalists by the pro-Boers. Once the leaders of the imperialist faction entered and gained control of the Imperial Liberal
Council, its form changed and it seemed to confirm their desire
to form a new, reconstituted Liberal Party. But their actions, at
least among the highest echelons, seem to belie this. It was not
they who were anxious to split the party, rather, it was the moral
righteousness and anger of the pro-Boers who were disposed to
purge heretics from the ranks.

It would be wrong to assume that the clash in the party prevailed merely in parliament; it extended to the grass roots.[124]
This was the case in Sheffield where both the nature of the
division and its effect upon the party as a political force were
revealingly illustrated.

The local Liberal Party was dominated by the presence and
family connections of H. J. Wilson, who sat for Holmfirth.[125] An
advanced Liberal who had entered politics under Gladstone's
awesome influence,[126] he opposed the war as 'a crime against
humanity',[127] and tried to use the local party machine as a basis
to denounce imperialism. Those Liberals opposed to him were
also a powerful group. They included the proprietor of the
Sheffield and Rotherham Independent and its editor, Derry; J.
Skinner, the agent for Hallam, Sir F. T. Mappin, MP for
Hallam; and J. B. Langley, member for Attercliffe. Thus,
Skinner wrote to Wilson on 17 January 1900, that 'the advis-
ability of holding public meetings during the war was discussed
at length and it was unanimously decided that it was best not to
hold any at present'.[128] And in a memorandum written in the
autumn of 1901, Wilson complained: 'Some of us wanted the
"1000" to meet nearly two years ago. Executive would not

[124] Some were more seriously affected than others; Leeds Liberal Federation
passed three resolutions in 1900 which supported Campbell-Bannerman as leader,
welcomed Rosebery back to politics and reiterated its faith in Peace, Retrenchment
and Reform. Leeds Liberal Federation, *Annual Report, 1900*, pp. 72–9.

[125] Wilson had been one of the founding fathers of the Sheffield Liberal Party
and he controlled Brightside Division Liberal Council where his fellow pro-Boer,
Maddison, was the member. His brother, Wycliffe Wilson, was closely involved
in Hallam politics. His wife was Chairman of the Woman's Liberal Council.

[126] His first involvement in national politics came, predictably, with the Bulgarian agitation which brought him into contact with Gladstone from whom he
derived his belief in the Christian duty of politics. Mosa Anderson, *H. J. Wilson:
Fighter for Freedom* (London, 1953), p. 39.

[127] *Ibid.*, p. 72.

[128] H. J. Wilson Papers, 1960 Deposit, Hallamshire Politics Bundle.

consent. . . . Everything we did was found fault with. . . . Nothing since except silence and boycott. Liberalism might not exist.'[129]

The dangers that the war presented to Liberal unity were illustrated by the first public meeting in connection with the war, held on 20 September 1899. Called by the Wilson faction, it was marked by 'stormy scenes—much controversy arising'.[130] An amendment was moved deprecating the fact that the meeting had been called and supporting the government in their peaceful efforts to secure rights for the Uitlanders. But this opposition was circumvented by a resolution which managed to express the sentiments of both factions.[131] Similarly, in March 1900, when a Cronwright-Schreiner visit was arranged, the *Independent* ensured that the invitation was widely known by printing a copy of a ticket for the meeting. The result was that the meeting was cancelled for fear of rioting.

Thus, after some further attempts to secure the acquiescence of the local Liberals in their anti-war agitation,[132] the Wilson faction retreated into their strongholds of Brightside and Holmfirth and created a local branch of the South African Conciliation Committee.[133]

Attempts were made to find some common ground between the two factions. But it proved impossible to obtain agreement on a unity resolution, involving, as it did, an expression of the positions of Campbell-Bannerman and Rosebery in relation to the leadership of the party. The result of these futile negotiations was almost inevitable. In April 1902, after the separation of the two previous years, a Liberal League was formed as a separate organization. Skinner, who had often acted as the sole Liberal agent, resigned to become agent to the League, and he refused to undertake unified party work for either parliamentary or municipal elections.[134]

The practical effects of the split were well illustrated by the 1900 General Election in Brightside. Skinner refused to act as

[129] *Ibid.*, Sheffield Politics Bundle, August-December 1901.
[130] *Ibid.*, Diary of Claude Moore, MD. 2467.
[131] *Ibid.*, MD. 2517, f. 1.
[132] A meeting was held in Eccleshall Liberal Club in October and another one planned for 10 November but this was later abandoned.
[133] Wilson Papers, MD. 2521, f. 10.
[134] *Ibid.*, Sheffield Politics Bundle.

an agent for Maddison, using ill-health as an excuse.[135] The isolation of the pro-Boers was illuminated: Claude Moore, Wilson's secretary, acted as agent. Perhaps more significant than this was the attitude of the Liberal newspaper. It had been made quite clear to Wilson that Derry intended to support Maddison 'reserving, however, the right to make his own position re war quite clear'.[136] On domestic policy the newspaper fully supported Maddison, but throughout the election period it continued to emphasize his anti-war opinions in a way which caused him to complain to Moore: 'If only Derry would cease that forced effort of his to attack the Tories and drop his half-apologetic style, confining what support they intend to give me to the non-editorial part of the paper, they might help us a little.'[137] Maddison was defeated in the election. The seat was not a safe Liberal constituency but the divisions within the party and the important effect that they had on the party machinery were all contributing factors.

Thus, the situation in Sheffield can be seen as a microcosm of the paralysis of the party as a whole. The pro-Boer efforts to use the Liberal Party as an organ of anti-war radicalism failed. But, more than this, they stultified the party as a whole and, in this sense, defeated their own ends. To conduct an anti-war agitation, a secure political base was essential. Because of the nature of the divisions within the Liberal Party and because their own efforts accentuated these divisions, they did not have, nor could they secure, this necessary base.

The failure of Radicalism was not, therefore, solely a matter of the irrelevance of peace during an era of imperialism. When the organs of protest are examined the scale of anti-war activity becomes impressive. None of the dissenting organizations was fitted to conduct a campaign designed to arouse the nation against the war. The South African Conciliation Committee was essentially a middle-class propaganda body which limited itself to the rational refutation of irrational arguments. It consciously restricted itself to shedding truth upon imperialist distortions. It failed to attract mass support because of this but also because it

---

[135] *Ibid.*, Hallamshire Politics Bundle.   [136] *Ibid.*, Brightside Politics Bundle.
[137] Maddison to Moore, 12 September 1900. In Vol. 1 of newspaper cuttings compiled by Moore on Brightside elections.

had no intention of becoming a mass political force. Its Fabian tactics revealed its limitations and also its political unrealism. The Stop-the-War Committee was, in a sense, more realistic. It recognized, drawing from the experience of 1877–9, that agitation to be successful must reach and be sustained by mass support. But this was as far as its realism went. It failed to recognize that agitation must also be 'moderate' in that it must encompass as many shades of belief and opinion as possible. This mistake was, perhaps, illustrated by its close alliance with the SDF which continued to be devoid of any large-scale popular following. Although the creation of small groups of enthusiasts all over the country was essential, it could help little if these were men and organizations who had patently illustrated their lack of popular backing. The extremism of the committee was its greatest handicap.

Further, the Liberal Party was hopelessly divided and, thanks to the personalities and issues, could not conduct any sort of 'new Midlothian'. The very nature of the divisions precluded any sort of unified policy arising while the war continued. The pro-Boers found, as Gladstone had found, that they could not force the Liberal Party to go in the direction in which they wanted it to go. Unlike the late 1870s, however, there was no Gladstone to rescue them.

This was important. For the moral issues raised by the war were issues which could have been exploited to the full by an experienced and popular figure like Gladstone. The failure to rouse the nation's 'moral conscience' was as much a failure of men. The leaders of the anti-war agitation, such as Courtney and Stead, were disqualified by their own personalities. Occasionally elements of later oratorical power can be seen in Lloyd George. But he was too young and, until the war, virtually unknown. The Gladstonian formula of uniting electorally the working-class and the middle-class Nonconformist conscience might have worked in 1900. What it really meant was that there was a lack of leadership which possessed a sufficiently wide and popular appeal. Keir Hardie recognized this. He wrote to Hodgson Pratt:[138]

[138] Hardie to Pratt, n.d. Quoted by Pratt at Annual Meeting of Club and Institute Union, 30 May 1900. See *Annual Report of Club and Institute Union 1900* (London, 1901), p. 92.

The working people do not think and have lost the power of asserting themselves in politics, have blindly followed leaders who found most favour with the aristocratic or moneyed classes. When they found nearly all those condoning the war they followed their lead. There has been no voice at Hawarden.

This was echoed by an editorial in *Club Life*, the journal of the Working Men's Club movement where Bradlaugh was the hero, written following the attempted break-up of an anti-war meeting at the Queen's Hall:[139]

It is at a time like this that we miss the power and influence of Brad-laugh, who would have made short work of the Stock Exchange bullies, or their friends the raw and ill-educated medical students . . . had he been alive few would have attempted to assault and maltreat a man who wished to speak his mind.

This then, was the second feature necessary to any successful political agitation which was absent from the situation. If the pro-Boers failed to convert the Liberal Party—at a national and a local level—to their policy then there was nothing else they could do. They had no political figure around whom they could centre, and, unlike Gladstone in 1877, they had no extra-parliamentary base from which to conduct their operations.

[139] *Club Life*, 22 June 1901, p. 9.

II

◇◇◇

Working-Class Attitudes
and Institutions

◇◇◇

I F the anti-war movement failed to appeal to working men because of its own intrinsic deficiencies, this does not imply that the issue of the war did not command the same attention and debate within working-class society that it did within the other classes of the nation. It was, without doubt, the issue of the day. Working-class newspapers, like the *Morning Leader* and *Reynolds News*, devoted as much of their space to the course of the war as did the *Daily Mail* or *The Times*. Of course, their emphasis was different. The working-class press was, on the whole, anti-war; it emphasized the casualties and printed many letters from soldiers which recounted in full the sufferings of the ordinary Tommy and the incompetence of the officers. Thus, wherever working men gathered, the topic could hardly be avoided. Awareness of this is tantalizing for the historian. The present-day sociologist interested in working-class attitudes is well equipped to investigate his subject. He needs only a tape recorder and an entrée into the confined circle of a working-class pub, and he can gather invaluable source material for the future historian. Our task is not so easy. We have to rely for our evidence upon the impressionistic printed word which reported the limited atmosphere of a lecture or public meeting within a working-class institution. The available evidence for determining the dominant characteristics of expressed working-class attitudes to the war is, of course, very scanty. And it is often uncertain just whose opinion is being recorded. Similarly, lack of evidence has prevented the development of an in-depth and

46

detailed profile of one or several representative working men's attitudes toward the war. What results is, therefore, subject to the severe limitations of the source material and methodology. Nevertheless, if these limitations are accepted, it is possible for us to identify some broad generalizations. That these generalizations have some validity is strengthened by the fact that they will be seen to be part of a pattern confirmed elsewhere in this study.

As has been noted earlier, virtually the only source that we possess for determining working-class attitudes is the working-class institution. Pride of place is given to the working men's club as our channel into working-class society, but reference is also made to Trades Councils and the working men's colleges where they are relevant to the discussion. The Club Movement was chosen because of its basically non-sectarian nature and because it reached a large number of working men. By 1903, about 900 clubs and 321,000 members were affiliated to the Club and Institute Union which was the central governing and coordinating organ of the movement. The clubs were, in origin, just one of many social-reforming institutions founded by the middle classes for the working classes in the middle of the nineteenth century. But unlike most other examples of this kind of social-reforming philanthropy they had retained their working-class character both in composition and in function. A few scattered examples will enable us to illustrate the working-class membership of the clubs. Thus, in 1866, the Wednesday Club was composed 'almost exclusively of bona-fide weekly wage operatives, the only person a little above that rank . . . being a clerk'. In the same year, the committee of Camden Town Working Men's Club was composed of three journeyman upholsterers, two piano-makers, three printers, a painter, tin-plate worker, tailor and seven other miscellaneous trades. The artisan class of the men who attended the clubs did not change throughout the century. In 1899, the Secretary of Boro' of Hackney Club revealed that the members reflected the dominant trades of the area; shoe-makers, cabinet-makers and woodworkers made up the majority of the membership.[1]

The clubs' success in attracting working men was, in part, a result of the conscious choice of the founders of the movement

---

[1] See the *Working Man*, 10, 17 March 1866, p. 151 and p. 174; *Club Life*, 29 April 1899, p. 1.

not to proselytize temperance and Christianity. The clubs were intended to provide alternative centres of social recreation to the pubs but were to do so by creating a different environment from them: an environment that was pleasant and comfortable, which provided all the necessary conditions of social intercourse, including alcohol, but where the 'temptations' and evils of the bar would be absent. There would, for example, be no pressure on working men to buy and drink 'for the good of the house'. Thus, the clubs were one of the few philanthropic efforts that were really accepted by the working men and were to become an integral part of the working-class society. Within the clubs there was a myriad of working-class activity. Designed to humanize the working men through the presence of a good environment, it was originally intended that formal education facilities would also be provided. Although this aspiration was seldom to be realized, the clubs were a useful meeting place for the politically and socially conscious working men and lectures of political and social interest were common. The issues of the day were always debated in the clubs. From these debates and lectures, recognizing the limitations mentioned above, the basic characteristics of working-class attitudes emerge.

There is, therefore, ample justification for a concentration on this particular movement. Unlike the historically more familiar ILP and SDF, it was a mass movement, with no political programme to propagate. Discussion and debate of issues was, therefore, not within any particular political framework. Nor was it something induced from a central committee, as was often the case with local ILP activities. Thus, the clubs can reveal attitudes and reactions that were typical of the working man better than most other working-class institutions can do.

It must be recognized, of course, that the movement did have an ideology: an ideology bestowed upon it by the founders of the clubs in the 1860s. The principles of the movement were fairly straightforward. It was designed to help create a temperate, moderate, working class interested in education and devoted to class mutuality. It was consciously designed as an agency of social control. These principles were impressed upon the movement by the constant periodical and pamphlet propaganda of its middle-class originators and by the policies of the Club and Institute Union until it underwent a change in 1884. Thus, it should be borne in mind that the attitudes expressed through the clubs were possibly influenced by the ideals and principles of the Club Movement. More important, however, the conflicts which were inherent in the differing functions of the clubs played an important part in determining the limits of discussion. The tensions between the educational, social and political aspects of the clubs will be seen to have influenced the nature of political activism and discussion in the clubs at this particular time. Thus, the ideals and principles of the movement and the tensions within it are all relevant to what the clubs reveal about working-class attitudes and reactions towards imperialism.

The origins of the Club Movement were a compound of middle-class philanthropy, an attempt to cure the intemperance and barbarism of working-class life, and a desire to elevate the intellectual achievement of the working men by providing 'healthy' recreational facilities until the state was reached when [2]

a large majority of the members of all social and political clubs prefer lectures, conversation, reading, recitations, and good music in their clubs on Sundays, to the empty headed nonsense and noise, however 'refreshing' the latter amusements may now be.

The man who wrote these words, the Reverend Henry Solly, founded the Club and Institute Union in 1862 and was the most significant figure in the early days of the movement's history. He had been inspired to create the Club Movement by the examples of William Lovett,[3] Frederick Robertson,[4] W. T. Marriott[5] and F. D. Maurice.[6]

However, it had taken Solly twenty years of association and

[2] *Our Magazine*, December 1891, p. 279.
[3] See Henry Solly, *James Woodford, Carpenter and Chartist* (London, 1881), II, p. 35, where Lovett is praised as an archetypal 'sensible' working man: 'He knew just what he wanted and what we working men wanted.'
[4] Henry Solly, *These Eighty Years* (London, 1893), II, p. 50, where he writes: 'Mr. Robertson's movement . . . brought the formation of Workmen's Institutes within the sphere of practical social politics all over the Kingdom.'
[5] Marriott was propagating the necessity of clubs in Manchester in the 1850s. See William Thackeray Marriott, *Some Real Wants and Some Legitimate Claims of the Working Classes* (London, 1860).
[6] Henry Solly, *Working Men's Social Clubs and Educational Institutes* (1st ed., London, 1867), p. 5, where he writes a dedicatory letter to Maurice: 'I saw in your endeavours what I had been groping after for years, and what supplied, in the work which I had long been trying to do myself, precisely those links without which it must always have been wretchedly inefficient and incomplete.'

contact with working men before he had been able to settle on the correct formula for establishing successful clubs. There had been experiments in working men's clubs at least since 1848 when Robertson of Brighton had played an important part in founding an institute for the working men of the town. Throughout the 1850s others had realized that if working men were to be weaned away from the pub an attractive alternative had to be offered. Clubs were established by social philanthropists like Mrs Bayly and Adeline Cooper whose separate institutions both propagated Christianity in an attempt to improve the conditions of working-class existence.[7] Mrs Bayly's analysis of working-class problems was typical of the presumptions that created the Club Movement. Drink was at one and the same time both a symptom and a cause of working-class distress. In common with the other initiators of the clubs, Mrs Bayly felt it to be the key problem. She calculated that one-fifth of the working man's weekly wage was spent on alcohol and that this was the margin between a healthy, sufficient life with a 'clean, neat home' and the squalor that characterized so many working-class residences.[8] She believed that working men behaved thus foolishly because they lacked the willpower and moral values to resist the temptations and sensual pleasures of beer. A change of character and life-style was necessary. For Mrs Bayly, the solution was to inculcate into the working man the moral and spiritual values of Christianity which would provide him with sufficient strength to resist the evils of drink.

To others, however, changing the character and life-style of the working man was not so easy. The inconvenient fact was that any attempt to christianize the working man usually met with a justified sullen resistance. A way had to be found which would have the same effect but which would not seem to be an overt attempt to impose a different and alien value system on working-class society. It was Henry Solly who successfully realized the potential of the clubs as agencies of social reform. And with the help of several prominent aristocrats and middle-class men he formed the Club and Institute Union with the

[7] For Mrs Bayly's Workmen's Hall in Kensington Potteries see Mrs Bayly, *Long Evenings and What to do in Them* (London, 1874), pp. 26–7. For Adeline Cooper's Westminster Working Men's Club see *Occasional Papers of the Working Men's Club and Institute Union* (London, 1863), No. 1, p. 5.

[8] Mrs Bayly, *Workmen and their Difficulties* (London, 1861), pp. 137–43.

object of propagating the idea of clubs and providing legal and moral advice to those trying to establish them. The big difference between the clubs as they emerged under Solly and those of the earlier proponents was that Solly was concerned to provide an alternative to the pub only in so far as the club would be comfortable, clean, warm, and would be devoid of the habits and customs of the public house. He believed that the association of working men with gentlemen who would visit the clubs, the better environment and the encouragement of middle- and upper-class patrons would all work to 'improve' the working-class mind and intellect. There was no need to apply a religious test. It was because of the absence of an overtly uplifting purpose that Solly was successful where others had failed. Although at first the Union discouraged the sale of beer in its clubs, by 1867 this policy was reversed—the better environment of the club, it was believed, would prevent drunkenness—and the clubs were assured of attracting large numbers of working men.

Henry Solly was a restlessly autocratic, hypersensitive individual. He found it almost impossible to work in harness with others. The only institution in which he retained an executive position for any length of time was the Artisan's Institute; and it is significant that it was the only organization over which he had absolute control. He had insisted upon this 'in consequence of seeing how all my other attempts had been taken out of my hands . . . to manage them . . . not according to my designs'.[9] Convinced of his own rectitude and confident that he alone knew what was wanted in any given situation, he would ride roughshod over the sensibilities of his colleagues and would then complain of being 'misunderstood' and of being ill-treated. The occasion of his final break with the Club and Institute Union in 1878 was illustrative of his arrogant and high-handed treatment of an organization which he considered his own but which refused to be subjected to his whim.

He had received information that the practice of tied clubs was becoming very widespread in London and was causing the inevitable abuses of brewers' control.[10] Solly, instead of going

[9] Solly, *These Eighty Years, op. cit.*, pp. 436, 443. The Institute was a combination of a club and a technical institute. For its early history see Solly Collection, Vol. 12, B. 11. And C. T. Millis, *Technical Education* (London, 1925), Ch. VI.

[10] Solly to Chairman of CIU Council, 23 April 1878, Solly Collection, Vol. 16, M.409.

straight to the Council of the Union with this problem, laid his allegations before the Earl of Shaftesbury and Samuel Morley— both Vice-Presidents of the Union—and, worst of all, before the Board of Inland Revenue, which administered the licensing laws. Two days after this he did inform Hodgson Pratt—then one of the Secretaries—of what he had done.

The Council was annoyed because of 'your course of action in bringing the matter before Lord Shaftesbury, Mr Morley and the Board without consulting your colleagues or giving them any intimation that you intended to do so'.[11] The next day a special Council meeting passed a resolution which stated that 'statements of an injudicious character' had been made but that 'no definite charge has been made and the Council consider they have no information to act upon'. A further resolution was passed which expressed the hope that Solly would apologize for the course of action he had adopted.[12] Heated words were spoken. Many of the Council who, like Thomas Paterson, were long-standing opponents of Solly, felt that he had deliberately tried to damage the movement. He, in his turn, felt that he had been ill treated because it had not been made sufficiently clear that he had, at the first opportunity, laid the matter before Hodgson Pratt and had given his consent to its being brought before the Executive Committee.[13] He therefore intimated his intention not to stand for re-election to the Council. But the mantle of a martyr seemed to fit comfortably upon his shoulders. He wrote to Shaftesbury in 1878 that 'some good appears to have been done by the move I made in the matter. . . . Martyr-dom is often useful, though . . . I shall always feel that I was treated by the Council . . . unfairly.'[14]

Solly's whole connection with the Union was short and stormy. He was Secretary from 1862–7 and again from 1871–2. And his failure to work well with men like Hodgson Pratt and Thomas Paterson was largely due to his personality. He had a great personal regard for Pratt, but felt that he did not make sufficient effort to understand him:[15]

---

[11] Pratt to Solly, 3 April 1878, *ibid.*, M. 403.
[12] Copy of resolution of Council meeting, 4 April 1878, *ibid.*, M. 407.
[13] Solly to Chairman CIU Council, 23 April 1878, *ibid.*, M. 410.
[14] Solly to Earl of Shaftesbury, 4 July 1878, *ibid.*, M. 313–14.
[15] Solly to Lord Lyttleton, 1 March 1872, *ibid.*, M. 313–14.

What I complain of is that instead of helping me to correct mistakes and faults and to some extent bearing with them for the sake of counter-balancing qualities, and for the regard with which I had treated him, he sanctioned . . . conduct on the part of those who wished to get rid of me that was both unjust and dishonourable.

It is probable that the main fault was on Solly's side. He was a 'hard working idealist . . . fond of his own authority',[16] who did not suffer fools gladly and who exhibited a complete lack of tact and judgment. James Hole, a member of the Council, wrote a frank, biting letter which illustrates Solly's complete inability to work with other people. Hole wrote referring to some fracas in a Council meeting:[17]

If you had followed my advice and kept quiet, the scene that followed would have been avoided. . . . You have yet to learn the value of *silence*. If Mr A. Hills remarks were worth nothing and in the matter of subscriptions absurd, why could you not trust us to find that out? You must think that we are all fools and that we could not come to right conclusions unless you showed us the way. You are without exception the most deficient in tact, that I ever saw in a man in a public capacity dealing with committees.

Thus, the failure of Solly was essentially a personality failure and the arguments within the Union in the early years were a reflection of this. They centred around finance and propaganda. Solly's restless personality and unbounded enthusiasm delighted at the thought of spreading the word about the clubs throughout the country and much of his time was spent on these travels and meetings, especially after 1866 when he became Travelling Secretary. But other members of the Council, led by Hodgson Pratt and Thomas Paterson, were afraid of the dangers of the movement becoming over-extended and felt that the time had come to consolidate their gains. In 1866, it was decided that the Union would henceforth direct more attention to the strengthening of the existing clubs rather than promoting the formation of new ones.[18] It was rationalized that 'the organisation should for a while rest content with its position and develop itself from within . . . it should begin to awaken sentiments of self-reliance and self-support'.[19] Solly, who was always paranoid, felt that

[16] George Tremlett, *The First Century* (London, 1962), p. 6.
[17] James Hole to Solly, 5 July 1872, Solly Collection, Vol. 16, M. 338-9.
[18] B. T. Hall, *Our Fifty Years* (London, 1912), p. 30.   [19] *Ibid.*, p. 33.

this move had been directed at him and he resigned in the following year. There was also the problem of money. Solly was not a wealthy man and felt that he should receive adequate remuneration which the Union could ill afford. He felt sure that the reluctance to grant him £150 per year plus his travelling expenses as a salary for the post of Travelling Secretary was motivated by personal animosity. This animosity came primarily from Thomas Paterson, the self-educated working man who was a member of the Union Council. It was Paterson's opposition and the antagonism of certain other members of the Council that forced Solly's resignation in 1868 and which prevented a successful reunion in 1871–2 when Solly, for a short time, formed a rival to the Club and Institute Union.[20] He remained a member of the Council until 1878 and was always active in the movement, but never again held a position of authority.

The most persistent problem that the Union faced, however, was not Solly: it was finance. The Club and Institute Union was typical of Victorian social-reforming philanthropy in that it was dominated and controlled by patrons from the upper and middle classes. The role of the 'gentleman' was an important one both at the local level and in the national organization. Their function was to guide the working men in the arts of committee work and business affairs, and to devote time and effort talking to and educating the club men. From the very beginnings of the movement it was regarded as essential that the clubs should be a joint effort between working men and the wealthier classes. Robertson at Brighton had hoped that the Brighton Working Man's Institute would induce more respect between the lower classes and the clergy and soon concluded that middle-class exclusion from the running of the institution was bad because it did nothing to improve the 'vicious state of relationship between class and class which is . . . the worst evil in our social life'.[21] The role of the gentleman was symbolic of the promotion of class mutuality that was seen as such a vital part of club work. There are many instances that could be used to illustrate this but two will

[20] Solly to Lord Lichfield, 27 June 1868, Solly Collection, Vol. 16, M. 193–200. For the reconciliation attempt and the rival organization, the Social Working Men's Club Association, see M. 260–87.
[21] Stopford Brooke, *Life and Letters of Frederick W. Robertson* (London, 1865), p. 238.

suffice. Hodgson Pratt who made a tour of the clubs in 1872, commented approvingly on one club which had circumvented the usual financial and organizational difficulties of a newly founded club by enlisting the aid of a 'man of superior education and position, [who . . .] was willing to meet the workmen on equal terms, giving them the benefit of his larger experience and information'. The real importance of this kind of co-operation was that it promoted 'that conciliation of the classes which the nation so deeply needs'.[22] Similarly in 1883 when the middle- and upper-class control of the movement was under attack and was about to be swept away, an editorial in the *Club and Institute Journal* warned[23]

The Union is in no respect a class institution, we have quite enough of them already. One of the best features of Union work . . . lies in the fact that it brings people of different grades and classes together, and helps to remove the idiotic and wicked class prejudices which are the bane and curse of society.

There was, however, a further, more practical reason why the respectable classes should be associated with the movement: the need for money. The smooth functioning of the Union depended on the generosity of men like Samuel Morley, James Hole and Richard Tangye. And this dependence upon donations was reflected in the fact that those who ran the Club and Institute Union until 1884 were those with the time and money to spare. But a reliance upon subscriptions from well-wishers was an insecure basis upon which to build a nation-wide movement and by the late 1870s the Union was caught in an ever-increasing deficit which various palliative measures, such as discontinuing the *Journal*, did nothing to resolve. This dependence upon sub-scriptions was also reflective of the patronizing character of the movement and of the control which was exercised over the Union and the clubs by wealthy philanthropists. Ultimate control of individual clubs was usually in the hands of Trustees who had raised the original capital for their foundation and although this control was seldom used in an arbitrary way, the fact remained that it was the Trustees who determined the nature and limits of the club's activity. It was in the government of the

---

[22] Hodgson Pratt, *Notes on a Tour among the Clubs* (London, 1872), p. 5.
[23] *Club and Institute Journal*, 23 November 1883, p. 69.

Union, however, that this control was most evident. The clubs had little voice in its deliberations: there were only ten representative members out of a total of forty-six on the Council of the Union, and these had only been obtained as a result of unrelenting pressure from the London clubs. Thus the questions of patronage and financial stability were very closely linked and were eventually to be resolved together.

From the mid-seventies demands for an increased club representation on the Council grew in strength. The Union met these demands with a series of palliatives which did little to solve the basic dissatisfaction with patronage that the working men felt.[24] It was during the early eighties, however, that the problem attained serious proportions. A conference in 1880 saw a resolution from the London club delegates urging the desirability of making 'the Union truly representative of the Clubs', and of maintaining the Union by fees from the clubs instead of from outside subscribers.[25] The Union reacted to these demands as if the problem was merely one of a failure of communication rather than a desire by the clubs to take control of the movement and suggested a series of measures which were designed to establish a closer and better understanding between the middle-class men of the Union and the working men of the clubs.

The prominent part played by the London clubs in these early initiatives was maintained in a series of conferences in 1883–4 which resulted in a change in the government of the Union, a secure financial basis being established and in the casting off of middle- and upper-class patronage. The Union innocently called a conference to discuss ways in which communication between the clubs and the Council could be improved. But they were more concerned at this time with the difficulties of ensuring that the wishes of the provincial clubs were fully represented.[26] From the very beginning, however, it was clear that the discussion was not going to be limited to the subjects that the Union had defined as crucial. A week before the conference was due to open

[24] The London Delegate Council was a result of this dissatisfaction. It was created in 1871 as the representative but powerless organ of the London clubs and intended as a means by which the Union could determine club opinion on particular issues.

[25] *House and Home*, 21 August 1880, p. 91.

[26] See Hall, *op. cit.*, p. 83; *Club and Institute Journal*, 28 September 1883, p. 41; 31 August 1883, p. 33.

the *Club and Institute Journal* noted that 'there seems to be a feeling, which we must admit to be well-founded, that the Clubs have not sufficient voice in the management of the Union affairs'.[27] The first session of the conference, on 10 November 1883, confirmed the suspicion that club men were anxious to make some far-reaching changes. Three papers were read, none of which attacked the problem of club representation and control of the movement. A paper by Solly illustrated how out of touch the 'establishment' were. He had recommended reviving the post of Travelling Secretary, the position that he had held so ingloriously twenty years before. Solutions such as this were clearly irrelevant to the needs of the Union in the mid-eighties. The ensuing discussion ignored the subjects and recommendations of the papers and concentrated on the problem of patronage. Mr Fuller of London Patriotic Club sounded the warning tocsin when he argued that 'outside subscriptions should cease, they were demoralising'. Mr Owen of Haverstock Hill Working Men's Club asserted that 'the working men have a right to work out their own aims'. The sentiment of the conference was quite clearly with these arguments and a resolution was carried which embodied the demands of the reformers and established a committee to draw up a scheme to implement its principles.[28]

These demands did not go unchallenged by the Union officials, and the committee, which held four meetings throughout January 1884, proved unable to recommend a unanimous report. As early as 23 November 1883, when the extent of the reformers' demands were apparent, the *Journal* had published a long editorial attacking the protest against patronage as preaching the message of class warfare. Henry Solly, at the first committee meeting, felt that 'there was no doubt that by doing what was proposed we should alienate our outside subscribers, who would leave unless they saw that they were wanted'.[29] That this was exactly the point does not seem to have penetrated Solly's consciousness. The officials of the Union used every weapon at their disposal to discredit and cripple the reform movement. Hodgson Pratt wrote many articles against it in the name of class mutuality; the *Journal* berated those who attacked

---

[27] *Club and Institute Journal*, 26 October 1883, p. 53.
[28] *Ibid.*, 16 November 1883 (special conference number), p. 2.
[29] *Ibid.*, 18 January 1884, p. 12.

the Council as acting solely in the interests of the London clubs. It claimed that to make the Union representative would mean to ensure the predominance of the clubs of the metropolis over those of the provinces and a consequent decline in its 'power of uniting all the clubs in the country in common action'.[30]

It was certainly true that the London clubs were the prime movers in the reform initiative. Mark Judge and Fletcher Pape, both of the St James and Soho Club,[31] were the leaders within the committee of the demand for the democratization of the Union. They opposed the majority report presented by the Chairman, W. H. Sands, which advocated that, for all practical purposes, one-half of the Council seats would be reserved for the subscriber patrons. Judge moved the adoption of the minority report which recommended that the Council be made fully representative. Deadlock ensued with the Union officials, such as Nash the Secretary General, opposing the implementation of this report because it would alienate outside subscribers. It soon became apparent, however, that the delegates to the conference were determined on accepting the minority report and the Union acceded to their demands. How or why is not evident from the *Journal* (the only account we have for this whole episode) for, although at a subsequent meeting called to settle details, procedural amendments were moved in a last attempt to stop the reform from going through, in the event the minority report was accepted unanimously.[32]

The details of the change in the constitution are unimportant; its practical results were to induce the 'nobles' to leave, to make the Council truly representative of the clubs, and to ensure the financial independence of the Union.[33] A remarkable transformation can be seen after 1884 in the proportion of total income received from the clubs.

Financially, the Union was now secure and it could continue its

[30] *Ibid.*, p. 11. That the clubs had never been united in 'common action' seems to have escaped the *Journal*.

[31] This was one of the oldest of the London clubs having been founded in 1862. It was also unusual because it was one of the few clubs which had never depended upon middle-class patronage.

[32] *Club and Institute Journal, op. cit.*, p. 12. See also 1 February, 10 March, 11 April editions for the reports of the committee's work.

[33] For this see *ibid.*, 1 February 1885, pp. 22–3; Hall, *op. cit.*, p. 85. A constitutional change abolished the office of Vice-President in 1886 and most of the nobles left the movement at this time.

work of propagating the ideals of the movement in complete
confidence. But what were those ideals and how successfully
were they attained?

TABLE 1

SOURCE OF CLUB AND INSTITUTE UNION'S INCOME 1881–90[34]

Year	£ from clubs	£ from subscribers	% from clubs
1881	201	334	37·5
1882	216	340	38·5
1883	241	331	41·2
1884	329	388	45·8
1885	459	279	62·2
1886	558	232	70·6
1887	682	215	76·3
1888	782	185	80·9
1889	1,063	178	85·7
1890	1,124	135	89·3

There were those like Charles Booth who were, by the end of
the century, disillusioned with the movement's progress.[35]
Booth's strictures on the clubs in his *Final Volume* are almost
certainly exaggerated, due to his concentration on two sets of
interested witnesses: the clergy and the police. Perhaps more
surprisingly, Cole and Postgate in their book *The Common
People 1746–1946*, reflecting that streak of puritanism which
runs through Labour politics and history, write of the clubs:[36]

It is a sign of the extreme narrowness and monotony to which working
class life had been reduced in the vast Victorian slum cities that the
formation of the bare and beery Working Men's club that still in some
places exist today [sic] should have been regarded as a major event.

[34] Table adapted from Hall, *op. cit.*, pp. 78, 105.
[35] Charles Booth, *Life and Labour in London* (2nd ed., London, 1902–3), 1st
Series, I, pp. 97–8; Final Volume, pp. 76–9. It is interesting to compare the
favourable report in the first volume with the unfavourable one in the last volume
of the work. In the former he wrote: 'Like cooperation and like socialism, though
in a less pronounced way, the movement is a propaganda with its faith and hopes,
its literature and its leaders . . . to many . . . club-life is an education.' In the latter
he has swung over in favour of middle-class superintendence quoting witnesses as
asserting: 'Working men are not capable of supplying the control needed.'
[36] G. D. H. Cole and Raymond Postgate, *The Common People 1746–1946* (2nd
ed., London, 1960), pp. 378–9.

In fact, most working men's clubs were neither bare, nor were they beery.[37] For the historian of the working classes they should be a rewarding institution to study. They represent the convergence of three institutional functions which were characteristic of middle-class philanthropy in the nineteenth century: the political, the social and the educational. Only in the clubs was it possible for these activities to be carried on concurrently and while there can be little doubt that the social function was dominant, the other two cannot and should not be ignored. Here, we shall deal briefly with the social and educational ideals that motivated the movement, evaluate their success and pay greater attention to the problem of political activity within the clubs.

In 1863, Solly wrote that 'the first want of working men . . . is that they should be gradually roused to a consciousness of the possession of the higher faculties of their nature, and of the duty of using them'.[38] He was horrified by the way in which the working man in modern society existed in a state of intellectual and moral degradation. Not all of the evils of working-class society were due to bad housing and working conditions. Much of the responsibility for their depressed conditions lay in the crudity of their social and political consciousness and the 'narrow and incomplete view many of them take of various questions'. Education, in the widest sense of the term, was the key to moral and intellectual reform; it was the 'light which enables men to understand *the true position* and relation of things'.[39] And one of the purposes of clubs was to develop an interest in education and culture, not in a formal manner but by the patient application of a 'friend' who would talk to working men and arouse their minds from the mental stupor in which they existed. The use of the 'inclined plane' was to be the mechanism of achievement and also the main point of difference with other reforming institutions, such as the Mechanics Institutes, which had often assumed too great a maturity on the

---

[37] Booth, *op. cit.*, 1st Series, I, p. 98, for the description of a very well-furnished club in Bethnal Green. And also Henry Mayhew, *Report Concerning Hours of Closing among Unlicensed Victualling Establishments open for Unrestricted Sale of Beer, Wine, and Spirits at certain so-called Working Men's Clubs* (London, 1872?).

[38] Henry Solly, *Working Men: A Glance at some of their Wants* (London, 1863), p. 4.

[39] Solly in the *Working Man*, 13 January 1866, p. 24.

part of the people for whom they were designed. Solly explained that[40]

You must make your machinery for elevating the people go right down to their actual condition, and then gradually apply whatever motive power you possess, to roll the burden 'up higher' . . . to heights which it would have been impossible to gain if you attempt to reach them all at once.

It was hoped that this method would produce 'scholars' who would then be equipped to tackle the more systematic education which was supplied by the Mechanics Institutes. It was also believed that colleges could eventually grow out of the clubs: 'If . . . the club be a living organism . . . it will infallibly grow, until . . . it develops into a college, while retaining its social club elements.'[41]

Such optimistic aims were, of course, doomed to disappointment. No club ever developed into anything approaching a 'college', although a few, such as Wisbech Working Men's Club, were culturally active.[42] Nor could the clubs realistically be expected to grow in this direction. B. T. Hall, writing of the 1880s, pinpointed the cause of the failure of educative activity as being 'the unwillingness of workmen to receive what was offered . . . there being no conscious need of education'.[43] At Tower Hamlets Radical Club, Frederick Rogers became disillusioned with the possibilities of education through the movement: 'When one morning, in the midst of a lecture on Shakespeare, I was asked to make a break to let the man come round with the beer, I knew my work at the clubs was drawing to an end.'[44] It was, of course, the wrong approach. Working men did not wish to suffer long discourses on subjects which were irrelevant to everyday life, and by the end of the century the idea of the lecture was under attack by those who wished to return to Solly's original conception of conversation by a cultured 'friend'.[45] It was recognized that the initial hopes that the clubs would develop into centres for technical training and liberal

[40] Solly, *These Eighty Years, op. cit.,* p. 51.
[41] Solly, *Working Men's Social Clubs and Educational Institutes, op. cit.,* p. 108.
[42] See F. J. Gardiner, *The Fiftieth Birthday of a Model Institute* (Wisbech, 1914). It should be noted, however, that this club was firmly controlled by the Peckover family.   [43] Hall, *op. cit.,* pp. 96–7.   [44] Rogers, *op. cit.,* p. 74.
[45] See S. Danziger, 'Clubs and Education', *Working Men's Club and Institute Annual Report for 1898* (London, 1899), p. 33.

studies would not be realized. Nor was there such a need for them once the polytechnics had been established.

There were exceptions. Frederick Rogers had noted, in the 1870s, the success of the Boro' of Hackney Working Men's Club in uniting 'intellectual training with amusements'.[46] In some clubs the libraries were well used, but principally for fiction. The librarian of Mildmay Club found that there was little interest until he started stocking novels and noted that 'directly a piece is played at the theatre, such as *The Only Way*, there comes a demand for *A Tale of Two Cities*'.[47] There were, in 1902, 500 clubs with libraries stocking a total of 187,000 books and this was in addition to the book boxes circulating from the Union.[48] Although information is scanty on the type of lecture and theatre production provided, a survey of the years 1899–1902 showed that over 300 lectures were listed as having been delivered, and this only takes into consideration those few clubs, primarily in London, that bothered to send in reports. The topics were wide-ranging: from Vivisection to Land Nationalization. Most theatre productions seem to have been the two- or three-act melodrama of the H. J. Byron variety. Often they were topical: a popular piece in 1900 was entitled *Jameson's Ride*. There is some evidence that the clubs were not so barren of culture as contemporary witnesses imply. In November 1900, the Mildmay Club staged a production of *Macbeth* which was reviewed by Charles Jones of *Club Life*. He noted that although the audience of 800 missed much of the pathos and meaning of the play, especially the complex character of Macbeth, 'it was impossible to see the hundreds of unrelaxed, almost grimly attentive, visages without being impressed'.[49]

Nevertheless, there can be little doubt that the main attraction of the clubs was their social function. Booth pointed out that although

the leaders may consciously realise the higher ideals of the movement . . . the rank and file are not above the average of their class, and usually join clubs with no higher motives than those which influence

[46] Rogers, *op. cit.*, p. 63. Interestingly enough, by 1901 this club was cited in *Club Life* as having a bad record of club work, the 'music-hall element' being too strong. See *Club Life*, 20 April 1901, p. 16.
[47] *Club Life*, 9 December 1899, p. 1.
[48] Club and Institute Union *Annual Report*, 1902, Table 1.
[49] *Club Life*, 3 November 1900, p. 2.

the clubgoer of any class, or would otherwise take them to the public house.

Solly explained that: 'The *main primary* feature of the club was to be social intercourse and recreation.'[50] But even here the 'uplifting' element was not ignored; for the object of the clubs was to provide a comfortable and relaxing atmosphere free from the pressures and temptations of the public house. The club atmosphere and 'club spirit', with its emphasis on mutual tolerance and discipline in the service of the club community, was reputed to have had a softening effect on many of the working classes.[51] Whatever spiritual benefits the clubs may have bestowed upon their members we cannot know. What is certain is that there was a continual conflict between the social and educational functions of the clubs. Frederick Rogers was partly right when he claimed that the workmen 'wanted amusement . . . and wanted it cheaply'.[52] They also wanted alcohol, and this was to provide much anguish in the early days among the patrons of the movement.

The expense of running a club was fairly substantial. While the initial capital to secure the building was usually provided by a wealthy benefactor and the furnishings often supplied by the members themselves, there was clearly a need for a constant source of revenue. The sale of alcohol was the most obvious way to ensure the solvency of a club and was also an assured means of attracting large numbers of working men.[53] In the early days, however, the Union had discouraged clubs from selling beer or spirits. Solly was adamantly opposed to it, fearing that the working men would be unable to resist imbibing to excess:[54]

I doubt very much if the men who would come merely because they could have beer would be likely to add anything to the general good of

[50] The *Working Man*, 27 January 1866, p. 51; Booth, *op. cit.*, p. 97.

[51] B. T. Hall (ed.), *Working Men's Social Clubs and Educational Institutes* (2nd ed., London, 1904), pp. 205–7.   [52] Rogers, *op. cit.*, p. 67.

[53] An example from the 1890s will illustrate the necessity of beer for the finances of a club. The North London Socialist Club tried to exist as a teetotal club unsupported, of course, from any patronage source, but was forced, in the spring of 1899, to admit the sale of intoxicating drinks. Immediately, the Stores Committee reported a profit of about ten shillings a week and by the summer of that year they were prosperous enough to buy a polyphone. North London Socialist Club Minute Book, Committee meetings, 18 April, 20 June, 1 August 1899.

[54] Solly in the *Working Man*, 16 June 1866, p. 378. See also Hall, *Our Fifty Years*, *op. cit.*, pp. 181–3.

the institute. . . . If the clubs are to be of any use at all, it will surely be by helping to raise the tastes and refine the habits of working men, and by supplying them with better amusements and excitements than they have hitherto depended upon.

Solly rapidly changed his mind, however, and one week after he had written the above, he conceded that 'where there is a dining or supper room in a club, I quite admit that those who wish it should have a glass of beer with their meals'.[55] This dramatic volte-face had been the result of two factors. In the first place, the Union's policy of dissuading the sale of alcohol had caused the failure of many clubs to attract sufficient numbers of working men—this was especially apparent in the iron districts of South Staffordshire. In the second place, there was the example of a club at Leicester which, ignoring the advice of its middle-class sponsors, had allowed the sale of beer in unrestricted quantities but which had experienced no cases of drunkenness.[56]

Solly was impressed with such a record but was still dubious until the results of a conference called at Oldbury made him realize[57]

what had not generally been realised by the original promoters of this movement, that there is a very large number of respectable working men who desire to have a pint of beer after a day's work . . . as much as a lady desires an afternoon cup of tea. . . . They wish for no more, but they will take no less.

By 1911, 96 per cent of all clubs supplied intoxicants and the few that were teetotal tended to be those run and superintended by wealthy individuals or by church organizations. They were generally concentrated in London and were organized into the Social Institutes Union and the Federation of Working Men's Social Clubs. It is noteworthy, however, that the latter organization was only financially solvent by virtue of an amalgamation with the Social Institutes Union which, although temperance by tradition and inclination, in 1910 allowed the sale of alcohol at the clubs it was establishing in the country districts.[58] When

[55] Solly in the *Working Man*, 23 June 1866, p. 390.
[56] *Occasional Papers of the Club and Institute Union*, No. 10 (London, June 1867), p. 8. Solly had met the President of this club sometime between 16 and 23 June 1866.   [57] See the *Working Man, loc. cit.*
[58] *Social Institutes Magazine*, September 1910, pp. 3–4; *Quarterly Newsheet of Federation of Working Men's Social Clubs*, 31 December 1914, p. 4; J. L. Paton, *John Brown Paton* (London, 1914), pp. 212–23. See Appendix I.

this working alliance ended with the dissolution of the Social Institutes Union, the Federation could only survive by drawing closer to the clubs dominated by religious bodies.[59]

If the sale of alcohol was the only realistic basis on which the clubs could exist, it was also the thin end of the wedge. For the club immediately became nearer to a public house than to a working men's college. Working men did not, and could not be expected, to join a club to be educated. They wanted the friendly, relaxed atmosphere and the facilities provided by the club which were absent at the public house.[60] This conflicted, however, with the idealism of the promoters of the movement who felt that too much emphasis was being given to this aspect of the club life. Exception was taken, in particular, to the problem of Sundays which Solly felt should be a day for[61]

refreshing and unfolding their higher desires, for nourishing those nobler and more spiritual faculties and desires which lead them to seek for a purer joy . . . than . . . the performance of comic dramatic entertainments, and the singing of comic songs.

Thus, there was a continuing and inherent conflict within the clubs between the ideals and purposes of the movement and its practical exigencies. The social-educational conflict was, however, only one facet of this. Of more relevance for our purposes was the manifestation of a similar conflict within the realm of the clubs and political activity.

The relation of the clubs to politics was never fully defined by the founders. Solly came nearest to it in his desire for the educative function of the clubs to combat 'party spirit' and 'irrational' political attitudes. Politics was perhaps the one area where the necessity of moderate and informed discussion was vital. He hoped that politics within the clubs would be discussed in an intellectual manner which would encourage the correct habits of thought by compelling[62]

men to reflect, to weigh arguments and evidence . . . stimulating a desire for information, and for acquiring the power of reasoning . . . to

[59] *Quarterly Newsheet of Federation of Working Men's Social Clubs, loc. cit.*
[60] The author's grandfather was an enthusiastic clubman who preferred the club to the public house because it provided a recreation room where games could be played. [61] *Our Magazine, op. cit.,* p. 275.
[62] Henry Solly, *Party Politics and Political Education* (London, 1879), p. 11. See also his *Working Men's Social Clubs and Educational Institutes, op. cit.,* p. 133 where he is adamant against political propaganda in the clubs.

apply the knowledge and convictions gained in the discussion meeting . . . to the great political questions of the day. Thus, the electors will begin to understand and act upon their perception of the true condition of the national well being and progress.

Of course, this was not to be the way politics were treated in the clubs. Typically, they became centres of working-class Liberal-Radicalism, and usually provided forums for Liberal candidates and organizational facilities at General Elections. They do not seem, however, to have applied a political test of membership. But the amount of political activity in the clubs was not consistent and the recurrent theme in club literature from 1890 onwards is that of the decline in political interest and activity compared with the 1880s. Notable achievements in the 1880s had included the organization of a meeting in 1884 when 80,000 had attended to vote in favour of the abolition of the House of Lords; and in 1887, when there had been the monster coercion protest meeting in Trafalgar Square. Many regretted that this activity was not permanent and that the clubs seemed to abandon political activity for social recreation.

The personal political beliefs of the founders and organizers of the movement were usually some form of Radicalism. Hodgson Pratt, for example, was a member of the International Arbitration and Peace Association and an archetypal advanced Liberal, as his presidential addresses to the Union in 1900 and 1901 indicate. His opposition to the Boer War (he was a member of the Transvaal Committee) was coupled with a strong demand for social reform and in particular, land reform, with its co-adjunct the reform of the House of Lords.[63] B. T. Hall was a member of the Fabian Society and Chairman of Deptford Labour Association; R. A. Cuereul, a prominent Council member in the late 1880s, was a republican Radical who later modified sufficiently to become the Liberal agent at Torquay.

In general, the Union as an organization steered clear of politics. The Boer War, arousing the feelings that it did, induced Pratt to raise the issue at the Annual Meeting in 1900 but he was opposed for bringing politics into the organization. From 1895–6, the Union contributed twenty-five shillings per month to the John Burns Wages Fund.[64] Delegates from the London

[63] Club and Institute Union, *Annual Reports*, 1900 and 1901.
[64] Hall, *op. cit.*, p. 122.

Trades Council attended the annual meetings of the Union and the two organizations sometimes formed joint deputations to press such matters as changing the School Board election day from Thursday to Saturday.[65]

Within the clubs, Gladstone and Bradlaugh were the most revered of the political leaders but how far this was a reflection of the greater political activity of the clubs in the eighties is not clear.[66] The whole problem of the political activities of the clubs during the 1880s is not very well defined. It is certain that they were caught up in the 'awakening' of that decade as the revolution within their own government alone testifies. It also seems to have been the time when many of them became occasional centres of working-class Liberal politics; certainly it was during the eighties that the words 'Liberal' and 'Radical' became common as part of the title of many clubs. Part of the problem of evaluating the political activism of the clubs in the 1880s is that for most of that decade there existed no equivalent to the journals *Club World* and *Club Life* of the 1890s and 1900s. On one thing, however, all writers were agreed: that by 1900 political life in the clubs had greatly diminished. And that although in many clubs there existed Political Councils, the mass of the membership could not be moved to any active political involvement: 'The cry is "We don't want to be bothered with politics after a hard day's work; what we want is recreation." There are many exceptions, but yet the fact cannot be ignored that this apathetic feeling is very strongly developed.'[67] This apathy was one of the contributory factors to the weakening of Liberalism in the London constituencies. The loss of Randall Cremer's seat of Haggerston in 1895 was attributed to 'apathy . . . nothing but apathy—no energy in anyone, not even the member'.[68] There were constant editorials exhorting the clubs to greater efforts in order to make their power in the country felt: 'If resolutions [on Old Age Pensions] were passed at every club connected with the Union and sent on to the Prime Minister, he would think twice before ignoring them.'[69]

[65] Hall to Secretary of London Trades Council, September 1894, LTC Minutes.
[66] *Club Life*, 27 May 1899, p. 1, for a poem in praise of Gladstone by a club man.
[67] Letter from C. Roquet of New Lansdowne Club, *ibid.*, 11 March 1899, p. 15.
[68] Interview with W. McNeill, *ibid.*, 29 April 1899, p. 1.
[69] *Ibid.*, 2 September 1899, p. 8; 7 September 1901, p. 9.

Attempts were made to alter this situation. The Metropolitan Radical Federation existed for just this very purpose. Defined as 'a combined Political Council of the Radical Clubs and Associations of the Metropolitan District',[70] its purpose was to press a more radical programme upon the Liberal Party which would include universal suffrage, old-age pensions, taxation of land values, and, if necessary, the abolition of the House of Lords. By the mid-1890s however, it had failed to move either the clubs or the Liberal Party. At a meeting in early 1895 only sixteen delegates from twelve clubs attended, showing how little interest there was in its activities. It was felt that 'the Federation has had its day and save for the purpose of visiting clubs each month it is of no value to those who wish to see improvement in the condition of the people'.[71] It continued to exist, however, and perhaps even underwent a mild renascence during the war years when there was some demand for speakers in the clubs and opportunities for it to organize in concert with others.

The issue was seen—probably incorrectly—largely in terms of a failure of organization; a failure to utilize the resources which existed within the Union. And the Union itself was blamed for this situation. Thus, in April 1901, *Reynolds News* began a campaign which aimed at the establishment of a Radical Union of clubs separate from the Club and Institute Union on the basis of the twenty-five most politically active of the clubs. It was claimed that although the 'social element' was a powerful deterrent to political activity in the clubs, the Union itself hardly set a good example:[72]

This organisation meets once a month for the purpose of affiliating clubs that wish to belong to the Union and disaffiliating clubs . . . which do not pay . . . their membership . . . after which the delegates . . . wind up with the eternal variety show. . . . They never discuss the questions of the hour, and beyond the fact that they form a backbone for . . . the social clubs . . . the work of the Club Union might be dispensed with with advantage . . . why should not these clubs [i.e. the politically active ones] form a 'Club Union,' with a Political Committee as much a consideration as the Management Committee and inde-

[70] Programme of the Metropolitan Radical Federation, 1897.
[71] *Club World*, 12 January 1895, p. 4.
[72] Letter written by 'A Reformer' to *Reynolds News* and reprinted in *Club Life*, 13 April 1901, p. 2.

pendent of that social cancer, the too much Social Club and 'Institute' Union?

At this attack all the people who usually berated the clubs for their lack of political activity suddenly became strangely resigned to the situation. A *Club Life* editorial remarked that agitation was a function of poverty and that nothing would change this all the time England was prosperous. 'The Stroller' in his column 'Club Gossip' remarked that 'politics forms no part of the Union's work. . . . You may lead a horse to the water but you cannot make him drink.'[73]

The idea of a Radical Union was attacked as impracticable. An attempt had been made in the late 1880s to found such an organization and had failed. It was concluded that the only way to deal successfully with the problem was a combination of adverse economic circumstances and 'for all earnest men of the respective . . . clubs to combine and force upon the Committees the need of giving up certain evenings in the week to the politically minded members'. This would induce 'an awakening of men to their responsibilities as Englishmen, and a return to the old principles which have always distinguished the Liberal Party: Peace, Retrenchment, and Reform'.[74]

The controversy had very little influence on the clubs as far as the Union and the Metropolitan Radical Federation were concerned. It did stimulate a conference at Southwark Liberal and Radical Club to consider the best means of organizing the political opinions of London clubmen, but it is noticeable that even here those who commonly regretted the political shortcomings of the movement were now more appreciative of the efforts that were made.[75] W. C. Wade, Secretary of the Metropolitan Radical Federation, stated that 'in spite of appearances a great deal of useful work was done by the Radical clubs today; that in many of them energy and public spirit was displayed . . . they proved a real need in keeping men together at election time'. He did, however, advocate that a federation of all the Radical Clubs in London be formed and a committee was established to report on this very issue, but nothing further

---

[73] *Ibid.*, 13 April 1901, p. 12.
[74] 'A Radical Union. Is it wanted?', *ibid.*, 20 April 1901, p. 1.
[75] W. C. Wade in 'Labour Letter', *ibid*, 27 May 1899, p. 14, where he laments the working man's indifference to politics.

materialized. Indeed, it is very likely that the whole campaign started by *Reynolds News* was all a part of its effort to stimulate the National Democratic League and in this respect it seems to have met with some success.[76]

The problem remained and it was, in essence, a problem of apathy. This should be emphasized. There was no basic change in the character of the clubs. The rising imperialist tide in the nineties could only be traced through the increase in plays and entertainments which used the Empire as a backcloth. Its political implications were completely absent. There was no drift away from a nominal Liberal-Radical position to an imperialist one and no working men's clubs were formed with the intention of propagating imperialism. Similarly with Socialism, whose impact on the movement was limited to the establishment of a few avowedly propagandist clubs.[77] The point was that political activism stood in the same relationship to the social functions of the clubs as did education. It was naturally inhibited by the conflicting ideals, principles and desires within the clubs. These tensions could only be transcended, if the 1880s were any guide, by the existence of issues, leaders and Radical politics, all of which were lacking in the late 1890s.

Those who were concerned about this situation recognized that the clubs themselves were not solely responsible for this situation; it was largely a reflection, they believed, of the parlous state of Radicalism in general. And many nostalgically looked back to the days of their imagination when under Gladstone the Radical Party had been strong and invulnerable.[78] But it was also correctly pointed out that such apathy was not an abnormal phenomenon among working men: 'The bulk of the members do not actively interest themselves in politics except at times of excitement. But this is . . . characteristic of the average working man—club man or not.'[79]

It was, perhaps, a result of this apathy that the most impressive feature of the clubs during the period of the war was the absolute lack of jingoistic excitement. Perhaps it also explains the virtual

[76] See pp. 92–4.

[77] There was a perceptible rise of interest in socialism in the early years of this century. See *Club Life*, 7 December 1901, p. 7.

[78] Mr H. Tibbits of Gladstone Radical, *ibid.*, 2 December 1899, p. 13.

[79] A. Dawes, North Camberwell Radical, *ibid.*, 21 July 1900, p. 2.

absence of any discussion in favour of the war. There were, no doubt, many who were in agreement with a correspondent from Newington Reform Club that 'Beware of the entrance to a quarrel; but, being in, bear it that the opposer may beware of thee'; and who were fatalistically resigned to the issue, regretting that there was war but seeing little possibility of stopping it.[80] This, after all, was the attitude of most Liberals. But the outstanding fact is that the discussion that did take place was almost entirely anti-war. There were, however, significant differences of emphasis between the working-class objections to the war and those which were expressed through the various anti-war committees.

Of all the arguments paraded against the South African War, that of morality was the favourite of pro-Boers of the middle class. The question of a just or unjust war was an essential part of their political philosophy, as also was their criterion of judging a war right or wrong: would it enslave or free a people capable of ruling themselves? In the working-class institutions such considerations tended to be less marked. They were most noticeable among the socialists. Thus, the Independent Labour Party regarded the war as an attempt to obtain the 'unfettered exploitation of the gold mines of the Transvaal' and drew the Radical conclusion that the 'war is an unjust war on our side . . . the Boers are in the right and we are in the wrong'.[81] This is why the Socialist societies were able to co-operate so easily with the Radicals of the Liberal Party. Both agreed in their analyses of the causes of the war. The greedy capitalists of the Rand were to blame and Chamberlain was their tool. The Socialists never attempted to place the war in any wider context; never regarded it as a result of the needs of British capitalism as a whole. The conspiracy theory appealed to both Liberals and Socialists.

It was similarly the case with arbitration. The idea of arbitration was at the heart of the case propagated by the Stop-the-War Committee. But there are only few occasions when arbitration can be seen to have affected working class thinking.[82] This lack of working-class enthusiasm for the principles

[80] *Ibid.*, 14 October 1899, p. 7.
[81] *ILP News*, November 1899, p. 2. Also, *ILP Annual Conference Report for 1900*, pp. 3–5.
[82] See resolution from Newington Reform Club to Colonial Secretary p. 14. Also, an editorial in *Club Life*, 28 October 1899, p. 8.

of arbitration was due, in part, to the source from which the Hague Conference emanated: the Tsar.

The call for a scheme of disarmament from the most auto-cratic monarch in Europe was met with universal suspicion from the working classes. The London Trades Council received a request from Stead's Peace Crusade to support a manifesto 'said to be issued with the consent of the Emperor of Russia'. While they were in favour of peace, they regarded the Tsar's initiative as an attempt to paint the wolf as a harmless lamb; conse-quently, they passed a resolution in favour of peace, but viewing with suspicion overtures in that direction 'made by an Emperor whose treatment of his own subjects is both brutal and in-human'.[83] Poplar Labour League explained that they had participated in the Crusade for Peace 'not because we love the Tsar and his proposal, but because we wanted to show the classes that the masses are in favour of the cessation of armaments'.[84] Similarly, in Morley and the working men's colleges, there was a suspicion of the Tsar's motive that prevented any whole-hearted support being given to the proposal.[85] This was the characteristic working-class reaction: the 1899 conference of the Independent Labour Party adopted a motion asserting a connec-tion between war and the competitive system but doubting the bona fides of the Tsar's offer.[86]

Thus, while it was true that considerations of the principles of arbitration and morality were not entirely absent among the working-class objections to the war, it must be recognized that unlike the middle-class pro-Boers, such arguments did not con-stitute the prime objections. Working men, on the whole, did not think in terms of right or wrong where such an issue was concerned, and any appeal to them based on such premises was bound to fail. It was this that puzzled most middle-class social observers. They interpreted it as being due to a lack of 'know-ledge' or lack of 'culture'. One such observer, resident at Toynbee Hall, complained that

certain words which had always to him signified clear and worthy ideas, such as honour, patriotism, justice, either form no part of the

[83] London Trades Council, *Annual Report 1898*, pp. 9–10.
[84] *Club Life*, 18 February 1899, p. 14.
[85] *Morley College Magazine*, December 1898, p. 20; *Working Men's College Journal*, January 1899, p. 10.　　　　　　[86] *ILP Annual Report for 1899*, p. 44.

working-man's vocabulary or are grossly and malignantly perverted from their true sense.

Similarly, the mere mention of the British Empire 'excites laughter as a subject to which no sincere man would dream of alluding'. His conclusion was that the masses needed to be humanized.[87] It was, thus, a combination of ingrained cynicism to anything 'official' and a lack of interest in any abstraction—both typical working-class characteristics—that explain why the issues of morality and arbitration were not taken up in the working-class institutions. Individual working men, such as 'The Seer' of the Mildmay Club were sufficiently politically integrated to accept the Radical argument against the war but, in general, the working classes could not be expected to follow the tortuous arguments of a moral law governing one nation's behaviour towards another. It is this which also helps to explain why the main objection of the articulate working man to the war was that imperialism conflicted with social reform at home.

The myth of a positive connection between imperialism and social reform has received an inordinate amount of attention when it is remembered that there was, in fact, very little lineal connection between the two.[88] Little attention has been paid to the negative aspect of the problem despite the fact that most anti-imperialists were also social reformers in a very real sense. The conflict between those supposed incompatibles permeates all the working-class institutions and provided the main objection they voiced to the issue of the war. Nor was it a new cry. As early as 1885, when the Pendjeh incident nearly precipitated a war with Russia, it was remarked at a working men's college that:[89]

A spirited Foreign Policy, they say, is good for the nation . . . to teach men they have one common foe is to level differences between them. . . . In their eagerness to keep back the oppressor abroad, whose oppression is felt by no one, they forget the oppressor at home whose oppression is felt hourly. . . . If our great moralists, our lovers of their country would appeal to men . . . upon these matters [i.e. social reform issues] . . . to produce a common unity against this common foe, much more would they be doing for the welfare of man than they do by

[87] H.E.S. (no name), in *Toynbee Record*, June 1908, p. 50.
[88] See Bernard Semmel, *Imperialism and Social Reform* (London, 1960).
[89] *Cheltenham Working Men's College Magazine*, July 1885, p. 211.

arousing enthusiasm upon matters so foreign to us as a scientific frontier.

The first resolution of the London Trades Council on the South African Crisis made the same point, if a little more directly:[90]

We further call the earnest attention of the working classes to the fact that we have always during this parliament a Foreign question thrust forward with the earnest intention of diverting the attention of the country from home affairs.

This reflected the attitude of Trades Councils all over the country. During a meeting of the Leicester Trades Council the Secretary, T. Carter, 'regretted that some Trade Unionists appeared to support the war and reminded delegates that the principles of Trade Unionism was to raise wages, whereas war would lower them'.[91] The Annual Report of Brighton Trades Council of 1901 pointed out that 'food, clothing, and all other necessaries of life are dearer today than they were before the war broke out'. It contrasted the deferment of old-age pensions 'on account of the cost to the nation, while untold millions that might have been used to brighten the declining years of those worn out workers are being squandered in blood shedding'.[92] The Annual Report of Peterborough Trades Council for 1902 lamented the accumulation of a war debt of £700 million which could have been spent on domestic reforms and 'which the British worker has to pay'.[93]

Such objections were strongest where, as in the case of Trades Councils, there was a close connection between the labour interest and politics. It is noticeable that the arbitration and morality range of objections tended to be more common in the clubs and colleges than in the Trades Councils. Nevertheless, the social reform versus imperialism theme also runs through club literature. W. C. Wade, in an article on Radicals and the Empire, emphasized the difference between the workman in Australia and New Zealand where 'there are no half timers . . . and an Old Age Pensions Act is in active force'. Writing of an

[90] London Trades Council Minutes, 10 August 1899.
[91] *Midland Free Press*, 3 March 1900.
[92] Quoted in *London Trades and Labour Gazette*, April 1901, p. 6.
[93] *Ibid.*, May 1902, p. 6.

argument in Paddington Radical Club, a correspondent re-ported: [94]

The relief of Mafeking has caused great enthusiasm in the club during the last few days . . . when I ventured to point out to one member that the cost of the present war would have put the Old Age Pensions on a sound basis, the answer I received was 'To Hades with Old Age Pensions.'

In *Club Life*, an editorial condemning the government for not using arbitration in an effort to avert the war was followed the next week by an editorial which lamented that 'the Government and the people do not see the necessity of spending their millions in times of peace, rather than defer the contribution till a time of war'. And it remarked on the changes the £30 million spent on the war could have wrought if it had been devoted to the housing of the people. [95] It was in the clubs that an interesting example arose of what the conflict could mean in practice.

The call up of Reservists had led to the creation of many Patriotic Funds, usually under the auspices of newspapers like the *Daily Mail* and *Daily Telegraph*, which were designed to provide support for the wives and children of those who had enlisted. One of the unfortunate results of this was that institutions that depended upon voluntary subscriptions, like some of the London hospitals, suffered a severe reduction in their incomes. The *ILP News* claimed that one such hospital, which it did not identify, was in danger of having to close as a result of this problem. [96] The Club Union, too, depended upon donations from the clubs to maintain a convalescent home which it owned at Pegwell Bay and which was used for club men who needed to recuperate after an illness. Early in November 1899, it was dis-covered that donations to the fund had dropped dramatically due to the appeals that were being made on behalf of the various Reservists Funds. And the clubs were exhorted to remember where their first loyalties lay. It is evident that many of the clubs were active in collecting for the Reservist Funds and it was quite natural that they should do so. Many of their members were in the Reservists; Mildmay Club reported that between forty and fifty of their club men had been ordered to the

[94] *Club Life*, 26 May 1900, p. 5.
[95] *Ibid.*, 28 October; 4 November 1899, p. 8.
[96] *ILP News*, March 1900, p. 3.

colours.[97] The situation was serious enough, however, for B. T. Hall to insert a special appeal expressing his concern lest the flood of charity should submerge the efforts being made on behalf of the convalescent home. He pointed out that 'thousands of pounds are wanted to pay off the debt on the building and money to pay current expenses'.[98] This was taken up in editorials several weeks in succession which warned that the home was in danger of financial collapse unless the money could be found to pay off the debt incurred in its building and running expenses. These appeals, coupled with several full-column advertisements, seem to have elicited a favourable response. Certainly, some of the clubs made a supreme effort: the Isle of Dogs Club, for example, raised £16 for the fund in the week before Christmas. By the New Year a change of editorial tone indicated that the appeal on behalf of the home had been successful. In November, a typically sour editorial proclaimed that[99]

the soldiers' wives and families will not starve even if clubmen withheld their donations for a twelvemonth, for there is plenty of money in this country coming from people who can well afford it and whose place it is to subscribe to those who guard and fight for their property.

But in January, the efforts of South Bermondsey Club in granting the wives of their Reservists eight shillings per week was extolled and favourably contrasted with the parsimonious attitude of the Charity Organization Society.[100] At the February meeting of the Union it was satisfactorily reported: 'The Committee were able to draw cheques and pay off the whole of the tradesmen . . . so they did not owe anything to anybody except those from whom money had been borrowed.'[101]

But in spite of the general apathy that reigned in the clubs towards political activity, an early awareness was shown of the dangers of the situation in South Africa. In May 1899 'The Seer', an extreme Radical named Jackson who was Secretary of the Political Council of the Mildmay Club—one of the largest[102] and most politically active of the London clubs—was writing of the enormous 'perfidy displayed by us in our dealings with the

[97] The Central Club collected £22 in one week for the Reservists, *Club Life*, 18 November 1899, p. 9; 25 November 1899, p. 16.
[98] *Ibid.*, 18 November 1899.   [99] *Ibid.*, 18 November 1899, p. 8.
[100] *Ibid.*, 13 January 1900, p. 8.   [101] *Ibid.*, 10 February 1900, p. 1.
[102] In 1901 it had 2,200 members and could afford to build a new club house.

Boers and natives, and . . . the unbridled lust and plunder shown by our so-called statesmen'.[103] By September, meetings to protest against the possibility of a war with the Transvaal were commonplace.[104] With the commencement of hostilities the topic became a regular feature of club meetings and took the form of addresses or lectures from two propaganda bodies: the Imperial South African Association and the Transvaal Committee.[105]

The Imperial South African Association had been formed in 1896 to propagate the need for a united British South Africa. Unashamedly Rhodesian in its sentiments, it consciously aimed at arousing attention to 'the iniquities and tyrannies under which their fellow subjects laboured' by disseminating 'literature and speeches calculated to bring conviction to the working classes'.[106] The Association's activities increased as the dispute became more acute; it sponsored three times as many meetings in 1899 as in 1898 and doubled its distribution of pamphlets.[107] But by 1901 the number of meetings and the number of pamphlets distributed had again dropped back to their pre-war averages. The work of the Transvaal Committee seems to have been almost entirely devoted to addressing meetings in the clubs. It had an obvious connection with the movement in that the Metropolitan Radical Federation had affiliated to the Committee in August 1899.[108] On the whole, however, its activities seem to have been slighter than those of the imperialist organization.

The Imperial South African Association had conducted a steady propaganda in the clubs since 1896 and long before there had ever been a prospect of war its lecturers were commonplace in the clubs of London. It felt that it was achieving success in its attempt to win over the working classes to an awareness of the

[103] *Club Life*, 6 May 1899, p. 14.

[104] *Ibid.*, 16 September, p. 3; 23 September, p. 3; 7 October 1899, p. 10. For meetings at Bethnal Green, Bow and Bromley, and Newington Reform Clubs.

[105] I have identified at least thirty lectures and meetings reported in detail in *Club Life* on this issue. There were certainly many more that were not reported. The majority of clubs did not send reports of any of their activities to the magazine.

[106] Speech by G. Drage, MP, chairman of Imperial South African Association, at Derby, 7 December 1899. *Imperial South African Association*, Pamphlet No. 21. See also *Annual Report 1897–98*, p. 6.

[107] Imperial South African Association, *Annual Report 1899–1900*, p. 2.

[108] See *Club Life*, 26 August 1899, p. 2.

importance of British supremacy in South Africa. In 1898, the Association's Annual Report claimed that there was an increasing demand for 'lectures, particularly from the Radical Associations in the Metropolis where the views of our speakers have won assent'.[109] In spite of its massive propagandizing effort in the clubs, however, the evidence disputes this assertion. An inescapable feature of the period is the absolute success of anti-war meetings within the clubs. A meeting addressed by Victor Fisher of the Transvaal Committee at the Boro' of Hackney Club was[110]

packed with working men of all shades of opinion, [who] listened with marked respect and order to the lecturer's address. Of course there were some paid rowdies present—one gentleman shouting 'The Queen, God bless her'—but when he heard the lusty voices of men of common sense and humanity shout, 'Put him out', he desisted.

A month later the same lecturer was received at Bethnal Green Club by 'a capital audience who listened with rapt attention while he described the . . . way in which the war had been brought about. . . . At the close a vote of thanks, . . . was carried unanimously.'[111] In February 1900, the same club carried an anti-war resolution by 'an overwhelming majority, an amendment was moved but . . . there were only about a dozen hands held up for it'.[112] Perhaps more surprisingly, the Mildmay Club was able to arrange a debate between H. F. Wyatt of the Imperial South African Association and Victor Fisher of the Transvaal Committee during the week following the relief of Mafeking where the audience 'were mainly against the war'. The most noteworthy feature of this meeting—considering the time that it occurred—was that 'the proceedings were very orderly and not the least disturbances took place. There was a little excitement at times, but none of the rowdy behaviour that has disgraced many of the meetings for or against the war.'[113]

This was a general feature of the clubs throughout the war. It was possible to hold anti- and pro-war meetings without fear

[109] Imperial South African Association, *Annual Report 1897–98, loc. cit.*
[110] *Club Life*, 4 November 1899, p. 13.
[111] *Ibid.*, 16 December 1899, p. 7.   [112] *Ibid.*, 24 February 1900, p. 6.
[113] *Ibid.*, 26 May 1900, p. 10. No other instance of any similar meeting has been found. It is almost inconceivable that such a debate could have been arranged in any other institution during the war.

that they would be disrupted; and this tended to be true of all
working-class institutions.[114] The emotive content of the issue
seems to have been very muted; lectures and addresses were
often regarded as having an educative function—fulfilling Solly's
aims of political discussion. Thus, Bow and Bromley received a
'highly instructive' lecture from T. R. Dodd of the Imperial
South African Association which enabled those who attended to
'discuss these questions with clearer opinions, and better judgement than they might otherwise have done'.[115] And a *Club Life*
correspondent remarked in 1901 that 'we are pleased to note
these lectures [at the Isle of Dogs Club] are being well received, for they largely tend to improve the tone of club life'.[116]
This is not to deny that sometimes the arguments were heated:
'On Sunday morning there was a very strong argument on the
Transvaal crisis . . . Teddy Cobb . . . got so heated . . . that he
nearly wanted seeing home.'[117] Nor does it mean that club men
unanimously opposed the war:[118]

We have a diversity of opinion on the Transvaal question in this club
[Gladstone Radical]. Some good and sound Radicals . . . support the
Government . . . [and] maintain intolerable injustice and oppression.
. . . Discussions of this character are healthy if carried out in the proper
spirit, viz. to obtain information and arrive at the truth.

The relevant thing to note is that there was complete tolerance. The Political and Educational Council of the Mildmay
Club was totally opposed to the war, but it organized a lecture
by T. R. Dodd and a discussion during which only 'Mr. Nicholls
. . . spoke in sympathy with the lecturer'. The correspondent of
Club Life noted that 'the Political and Educational Council on a
burning question like to afford facilities for both sides of the
question to be presented'.[119] Similarly, the Isle of Dogs Club
organized many lectures on the war from both viewpoints. One,
given by an Imperial South African Association delegate was
'listened to with the deepest interest by a very appreciative
audience and . . . the speaker was treated with the greatest
courtesy with one or two exceptions'.[120] The same sort of

[114] S. C. Cronwright-Schreiner, *The Land of Free Speech* (London, 1906), p. 18,
for an anti-war meeting in Mansfield House, University Settlement.
[115] *Club Life*, 14 October 1899, p. 5.   [116] *Ibid.*, 23 March 1901, p. 10.
[117] *Ibid.*, 14 October 1899, p. 7.   [118] *Ibid.*, 14 October 1899, p. 6.
[119] *Ibid.*, 21 October 1899, p. 2.   [120] *Ibid.*, 23 March 1901, p. 10.

reception greeted J. M. Robertson, a pro-Boer, who was 'listened to with rapt attention, and at the conclusion received an ovation and well-merited vote of thanks'.[121]

Similarly, with a series of speeches at the Boro' of Hackney Club in October 1899 where Randall Cremer evoked the memory of Charles Bradlaugh in support of the anti-war campaign. It was noted, with approval, that the speeches were listened to quietly and respectfully and this was contrasted with the behaviour of the 'top hat, cuff collar brigade that yelled for the blood of their fellow countrymen' in Trafalgar Square a few weeks previously.[122]

It should be understood, however, that this does not imply that working-class institutions were devoid of the customary forms of patriotic rejoicings. When the City Imperial Volunteers arrived back in England there were reports that many club men went to 'swell the crowds assembled to see C.I.V.'s, and in the evening were pretty merry and gave forth sounds of harmony of a patriotic character'.[123] Mafeking Night, too, was celebrated. At Willesden Radical it 'seemed to have . . . disorganised our officials', and at East St Pancras Reform, 'our people rejoiced at the news of the release of Baden-Powell'. Members of the West Southwark Radical put their drum-and-fife band to good use, marching 'round the neighbourhood playing patriotic airs and got a glorious reception from the multitude'. But even on this occasion it was noted that 'although patriotism was great, great order prevailed'.[124]

The same kind of seemingly contradictory attitude could be seen even before the war began. In September 1899, a correspondent of *Club Life* at the Bow and Bromley Club was puzzled by the willingness of the club to pass a 'strongly worded' resolution against the prospect of war and their acceptance of jingo entertainment. He noted that at a recent concert derogatory references to Kruger and the Boers were received with the greatest applause and found it incomprehensible how the two positions could be reconciled.[125] The same theme can be illustrated by even more innocuous examples. Thus, at the Central Club's fifth anniversary dinner, in October 1899, the

[121] *Ibid.*, 20 April 1901, p. 14. [122] *Ibid.*, 14 October 1899, p. 10.
[123] *Ibid.*, 27 October 1900, p. 8. [124] *Ibid.*, 26 May 1900, p. 11.
[125] *Ibid.*, 23 September 1899, p. 3.

menu included such delicacies as 'Boers Head' and 'Chamberlain Hash' and the club room was decorated with the flags of all the contestants.[126] Light-hearted though this may have been, the spectacle of the Transvaal Veikleur in the West End clubs would have been unthinkable.

The real difference in the political activism of the clubs at this time as compared with the 1880s was illustrated by their lack of participation in public demonstrations against the war. The only one where clubs seem to have been involved as institutions was the disastrous Trafalgar Square demonstration of 24 September 1899. This meeting, which symbolized the unity of the left that was to characterize the anti-war movement, was called on the initiative of F. W. Soutter and the Bermondsey Labour League. A manifesto was issued from the League at the beginning of September[127] which called on its

fellow workers . . . to express at public meetings their opinion that all questions at issue between the two Governments are questions which can only be settled by arbitration, and that a war between the two countries would be a national crime by whomsoever provoked.

There was an immediate response from the Liberal Forwards, the International Arbitration and Peace Association, and the Social Democratic Federation. An approach was made, in September 1899, to the Council of the Metropolitan Radical Federation. The deputation urged the delegates of the Federation to 'go back to their clubs . . . and do everything in their power to make their demonstration a success'. The Council expressed its agreement with the objects of the demonstration, donated a sum of money towards its expenses, and promised to provide a speaker for one of the eight platforms which were to stand in the square.[128]

Exactly how many clubs responded is not clear, but at least two organized groups of members were known to attend in support. From Paddington Radical Club, it was reported that 'our members were in strong force in Trafalgar Square. Our President was protected from being assaulted by the police from a gang of well-dressed roughs who had set upon him with sticks

[126] *Ibid.*, 21 October 1899, p. 2.
[127] Francis William Soutter, *Fights For Freedom* (London, 1925), p. 210–12.
[128] *Club Life*, 23 September 1899, p. 2.

and umbrellas;' and the Political Council of the Mildmay Club organized a 'brake outing to Trafalgar Square'.[129]

The meeting was a fiasco; there was continuous shouting which prevented all but one of the platform speakers from being heard. All kinds of missiles were hurled at the speakers, especially Hyndman, and afterwards there was the usual suspicion of organized opposition.[130] It all contrasted unfavourably with a meeting held in Newington Reform Club that same week where Dr G. B. Clark, who was one of the most extreme of the pro-Boers and who had been a special target of the patriots at Trafalgar Square, received an ovation and where[131]

in one of the most crowded halls we have ever had—last Wednesday was a genuine record one—our meeting against war in the Transvaal was unanimous in its resolution passed. . . . Although many of the public were admitted utter silence and respect to the speakers was in evidence the whole three hours.

A notable feature of the issue of the war in the clubs was the way in which anti-war sentiment, or at least a passive tolerance of all range of opinions, combined with participation in jingo celebration on occasions such as Mafeking Night or the return of the City Imperial Volunteers. The same kind of dichotomy can also be illustrated by the experience of the few Trades Councils who took a stand on the issue of the war. Their activities were reflective of their role as the collective organs of local Trades Unionism. They tended to be more interested in politics than the individual unions and in several towns during the war they represented the working-class wing of the peace movement.

The activity of Aberdeen Trades Council provides us with an example of how there were two seemingly contradictory attitudes involved in working-class anti-war sentiment. The first was a fairly clear and recognizable Radical antipathy to imperialism: an antipathy around which both the Socialists on the Councils and the declining, but still predominant, Lib-Labs

[129] *Ibid.*, 30 September 1899, pp. 5, 9.
[130] *Morning Leader*, 26 September 1899, where the Secretary of the Demonstration Committee alleged that 'several working men from Smithfield market had written to her to say that touts had been going round the market at the end of last week inducing men by promises of plenty of beer to go to the square to make a disturbance'.   [131] *Club Life*, 7 October 1899, p. 10.

could unite. Aberdeen Trades Council was one of the few councils to protest against the war early in its course.[132] In October it passed a resolution which condemned the government for 'forcing a war with the Transvaal Republic in the interests of Jewish and British speculators', and urged the local members of parliament 'to raise their voices in the House . . . against the granting of additional supplies to carry on a war so unjust and iniquitous'.[133]

The issue for the first year of the war focused on this question of Trades Council attitude toward the local Liberals, Pirie and Bryce. Relations between the Liberals and organized Labour had never been very easy. Bryce's attitude towards the eight-hour day had, in particular, been a cause of considerable friction in the 1890s. And during the 1895 election several prominent Council members had addressed meetings in favour of the Liberal Unionist candidate because he was more sympathetic towards the eight-hour agitation. In the by-election in South Aberdeen in 1896 the Socialist candidature of Tom Mann had been supported against that of Pirie, and Mann had come within 400 votes of victory.[134] Socialism was strong in Aberdeen, generated by the thriving SDF branch in the town, and although the Socialists on the Trades Council could not yet overwhelm the Lib-Labs, they were the prime movers in its anti-war activities.

Thus, in the summer of 1900, there was considerable discussion as to the attitude that should be taken towards the Liberals. The possibility of running a Labour candidate was raised in June and July but no satisfactory decision could be made. While there were doubts about supporting the two Liberals they did not want to let the Tories gain the seats, nor did they want to revive painful memories of Hyndman's attempt to foist a Socialist on the South constituency without consulting other Labour bodies.[135] Their doubts about Bryce not only involved his

---

[132] Other Councils to take similar action included Bradford which sent a resolution to the Colonial Secretary condemning his attempt to foment war. Others that sent similar resolutions included Keighley, Reading, Southport and Darwen. See Colonial Office Papers, C.O. 417/277 ff. 212, 501, 804–807, C.O. 417/278, ff.127. For Bradford see also *Bradford Labour Echo*, 16 September 1899.

[133] *Daily Free Press*, 5 October 1899. Also K. D. Buckley, *Trade Unionism in Aberdeen* (Aberdeen, 1955).

[134] Buckley, *op. cit.*, pp. 175–6.   [135] *Ibid.*, p. 186.

attitude to Labour questions but also his lukewarm opposition to the war and were indicative of the strength of Socialism on the Council. William Diack expressed the feelings of the Socialist group when he said:[136]

It might be right to give Mr. Bryce a certain measure of approval for the course he had taken in connection with the Imperial question. . . . Mr. Bryce had wobbled a good deal, however, and if Mr. Bryce had taken up the decided stand . . . that the member for Banffshire or Mr. John Morley had taken he would not have the slightest hesitation in advising the Council to take no action in the matter . . . but he did not know if Mr. Bryce's position was such as to warrant them considering him worthy of their support.

An amendment to call a conference of Labour groups to consider the situation was carried and the conference met on 5 September. Its outcome was fairly innocuous—merely to recommend that a small committee interview the candidates with a view to deciding which should be given Labour support. Later in the month after the candidates, excepting Pirie who was in Spain buying horses for the army, had been interviewed, the decision was taken to support the Liberals.[137] This rather reluctant decision was motivated solely by one factor: that of the war. At the Trades Council meeting of 1 October, J. Elric, in seconding the resolution of confidence in Bryce and Pirie, claimed that the working men of Aberdeen had no choice but to support the Liberals: 'The reason why the Labour party were prepared to support Mr. Bryce was . . . because of the position he took upon the war.' Similarly, the Social Democratic Federation supported the decision of the Labour conference that support be given to the Liberal Party in Aberdeen, 'so far as its attitude on Imperial questions is concerned'.[138] When the election resulted in the return of two Liberals the Trades Council was anxious to emphasize the purely transient nature of its support. The President, J. H. Elric, 'was pleased to think that the organized workers accepted the recommendation of the Trades Council and that they had returned both Liberal members', but he emphasized that Labour held the 'balance of political power in both divisions'. A unanimous resolution, proposed by Mr Green of the shoemakers,[139] explicitly stated that

[136] *Daily Free Press*, 26 July 1900.   [137] *Ibid.*, 26 September 1900.
[138] *Ibid.*, 2 October 1900.   [139] *Ibid.*, 4 October 1900.

our action in voting for the Liberal candidates as against the Imperial policy for the Government in no way nullifies our oft-repeated resolution in declaring ourselves in favour of independent political action on the part of the workers of the city of Aberdeen.

In fact, the Trades Council appears to have only just preserved a precarious unity over this problem. Many individual members had supported Bryce on the platform, including George Garden who was Secretary of the local Independent Labour Party. He seconded a motion thanking Bryce for his services to Liberalism and pledging to support his return to parliament. In his speech, he stated that the only reason the Trades Council had agreed to support Bryce in the contest was because of the attitude on the South African War. At the same meeting, however, another Trades Council delegate, a Mr Kemp of the Baker's Union, was to be found seconding an amendment which declined to give Bryce any support.[140] The unease of the delegates was illustrated when Councillor Johnson, a Trades Council member speaking at a Bryce meeting, said that 'of the two evils he was determined to choose the least. Although he could not say that either of the Liberal candidates exactly came up to his standard, still he would take them both before Mr. Smith and Mr. Williams', the Conservative and Liberal Unionist candidates.[141]

It had been fairly easy for the active Socialist members to persuade the Trades Council to take a strong stand on the political issue of the war. The resolution of October 1899 had been unanimous, and most of the Council had supported Bryce and Pirie albeit with varying degrees of enthusiasm. But it was one thing to condemn the justice and morality of the war and quite another to take a determined stand on an issue that was far closer to working-class society and life. Throughout the winter of 1901 attempts by Diack and others to obtain a condemnation of the 'methods of barbarism' dominated the Council meetings. As far as most working men were concerned this issue was a question of whether the British soldier was to be held responsible for the farm burnings and other atrocities that had been committed by the army in South Africa. And the reaction of the Council to this issue provides another example of the dichotomy

[140] *Ibid.*, 1 October 1900.   [141] *Ibid.*, 3 October 1900.

which penetrates virtually all working-class attitudes and reactions to the war and which we noted in the clubs. Those opposed to the resolutions were quite happy to acquiesce in any measure which trounced the politically safe target of the Tory government, but the identification with the working-class soldier was too strong for them to welcome any implied slur on his character and behaviour.

The issue was precipitated by a motion proposed by Diack protesting against the 'brutalities now being perpetrated in South Africa . . . the burning of homesteads . . . the destruction of property . . . the turning of women and children destitute into the veldt'. The meeting was adjourned before the resolution could be discussed and at the following meeting an amendment, moved by Garden, proposed to strike out all references to explicit brutalities and substitute a more general statement which expressed the opinion that the war was unnecessary and unjust and urged the local members of parliament to renew their efforts in pressing the government to offer terms of peace which would be acceptable to the Boers. Once again the meeting was adjourned.[142]

When, at the meeting of 20 February 1901, the motion was eventually discussed it was evident that Garden's amendment was designed to prevent any suspicion of blame being attached to the soldiers and to preserve unity. He 'would not believe, except on the strongest evidence, that the soldiers were guilty of the cruelties alleged against them', and urged a moderate resolution 'in order that they might carry the bulk of the people with them in their crusade'. Diack denied the charge that he slandered the soldiers, claiming it was the policy he condemned; and it is significant to note that the theme of the speech he made justifying this motion was that the war detracted from social reform.[143] His resolution certainly condemned the soldiery by implication, and the topic was an emotive one at this particular time when the full extent of Roberts's original proclamations were just becoming known. The debate was again inconclusively adjourned.

The next two meetings revealed the full extent of the split. On 6 March, the debate ranged widely over the war issue and

142 *Ibid.*, 24 January, 7 February 1900.
143 *Ibid.*, 21 February 1901; *Peoples Journal*, 23 February 1901.

was again adjourned until 20 March when the most heated discussion yet occurred. Speeches were delivered 'denouncing those who sullied the soldiers in South Africa' and 'who called themselves democrats and yet denounced their own kindred'. Equally strong were the speeches on the other side. Mr. A. M. Craig referred

with sarcasm to the emotional enthusiasm which had characterised Mr. Milne's speech. The war he described as unnecessary and unjust and observed . . . that when Mr. Stead was in Aberdeen supporting the ideals of arbitration the man who was on the platform and seconded one of the peace resolutions was the mover of the previous question.

The President tried to conciliate the two factions wondering 'how working men could hesitate for a moment in deciding whether they should or should not vote in favour of the speedy ending of the war'. He announced that Mr Livingstone was prepared to withdraw his amendment that no action be taken in the matter, if Diack withdrew 'all that rubbish about atrocities and brutalities committed by the British and proposed simply that the Government should offer the Boers reasonable terms of peace'. This Diack refused to do and the motion was lost by 34 to 37 votes.[144]

This was the last attempt made by the anti-war party to bring the Trades Council into a further condemnation of the war than had been made in 1899. Even this had not been passed without some minor trouble. Arthur Bain spoke of the 'unfortunate language used by important officials . . . at the commencement of the war' which had 'very nearly prevented his association being represented'.[145] However, it is significant that unity could be maintained until there was an attack upon the conduct of the British soldier. Later in the year there was no response to Campbell-Bannerman's 'methods of barbarism' speech or campaign. It is therefore clear that while members were willing to condemn the government, they were not willing to do anything which might reflect upon the working-class soldier. The association between the institution and the class was too close for them to do so—either through fear of their members' reactions, or because of an instinctive reaction to an implied assault on the standards of behaviour of that class.[146]

[144] *Daily Free Press*, 7 March, 21 March 1901.
[145] *Peoples Journal*, 23 March 1901.   [146] *Ibid.*

The Northampton Trades Council adopted a similar position to that of Aberdeen. They refrained, as was their usual custom, from giving official support to Labouchere, but they approved of 'the attitude taken by Mr Labouchere with regard to the Transvaal war'.[147] As individuals, they too were closely involved in the anti-war movement which in Northampton, as elsewhere, was an amalgam of the left. On this issue, they were united in their support of Labouchere; it was J. G. Gribble, Secretary of the local Social Democratic Federation, who moved the resolution of approval of Labouchere's attitude to the war and there was an impressive attendance of Trades Council members at the anti-war meeting of 7 February 1900. This meeting, disrupted by organized rowdyism, was discussed at the following Trades Council meeting where a resolution was passed which expressed regret that free speech had been prevented and confirmed their support for Labouchere. They felt strongly that Northampton, with its Radical tradition, should not be subjected to 'this spirit of jingoism which was not confined to one party, but to the young bloods of each party'.[148] Only slight opposition was offered to the proposal which gave support to Labouchere; it was felt necessary to counteract Chamberlain's taunt that 'his constituents had . . . not been willing to hear him'.[149] During the General Election this support was recalled and many members of the Council attended and spoke at his meetings. There can be little doubt that he had the unofficial support of the members. Thus the Secretary of the Council, W. H. Reynolds, urged all 'friends of labour to vote for Mr. Labouchere'.[150]

An even closer connection between the Trades Council and the anti-war movement can be discerned at Leicester. At a meeting called to protest against the war on 20 February 1900, the Chairman and Secretary of the Council moved and seconded a resolution 'amid scenes of the greatest disorder', that: 'The present war in South Africa is a scandal to Christendom and a disgrace to civilisation which it is the duty of all good citizens to endeavour to stop.'[151] Altogether there were twenty-three

[147] *Northampton Daily Reporter*, 25 January 1900; Northampton Trades Council, *Annual Report 1900*.   [148] *Northampton Daily Reporter*, 8 February 1900.
[149] *Ibid.*, 22 February 1900.   [150] *Ibid.*, 27 September 1900.
[151] *Midland Free Press*, 24 February 1900.

members of the Council at this meeting and once again they clearly felt involved as a body. At the delegate meeting on 27 February, the Chairman said: 'He agreed to propose the resolution he did at the meeting, without any fear and he was not ashamed of the ground he took up on the question. . . . It was not the working men of Leicester who disgraced that meeting (hear, hear).'[152]

In Sheffield, Charles Hobson, Thomas Shaw, Stuart Uttley, J. C. Whitley and T. W. Holmes—all members of the Trades Council—were associated with H. J. Wilson in his anti-war campaign. Holmes had written to the *Sheffield and Rotherham Independent* on 26 September 1899, protesting against the 'worthlessness of that trained diplomacy which costs the nation so much money if it cannot find some honourable way out of the present difficulty without war'. Throughout the nineties the Council seems to have confined itself essentially to Labour questions and there does not appear to have been any moves to commit the Council as a whole to the anti-war sentiment;[153] but the connection between individual members and the peace movement was significant.[154] And, as this short survey indicates, the active participation of Trades Unionists was a general feature of the peace campaign throughout the country.

The conclusions that can be drawn from the evidence reviewed in this chapter are twofold. In the first place, the failure of a mass opposition to emerge during the war is illuminated; in the second place, working-class reactions and attitudes are characteristically shown to be more complex and interesting than a simple and mindless jingoism.

To the failure of Radicalism another dimension must be added. There were, it has been indicated, far more vocal anti-imperialists among the working classes than vocal imperialists. The potential of this anti-imperialist sentiment was not exploited. Possibly they could have formed the base for a large-scale agitation. That they could not be so moved was due, in

---

[152] *Ibid.*, 3 March 1900.

[153] The newspaper reports of the meetings do not mention any attempt. The records of Sheffield Trades Council are missing for this period.

[154] See an anti-militarist speech at 1898 Labour Day held under the Council's auspices. Sheffield Federated Trades Council, *Annual Report 1898*, pp. 7–8.

part, to the prevailing apathy to political involvement which was not conducive to an anti-war movement. But the failure to conquer this apathy was in itself a comment on the efficacy of the anti-war organizations and upon Radicalism in general. The only anti-war committee that made any effort was the relatively unimportant Transvaal Committee. But this apathy can also be attributed to the demoralized state of Radical politics as a whole, and so one factor reinforced the other. Within the clubs, it was also a result of an inherent conflict between the social, educational and political functions of the institution. If, once the Union had been 'democratized', the sole financial basis of the club was the sale of alcohol, then it was inevitable that the social function should dominate. While the clubs were at times capable of acting as a strong political force, without the stimulation of a programme or an issue which could appeal to working men they represented *par excellence* a typical working-class disinterest in politics. If the 1880s had been different—and it seems likely that they had—it was only because there were issues, leaders and organizations which could interest, arouse and mobilize working-class political instincts. At a time when none of these elements was present, as during the Boer War, the social function of the clubs predominated. Paradoxically, this is even more interesting and relevant for this study. For it is clear that if the club could encompass working men with political and recreational interests, then the lack of jingoism is even more impressive. The fact that anti-war meetings could be held where all kinds of working men were gathered must surely disabuse the myth of working-class jingoism. It also suggests that there was, in fact, the basis for a stronger opposition to the war than resulted and that its failure to emerge was more a failure of the organizations formed to arouse it. It is clear from the number of anti-war meetings we know to have been held in the clubs that there were many working men who were politically aware and were opposed to the war. It is also clear that the vast majority of club members were quite prepared to tolerate anti-war meetings and this alone was an unusual phenomenon in the years 1899–1902.

But if Radicalism failed in its anti-war efforts this did not imply a rejection of Radical politics by working men. It has been shown that where the working classes expressed objections to imperialism they did so using the language of Radicalism.[155] The war was condemned because it detracted from social reform and (less often) because it threatened the independence of the Boer states. The Rand capitalists were denounced because they had 'greedily conspired' against the Boer governments for their own selfish ends, not because they were representative of a system which demanded the annexation of exploitable lands.

The Radical base that the clubs provided for political action is illustrated by the support given the left-wing Liberals during the Khaki Election. The Boro' of Bethnal Green Club pledged itself to fight for the return of Liberals in both local divisions and especially for the return of E. H. Pickersgill, an advanced Liberal who was closely associated with the club. After his defeat, due it was claimed to the 'Kharki' and 'beer', a correspondent wrote that 'there was one pleasant feature, and that was the club members [who] did good work in canvassing . . . they turned up and worked with a will'.[156] The Boro' of Shoreditch Club suspended all communication and contact with other clubs because of the work they were doing in the constituency for Professor Stuart. South West Ham Club resolved that 'we support the candidature of Mr. Thorne and do our utmost to get him returned'. More successfully in terms of election results, North Camberwell Radical worked for Dr T. Macnamara, East London for Steadman, Boro' of Hackney for Cremer and Newington Reform for Cecil Norton.[157]

The organizations that were designed to exploit this Radicalism, however, were seldom equipped to relate to the working men. None of the eighty or so pamphlets issued by the South African Conciliation Committee mentioned the cost of the war to social reform. The vast majority of Conciliationist propaganda was concerned with legalistically showing the duplicity of the government's diplomacy, with refuting the myth of an Africander conspiracy and with protesting against the imposition of martial law and the methods of barbarism. Likewise, the Stop-the-War Committee's conglomeration of pacifism, arbitration

[155] Anti-imperialist Radicals were asserting the contradiction between imperialism and social reform: C. F. G. Masterman (ed.), *The Heart of Empire* (London, 1901); F. W. Hirst, 'Imperialism and Finance', *Liberalism and the Empire* (London, 1900).
[156] *Club Life*, 13 October 1900, p. 5.
[157] *Ibid.*, 22 September, p. 4; 29 September, p. 5; 6 October, pp. 4–10.

and Christianity said absolutely nothing to working men. The fact was that neither group talked the language of working-class Radicalism; nor did many politicians—and we shall see that the exceptions were usually those who were most successful in their electoral appeal to working men.

That working men could respond to the relevant programme and rhetoric is illustrated by the relative, though brief, success of the National Democratic League in the clubs.[158] The League was the direct result of the desire of left-wing Radicals to create a revived Liberal Party purified of its 'whig imperialist' elements. John Morley had spoken to the Oxford Eighty Club of how, if he had to choose between Socialists and imperialists, he would choose the former. This was seized upon by the magazine *New Age* and by W. M. Thompson of *Reynolds News* to presage the desire for co-operation between all leftist organizations on an anti-imperialist and social-reforming platform. Just before the election *New Age* urged that all 'radicals and socialists sink minor differences and vote for each other'.[159] That journal had long expressed the desire of pro-Boer sentiment within the party to get rid of the Liberal imperialists. In August 1900 it had editorialized that[160]

there is practically no difference between Tories and those so-called Liberals who shout with the jingoes. It is high time those Liberals whose policy is fundamentally different from that of the Tories should declare themselves. . . . The Whigs are essentially Tories. Let them go into Tory camp.

And the desire of *New Age* to cast off the Liberal imperialists was motivated in part by its 'Gladstonian' belief in the immorality of the war, but mainly because it believed that it would facilitate the co-operation of all 'advanced' men in uniting on an anti-imperialist and social-reform platform.[161] The National Democratic League was the outcome of such a mood.

Formed by W. M. Thompson, who previous to the election had published a 'white list' of candidates who were 'straight' on the war and 'sound' on social issues, the League managed to rally impressive support. It was clearly intended to be the embryo of the working-class wing of a revitalized left-wing

[158] See Appendix II.   [159] *New Age*, 2 August 1900, p. 482.
[160] *Ibid.*   [161] *Ibid.*, 18 July 1901, p. 449.

Radical Party. Tom Mann was Secretary, John Ward of the Navvies Union was on the executive, Lloyd George was a Vice-President and those associated with it included Robert Smellie, A. E. Fletcher, Charles Fenwick, Sam Woods and T. F. Macnamara. For a while it seemed to be a successful rival to the Labour Representation Committee and was, in essence, an 'attempt to revive Radicalism on the old lines with Labour support and to remove from the Lib-Lab attitude the taint of merely passive subservience to the Liberal Party'.[162]

It is interesting to note the attention paid to the League in the clubs. The formation of the Labour Representation Committee had gone by without a mention. There is no evidence that the clubs took any notice of its existence. And while it is true that the Committee was essentially Trade Union orientated, the failure of *Club Life* to devote an editorial to its formation is significant. The formation of the National Democratic League was immediately reflected in the clubs helped, no doubt, by Thompson's offensive to rouse them to a more active political role.[163] By 3 March 1901, of the twenty-eight branches of the League in London, one-half had been formed in the clubs.[164] One of the most active was the branch formed at Bow and Bromley Club early in the year. The club promised to support the League's nominees at the London County Council elections and urged the Political Councils to meet together to formulate 'some scheme to secure the return of as many Progressives as possible'.[165] That the National Democratic League was in harmony with the political ideals of the clubs is indicated by an editorial on Labour Representation mentioned in *Club Life* for the first time in November 1901. It welcomed the fact that the subject was being discussed in the clubs—perhaps due to the work of the NDL—and gave its blessing to the 'principles of extended labour representation'. But it noted in an oblique reference to Independent Labour representation that[166]

as soon as the matter is put forward sectionally a great move forward is apparent . . . what is wanted . . . is someone to weld all the elements into a powerful and coherent whole and prevent them from becoming

[162] G. D. H. Cole, *British Working Class Politics* (London, 1941), p. 165.
[163] See pp. 68–70.   [164] *Reynolds News*, 3 March 1901.
[165] *Club Life*, 23 February 1901, p. 10.
[166] *Ibid.*, 16 November 1901, p. 8.

mere sectional units. True progress . . . lies in that direction, and self-interest will indicate the . . . necessity of general cooperation.

And the NDL was later given editorial support as a body which 'has not as yet received the attention it deserves' but whose programme 'will almost certainly in time be adopted by a reformed energetic Radical Party'.[167]

Apart from illuminating the failure of Radical politics during this period, however, the most important feature of the evidence presented is the noted absence of that jingoistic intolerance that characterized other sectors of society. G. P. Gooch has related how his family were very seriously split over the war and how he was ostracized for his pro-Boer views.[168] G. W. E. Russell recounted how it was not until the middle of 1901 that middle-class suburban society would tolerate a pro-Boer speaker at any of their meetings.[169] This was in marked contrast to the clubs and other working-class institutions where pro-Boer speakers were always assured of a fair and quiet hearing. Morley College, whose enrolment suffered from a lack of public interest, noted that 'the general public took no . . . interest in anything except news from the seat of war' but added significantly: 'Not that the war spirit prevailed inside the College—it was its prevalence outside which was for a time somewhat of a drag on our prosperity.'[170] The same was true of the Working Men's College[171]

No one feels out of it for being a pro-Boer . . . I have been through the war at the College, and can witness that it was one of the few places where it was possible to be happy for a few minutes together. I think weekly visits to the College during the war saved several from the madhouse.

This could combine with a 'ramping, roaring Jingo evening' where 'Absent Minded Beggar' and 'Soldiers of the Queen' were sung and where 'young blood in its frankest, noisiest,

[167] *Ibid.*, 8 March 1902, p. 8. The absence of any mention of the LRC is puzzling. The following week, 15 March, an editorial devoted to the question of the representation of Labour mentioned it for the first time but in a completely neutral sense, congratulating it on its progress during the past two years.

[168] G. P. Gooch, *Under Six Reigns* (London, 1958), pp. 77–8, and information gathered from a personal interview.

[169] [G. W. E. Russell], *A Londoners Log-Book 1901–1902* (London, 1902), pp. 84–5.   [170] Morley College, *Annual Report 1900*, p. 2.

[171] J. L. Davies, *The Working Men's College* (London, 1904), p. 193.

happiest mood was there, but to the best of my knowledge no transgression of the laws of good taste or good sense took place'.[172] When those who had volunteered from the College returned home in September 1901, the unofficial magazine organized a welcoming dinner: 'The walls of the room were gaily decked with bunting, and a portrait of B-P surrounded by laurel leaves, gave the keynote to the enthusiastic patriotism that distinguished the proceedings.'[173]

The same kind of dichotomy has been noted in the activities of Trades Councils, and illustrates the lack of identification of one's comrades with the wider issue of imperialism. Such demonstrations did not necessarily imply support for the war, they were an exhibition of support and sympathy for fellow working men who had braved the dangers of war and who were glad to be home. To most working men, the issues were quite simply not related. The war, to them, meant friends and relatives joining the army and risking their lives, perhaps returning home injured or crippled. Their celebrations, when soldiers did return home, were indicative more of relief and pleasure that the hazards of war had been survived than they were of support for the war itself.

Furthermore, while these demonstrations were certainly patriotic, they exhibited none of the ugly features of jingoism. It is, in this context, interesting to note a dialogue between a working man and a middle-class man on the problem of South Africa which was published in *Club Life*. It was occasioned by an article written by 'The Seer' during July 1899 which asserted that 'we have always been the aggressors' in our relations with the Boers who 'three times have gathered their herds and household goods together and with their wives [gone] into the wilderness'. The root of the problem was 'the accursed lust of wealth [which] has driven us to break our pledges', and the fact that the Beits, Rhodes and Jamesons desired nothing less than entire control of the country.[174] The following week a Captain Duncan Presgrave, late of the 9th Lancers, an ex-Uitlander and a member of the Shakespeare Club, replied in a letter which not

[172] *Working Men's College Journal*, February 1900, p. 203.
[173] The *Vagrant*, September 1900. There were only two issues of this magazine which is unfortunate because it is more helpful in telling us what the men were interested in than the official publications of the college.
[174] *Club Life*, 1 July 1899, p. 13.

only illustrated the brashness of the pre-war period but which contrasted with the rational arguments put forward by 'The Seer'. He argued that there would not be a war and that the situation was analogous to 'sending a child to bed without its supper for being disobedient; . . . our much beloved Queen will see it is done. She has only to squeeze, and old Kruger will have a fainting fit.'[175]

It is thus evident that the most significant feature to emerge from a study of these institutions is the lack of jingoism. There were, it would be true to assume, a large number of working men opposed to the war. But the direct evidence for any kind of working-class attitude or opinion is scanty. It is clear that those who did oppose it did so because it detracted from social reform and aimed at the extermination of the Boer states. It was this range of beliefs that induced the Trades Councils to support pro-Boer members of parliament. It was, however, to be the last time they were to support the Liberal Party[176] and to that extent the war bolstered the Radical traditions of the working class.[177] However, this feature is overshadowed by the absence of the manifest forms of jingoism which seemed to infect the whole of society at this period. Public meetings against the war, as will be shown in Chapter IV, were only held with the greatest difficulty; and while it was easier to hold a meeting in a club which can exclude non-members, it was also a more significant test case—for they were specifically working-class institutions. It is noteworthy that there were no reports of meetings being broken up in the clubs and none had to be cancelled because of the fear of rowdy opposition.[178]

[175] *Ibid.*, 15 July 1899, p. 15.
[176] By the end of 1901 thirty-four Trades Councils had affiliated to the LRC. See Minutes and Letters of the LRC f. 78.
[177] Thus, Aberdeen Trades Council support of socialists in 1896 and opposition to the Liberals in 1895. And also the success of the NDL in the clubs.
[178] There was a report that 'a club meeting was broken up the other evening and several clubs have postponed their intended gatherings lest a riot should take place'. But this proved later to be untrue. See *Club Life*, 17 March 1900, p. 8; 24 March 1900, p. 11.

III

The 'Khaki' Election
of 1900

T H E General Election of 1900 resulted in a Conservative majority of 134 seats over the combined Liberal and Irish parties. This
victory, large by any standard, was especially unusual because,
defying the 'swing of the pendulum' theory, it was the second
successive victory for the Unionist cause. Fought nationally on
the platform of the government's policy in South Africa, it has
been ignored by historians perhaps because it was such an obvious
vindication of that policy. And while it is true that imperialism
was one of the first truly national issues,[1] it is not true that this
meant that local issues were no longer significant in influencing
the course of the election. Many constituencies can be distinguished where the significance of agricultural issues, ritualism
and social reform were dominant themes of the campaign.[2] It is
with the latter that this chapter is primarily concerned; for there
is a natural correlation between working-class constituencies
and social reform as an issue.

Elections present difficult problems for the historian. His
source material must be primarily the newspapers of the time
with their obvious limitations. Certain statistics can be mis-
leading,[3] especially in a work of this nature where we are trying

[1] As advanced by Asa Briggs in *Victorian Cities* (London, 1963), p. 370.

[2] A survey of the whole election revealed about 12 seats where agricultural
issues were significant, 9 where ritualism was dominant, and at least 43 where
social reform was important. Undoubtedly there were others that could have been
added to the list.

[3] For an example of this see F. Bealey, 'Les Travaillistes et la Guerre des
Boers', *Le Mouvement Social* (October-December, 1963), p. 66, where he illustrates a point by use of swing figures. Thus, Burns had a 1·6 swing in his favour but
his majority only increased by ten votes.

to determine attitudes. Where the major problem is one of trying to determine the size of the working-class vote in any particular constituency they must be used with the greatest of care owing to the fact that the census reports were based upon administrative counties and not on constituencies. It is thus necessary to try to use a judicious combination of the newspaper and the statistic and this is the pattern followed here.

The chapter—limited for obvious reasons solely to England, Scotland and Wales—falls into two main sections. In the first, a brief background to the election will be recounted which will illustrate the basically unchanged result of the contest. In the second, working-class attitudes towards the election and its issues will be examined. To illustrate this, two significant features will be considered: firstly, that of the constituencies which returned pro-Boer members of parliament; and secondly, the importance of social issues in certain working-class constituencies.

It was almost universally agreed that the election of 1900 was one of the most unexciting in recent memory.[4] Undoubtedly, this was partly because 'the general result was unquestioned from the first';[5] partly it was because in this year of the Scarborough riots and Mafeking Night, rowdyism was at a premium —even in the pro-Boer constituencies.[6] But it was also because the Liberals failed to put up much resistance. The party was, as has been shown, demoralized and rent with dissension. It never expected to win the election and it never really tried. An indication of its ineffective opposition were the 143 seats it allowed to go uncontested. This compared unfavourably with the 109 it had failed to contest in the *débâcle* of 1895.

This large number of uncontested seats precluded a Liberal victory under any circumstances. They were, in effect, a result of the disorganization and demoralization within the party. The

[4] An 'old campaigner' in Nottingham said that 'It was . . . the quietest election I remember'. Quoted in A. C. Wood, 'Nottingham Parliamentary Elections 1869–1900', *Transactions of the Thoroton Society* (1956), p. 64.

[5] James F. Hope, *History of the 1900 Parliament* (London, 1907), I, p. 2.

[6] Sir Alfred Newton's son was assaulted at Southwark West which his father was contesting. Probably the rowdiest constituency was Camborne in Cornwall, where the supporters of W. S. Caine on several occasions upset the meetings of the Liberal Unionist Candidate and on one occasion stoned his coach. See *Cornish Post and Mining News*, 27 September, 4 October, 11 October 1900.

TABLE 2

UNCONTESTED UNIONIST SEATS, 1895 AND 1900[7]

	1895	1900	Change 1900
Counties	74	83	+ 9
London	11	14	+ 3
Cities	20	43	+23
Wales	—	—	0
Scotland-counties	3	2	− 1
Scotland-burghs	1	1	0
TOTAL	109	143	+34

Secretary of the National Liberal Federation, Robert Hudson, wrote to Herbert Gladstone on 29 August 1900: 'If the election is coming in four weeks time I'm afraid there will be an awful scramble to get things into shape.' In reply, Gladstone blamed the leaders of the party for failing to give the 'lagging constituencies' a lead and gloomily concluded that 'we must scramble through the best we can'. After the election, Gladstone explained that he had 'ransacked the country' and 'run dry' the National Liberal Federation and the Eighty Club but that it was useless as 'some constituencies refused to fight'.[8] Ronald Munro-Ferguson, in charge of the Scottish organization, wrote to Campbell-Bannerman in June complaining of the shortage of money and the fact that 'I am at my wits end for good men'. Explaining the Liberal losses in Scotland he wrote that 'much more than usual depended on the candidates—T. Shaw had about the worst register on the list and won a brilliant victory on it. . . . The west went to pieces partly for the want of outstanding men.'[9]

A typical consequence of this disorganization was the loss of the second Sunderland seat. In 1895, Sir W. Doxford, Conservative, had captured one seat from the Liberals. In 1900, the retiring Liberal, Sir E. T. Gourlay, claiming that he had 'no wish to risk another contest', tried to persuade the local party

[7] Table adapted from *Constitutional Yearbook* (London, 1906).

[8] Philip Poirier, *The Advent of the Labour Party* (London, 1959), p. 123.

[9] Ferguson to Campbell-Bannerman, 9 June, 24 October 1900, Campbell-Bannerman Papers, Add. MSS. 41222, ff. 321, 330.

not to run another Liberal in the hope that the Conservatives would allow himself and Doxford an unopposed return.[10] The Liberal 900 first proposed that a local Liberal, Mr Standish, should run in harness with Gourlay. Standish, however, refused. The local Chairman, Samuel Storey, then obtained the nomination, stipulating that his running partner should be Standish.[11] The Executive Committee, meanwhile, felt that A. Wilkie, the Labour candidate, would be a better partner and so this proposal collapsed. At this point Storey declared the party to be 'helpless and useless'.[12] Eventually a satisfactory candidate was found in a Mr G. B. Hunter, but by this time there were only a few days to go before the election and the Conservatives obtained an easy victory.

Sunderland was also typical in that it represented an urban gain for the Conservative Party. The most outstanding feature of the election was the way in which the Conservatives emerged as a party of urban strength. They gained in all thirty-eight seats but two of these were from the Irish nationalists. Both parties lost the same number (thirty-six) of seats to each other but of the thirty-six seats gained by the government twenty-two were large borough constituencies. The Liberals tended to gain seats in the counties, and small boroughs and to consolidate their hold on Wales, where only four of the nineteen seats contested by Unionists failed to show a pro-Liberal swing.

The war probably played a part in the Liberal successes in Wales, the only area where they made positive gains. Certainly there was a heavy concentration of Liberal MPs who were avowedly anti-imperialist; but sentiment against the war seems to have operated most forcefully in the rural areas where Welsh nationalism was important and these areas were safe Liberal seats without the war.[13] In other parts of Wales the picture was more ambiguous; many of the local Liberal Associations in South Wales were under the domination of Liberal imperialists, and even Keir Hardie's victory at Merthyr cannot be explained

[10] *Sunderland Herald and Daily Post*, 19 September 1900.
[11] *Ibid.*, 21 September 1900.   [12] *Ibid.*, 22 September 1900.
[13] H. Pelling and K. O. Morgan, 'Wales and the Boer War', *Welsh History Review*, December 1969, p. 373. The strongest opponents of the war in Wales— Bryn Roberts, Arthur Humphreys-Owen, J. A. Bright—all sat for purely rural constituencies. And Lloyd George—the most infamous pro-Boer of them all—sat for a mixed constituency, Carmarthen Districts.

solely in terms of the anti-war miners but rather in terms of the unpopularity of Pritchard Morgan, D. A. Thomas's running mate.[14] The most important factor, however, in explaining the swing to the Liberals throughout the whole of Wales—a swing of 8·6—was the recovery that took place from the near break-up of the party in 1895 when *Cymru Fydd*, a Home Rule group, had shaken the traditional loyalty to Liberalism.[15]

The crucial area for the Conservatives was Scotland. Neither they, nor their allies, the Liberal Unionists, did very well in England as a whole and in Wales they were all but exterminated. The Liberals gained ten seats in England but lost ground heavily in Scotland. They seem to have done especially well in the counties of England, gaining seats at a greater rate than they lost them in the boroughs. But it was here that the largest number of seats were allowed to go uncontested to the Unionists.

Thus, the crucial factors of this election were the small but sufficient gains that the Conservatives made in the boroughs and Scotland and the failure of the Liberals really to resist the Conservative attack.[16] This election saw the Conservatives at their peak as an urban party before they were challenged in the towns by social democracy. The Liberals to a certain extent were driven back to the bedrock of their support—especially noticeable in their success in Wales. And it was noted that the real Liberal strength lay in the small boroughs: 'Excluding Derby . . . the Liberal borough gains are all in little urban constituencies averaging 9,000 voters.'[17] The distribution of the seats is illustrated in Tables 3 and 4.

Glasgow was a characteristic example of the urbanization of the Conservative Party. In 1900 the two remaining Liberal seats were lost to the Tories and only one of the seven divisions did not conform to the pattern of an increased Conservative vote —this was College division, where Stirling-Maxwell was strongly opposed by R. Paterson, a fervent follower of Lord Rosebery. In one further seat, Central, the Conservative was returned unopposed.

---

[14] *Ibid.*, pp. 372, 377.   [15] *Ibid.*, p. 378.

[16] In one sense the 1900 election rhetoric bears a resemblance to the 1970 mid-term elections in the United States. In both cases the publicity offensive was dominated by vicious rhetorical attacks on Liberals who dissented for one reason or another from the national policies. In both cases, however, this rhetoric seems to have had little effect.   [17] *Labour Leader*, 13 October 1900.

TABLE 3

PARTY DISTRIBUTION OF PARLIAMENTARY SEATS IN ENGLAND,
SCOTLAND AND WALES BY REGION[18]

	England			Wales			Scotland		
	Cons.	L.U.	L.	Cons.	L.U.	L.	Cons.	L.U.	L.
1895	298	51	116	7	1	22	19	14	39
1900	292	47	126	4	0	26	29	17	34

TABLE 4

PARTY DISTRIBUTION OF PARLIAMENTARY SEATS IN ENGLAND,
SCOTLAND, WALES BY COUNTIES AND CITIES[19]

	1895			Dissolution 1900			Election 1900		
	Cons.	L.U.	L.	Cons.	L.U.	L.	Cons.	L.U.	L.
England									
London	50	3	8	50	2	9	52	1	8
Boroughs	101	21	42	100	21	43	105	20	39
Counties	142	27	65	138	24	72	132	24	78
Wales									
Boroughs	5	1	5	5	1	5	3	—	8
Counties	2	—	17	2	—	17	1	—	18
Scotland									
Burghs	5	9	17	5	7	19	8	8	15
Counties	12	5	22	12	5	22	11	9	19

The two seats of Bridgeton and Blackfriars that fell to the
Conservatives in 1900 were the last remnants of a town that had
been totally Liberal in 1885. Blackfriars had reached the high-
water mark of its Liberalism in 1892 when the majority reached
1,081. The election of 1895 cut it down to 380 and in 1900 Bonar
Law converted this into a Conservative majority of 1,000.
Bridgeton reflected a similar pattern. Liberal in 1885, the
majority of 121 rose steadily to 1,440 in the 1887 by-election.
It then began to fall until by 1897 it had sunk to 125 and in 1900

[18] F. H. MacCalmont, *Parliamentary Poll-Book of all Elections* (7th ed., Nottingham, 1910), p. 237.
[19] From Augustine Birrell, *The Election of 1900*, Liberal Magazine Extra No. 1
(London, 1901), p. 5.

Scott Dickson, the Conservative, obtained a majority of 991. Calamachie, strongly Liberal in 1885, had been shaken by the split of the following year and had been held by the Conservatives since 1892. Similarly, in St Rollox, the Liberal Unionist split had shaken the large Liberal majority and in 1895, helped by a Labour candidate who split the Liberal vote, the Conservative captured the seat. The absence of a Labour candidate helps to explain why this seat was held with a reduced majority in 1900. Thus, in the long-term perspective, the failure of the Liberals to hold Blackfriars and Bridgeton was part of a long-term failure to retain their urban appeal in the face of the challenge represented by Liberal Unionism and Conservatism.

The more immediate reasons, however, for the defection of Blackfriars are interesting. Although both Bonar Law and Provand, the Liberal, fought the campaign solely on the imperial issue,[20] the operative factor was the Irish vote. Wherever there were Irish voters in 1900 the question of a Catholic University for Ireland was an important issue. Provand, a follower of Lord Rosebery, refused to commit himself either on Home Rule or on the university question.[21] As a result, the Irish decided to support Bonar Law[22] and it was to this that Provand attributed his defeat.[23] This is significant, for it illustrates how important local interests could be. The Irish group in parliament were the most violent opponents of the government's policy in South Africa, yet the Irish voters of Glasgow were prepared to support a Conservative candidate.

There were other constituencies which also illustrate how important local issues could be. At Hastings, the Liberals gained the seat as a consequence of disorganization in local Conservative circles caused by the resignation of the retiring member, Lucas Shadwell, over the question of ritualism in the Church of England.[24] Boyle, the Conservative candidate, did his best to divert attention away from this divisive issue by his adulation of

---

[20] *Glasgow Evening News*, 27 September 1900.
[21] *Ibid.*, 26 September 1900.
[22] *Ibid.*, 1 October 1900.   [23] *Ibid.*, 5 October 1900.
[24] That this issue caused a considerable disturbance in the local Conservative Party can be seen from a letter written by Mrs Lucas Shadwell to the *Hastings and St Leonards Observer*, 6 October 1900.

the Khaki spirit, 'which got us out of the war'.[25] But the potency of the ecclesiastical question in this constituency was obvious from the many questions at his meetings on the problem of ritualism in the Church of England. Anxiety was not allayed by his claim that 'the Church of England is large enough to embrace us all'.[26]

In Torquay, too, the issue of ritualism proved to be of greater importance even to Conservatives than imperialism. Normally a safe Conservative seat, it was lost to the Liberals in 1900, in spite of the fact that the Conservative candidate had the highest imperial credentials. Reginald Rankin had served with Remington's Horse in South Africa,[27] but ritualism proved to be too much of a 'thorny subject'[28] to enable him to win the seat.

The issue of ritualism provides some interesting sidelights on the election of 1900,[29] but it was only of very local and minor importance. In ten constituencies only can it be seen to have materially affected the result.[30] The fact was that this election was very boring. Unlike the Khaki Election of 1918, the troops were not home; there had been no peace celebrations, there was no sense of achievement and of tasks ahead. The government's campaign was unexciting and unvarying. It was asking for an endorsement of what had gone before. It received an endorsement, but with no great enthusiasm. Conservative candidates complacently assured the public that the war was over. They stood on imperial platforms and unless faced with a sharp Liberal challenge, ignored the issues. Their political speeches consisted largely of extolling the virtues of Tommy Atkins and elaborating on the necessity of the war. Most paid lip service to the idea of Empire Federation which they believed the war had made practicable; few noticed the far more significant federation of the Australian colonies. In spite of the efforts of Chamberlain

[25] *Ibid.*, 22 September 1900.
[26] *Ibid.*, 22 September 1900, Election Manifesto.
[27] See *A Subaltern's Letters to His Wife* (London, 1901).
[28] *Torquay Times*, 28 September 1900.
[29] In some places—Ashford, Kent and Brighton—Independent Conservatives stood against the official candidates on this issue. An interesting feature of the ritualistic issue was that it was concentrated largely in the South-east of England. It was an operative issue in Ashford, Brighton, Tonbridge and Hastings in this area.
[30] They were Bristol South, North Hunts., N.W. Lanarkshire, Walsall, Blackfriars—Glasgow, Ashford, Brighton, Tonbridge, Hastings and Torquay.

to make 'patriotism' the test of a candidate's acceptability,[31] there is very little evidence to suppose that this was the case. In fact, most Conservatives did not fight a 'Khaki' Election. They tended to point out, quite reasonably, that a disunited Liberal Party could not be trusted to carry out an effective settlement in South Africa. The impression was that this was the issue at hand and that having carried the war through to a successful conclusion the government should now be allowed to proceed with the settlement.

The Liberal campaign aimed at the consideration of domestic issues. It pointed to the Agricultural Rating and Church Benefices Bills as evidence of the 'class' nature of Conservative legislation, made fun of the Workmen's Compensation Act, and denigrated the Housing Act passed by the government. Candidates attacked the failure of the administration to redeem its hint of 1895 that old-age pensions would be introduced and although this did make some impact—in conjunction with the Browning Hall Pensions Committee set up in 1899 to agitate this issue—there was no burning social issue which could be used to indict the government and arouse voters from their apathy. It was only in this negative sense that the war issue dominated the election.

The overwhelming feature of the election was voter apathy. This cannot be emphasized too strongly because it helps to give the lie to the belief that 1900 was a 'Khaki' Election dominated by a patriotic concern and won by the Conservatives by a successful, though shady, manipulation of this war fever. Nothing could be further from the truth. Voters were, on the whole, not interested. Most turn-outs were down, and more than one million fewer voted in 1900, compared with 1895.[32]

This voter disregard of most of Chamberlain's patriotic exhortations is also illustrated by the survival of the pro-Boer section of the Liberal Party. The Colonial Secretary had asked

[31] Chamberlain's famous telegram: 'Every vote given against the Government is a vote given to the Boers' caused some embarrassment in Conservative circles, as also did his speech at Birmingham when he said that 'There is nothing going on now but a guerilla business which is encouraged by these men; I was going to say traitors, but I will say instead these misguided individuals'. See Birrell, *op. cit.*, pp. 19–21.

[32] In 1895 the total votes cast in England, Wales and Scotland numbered 3,409,711. In 1900 the total was 2,133,622.

for an overwhelming majority. In fact neither the Liberals nor the pro-Boers were overwhelmed. The government's majority was 18 seats down compared with 1895 and was only increased by 2 over what it had been at the dissolution. The pro-Boers lost 19 of their supporters but gained 5 new members, making their total strength in parliament about 52 which was almost one-third of the Liberal Party.[33] Neither was it any great advantage to be a Liberal imperialist follower of Lord Rosebery in 1900. They were usually attacked by Conservative candidates as being men who did not really have the courage of their convictions and as being part of a party that because of its anti-imperialist wing, could not be relied upon to carry out the imperialist mission. Thus, Liberal imperialists did not benefit from the Conservative attack on the pro-Boers; of the 62 Liberals who actively supported the government 14 failed to gain re-election. Of the 30 candidates who were specifically pledged to work for a return of Rosebery to the leadership, half failed to get elected.

Only in the pro-Boer constituencies was the war a live issue in so far as it provided the main and often the only topic to be discussed. The characteristic feature of the election as it was fought in many of these constituencies was that of a defensive Liberal campaign.[34] The Liberals were largely restricted by the various attempts the Conservatives made to arouse patriotic feeling against them.[35] And many of the Liberals responded to the Conservative's use of patriotism by softening their opposition to the war. This usually took the form of criticizing the way in which the negotiations had been conducted and by arguing neutrally that once the war had been declared then the incorporation of the Boer Republics into the Empire became inevitable.

[33] The method used for distinguishing the various factions of the Liberal Party is based on the categorization given in *The Times*, 31 July 1900, p. 8. This divided the party up according to the way each member voted in four test divisions. The divisions were: Dillon's amendment to the address urging arbitration; Stanhope's amendment in October 1899 disapproving of the conduct of the negotiations; Redmond's amendment to the address in February urging the cessation of hostilities and recognition of the independence of the Boer states; and Lawson's move to reduce Chamberlain's salary by £100 which produced the famous three-way split in the Liberal Party of 25 July 1900.

[34] See Appendix III for a list of pro-Boer members and constituencies.

[35] For example, a poster was issued in F. Cawley's constituency which pictured him kneeling before Kruger handing him a £20 cheque and referred to a subscription he was supposed to have sent an anti-war committee.

This approach was illustrated by T. G. Ashton, member for South Bedfordshire, who argued in his election address:[36]

I have never concealed my opinion that, but for the blundering diplomacy and unworthy influences this war might have been avoided . . . by voice and vote I condemned the blundering. But, with the outbreak of the war, with the changed circumstances, a change of policy became necessary, and I have constantly advocated the necessity of the unqualified supremacy of the British flag in the Boer states. Their incorporation in the British Empire must be irrevocable.

The defensiveness of this group of pro-Boers was illustrated by their sensitivity about the votes that they had registered in parliament. Thus, Charles Fenwick emphasized that his votes against the government were not intended to comment on the virtues of particular measures, but as a protest against governmental policy as a whole.[37] F. Cawley, MP for Prestwich, felt obliged to explain a letter he had written to the Manchester Transvaal Committee one month before the war broke out. He claimed that he believed that 'certain unscrupulous men' had worked for war and that he had tried to combat this, but once war had been declared he had constantly voted with the government and had supported annexation.[38]

There were others, however, who took a more aggressive stand. Thus C. H. Wilson, the Hull ship-owner and member for the Central Division of that city, stated:[39]

The war I have entirely disapproved of as a result of a bungling diplomacy and an awful waste of the lives of our splendid soldiers, through incompetancy in its conduct. . . . We have this loss of life and we annex two practically free Republics.

Similarly, M. Levy—one of the pro-Boer gains—who was fighting Loughborough, asserted that 'from his point of view there were no merits in this war at all. It was forced upon us by the hasty and capricious tactics of Mr. Chamberlain.'[40]

Those who were not prepared to make any excuses for their pro-Boer votes in parliament usually linked their opposition to their progressive social attitudes at home. They tended to

[36] *Bedfordshire Mercury*, 5 October 1900.
[37] *Newcastle Daily Chronicle*, 4 October 1900.
[38] *Middleton Guardian*, 29 September 1900.
[39] *Hull Daily News*, 26 September 1900.
[40] *Loughborough Herald*, 27 September 1900.

emphasize the way in which the expenditure on the war detracted from social reform. Thus, C. P. Scott pointed out that the £20 million spent on the war would have enabled the government to give an old-age pension to every man and woman in the country.[41] The same theme could be found in Burt's contest at Morpeth; he believed there was too much to be done at home to justify imperial ventures.[42] And although this was a common Liberal charge, the anti-war candidates were unusual in that they were doctrinally concerned with the two apparent choices of the expansion of the Empire and social amelioration at home.

But the vast majority of Conservative attempts to unseat pro-Boer members failed. Where they were successful or where the loss of a Liberal seat was directly attributable to the presence of a pro-Boer candidate was usually in constituencies which had only a very uncertain allegiance to Liberalism. Of the nineteen seats lost by the pro-Boers, twelve were of this nature. Six were lost because the sitting member retired and was replaced by a Liberal who was not pro-Boer, and one was lost through the defeat of Dr G. B. Clark by the official Liberal at Caithness.[43]

Of the twelve pro-Boer seats lost to the government, six were constituencies which during the 1890s had exhibited a definite swing away from Liberalism. This is illustrated in Table 5, which shows the Liberal share of the vote in each election from 1885 to 1900. It will be noted that in every case 1895 rather than 1900 seems to have been the crucial year. The decline in the Liberal share of the vote was greater between 1892 and 1895 than between 1895 and 1900 except in the case of Eskdale. These seats were constituencies which had been, with the exception of Cockermouth, safe Liberal seats in 1885 and had shown a recovery from the trauma of 1886 in the election of 1892. It is noticeable that four of the seats were urban constituencies and the process of the growth of urban conservatism throughout the nineties is illustrated here. The result of 1900 only completed a process the dangers of which 1895 had illustrated with alarming clarity.

[41] *Leigh Chronicle*, 28 September 1900.   [42] *Morpeth Herald*, 29 September 1900.
[43] R. L. Harmsworth, a Liberal imperialist, was adopted by the local party in preference to Clark. Clark fought the election and finished third in a pool of four. His main support came from the crofting community. See *Caithness Courier*, 7 and 28 September 1900.

TABLE 5

CONSTITUENCIES OF DECLINING LIBERAL INFLUENCE LOST BY
PRO-BOERS

Constituency	1885	1886	1892	1895	Change over 1892	1900	Change over 1895
S.W. Bethnal Green	58·4	55·9	59·5	52·8	−6·7	46·7	−6·1
Burnley	53·7	49·7	56·1a	51·0	−5·9	48·1	−2·9
Cockermouth	49·9	58·2	54·5	51·4	−3·1	48·7	−2·7
Cumberland-Eskdale	60·0	56·0	55·6	51·0	−4·6	45·2	−5·8
Newcastle-u-Lyme	58·5	48·7	57·8	50·7	−7·1	48·7	−2·0
Sheffield-Brightside	57·7	55·7	57·4	b	—	44·7	—

a. In the by-election of 1893 the Liberal share of the vote was 52·9.
b. There is no real basis for comparison: the Liberal was unopposed in 1895. In the by-election of 1897, the Liberal share of the vote was 52·3.

Out of the remaining six seats, four were constituencies where Conservatism or Liberal Unionism had gained an earlier hold and where the victory of a Liberal candidate was an unnatural result. Middleton provides an interesting example of responsiveness to the national mood. It was a 'see-saw' seat which reflected the voting of the country as a whole. Thus in 1897 when the Liberals were beginning to make a recovery at the polls, Middleton faithfully recorded this in the return of James Duckworth. The by-elections of Edinburgh and Stepney also illustrate this. Table 6 illustrates the Liberal share of the vote in these marginal constituencies.

TABLE 6

MARGINAL LIBERAL CONSTITUENCIES LOST BY PRO-BOERS

Constituency	1885	1886	1892	1895	1900
Dumfriesshire	57·6	44·1	48·2	50·02	47·1
Edinburgh South	No Cons.	63·2	52·4	49·5[a]	49·5
Middleton	54·6	48·5	50·5	46·0[b]	49·4
Stepney	50·1	43·7	48·9	44·4[c]	38·1

a. In the by-election of 1897 the Liberal share of the vote was 53·8.
b. In the by-election of 1897 the Liberal share of the vote was 51·2.
c. In the by-election of 1898 the Liberal share of the vote was 50·2.

The two remaining seats of Aberdeenshire East and Sutherlandshire were the only seats where Liberalism could have been expected to survive. Sutherlandshire, with its small electorate of 2,800 in 1900, had returned a Liberal since 1885, each time with safe majorities and with a share of the vote that had never fallen below 60 per cent.[44] Similarly, Aberdeenshire East had been regarded as a safe Liberal seat and had never had a majority for the Liberal candidate of below 1,400. The rejection of T. R. Buchanan was, therefore, unexpected and Ferguson attributed it to the fact that ' "Khaki" feeling is very strong in the Moray Basin'.[45] However, these were the only seats which the Conservatives captured solely as a result of the war: they were the

[44] The majorities were: 1885, 643; 1886, 880; 1892, 846; 1895, 495.
[45] Ferguson to Campbell-Bannerman, 24 October 1900, Campbell-Bannerman papers, *loc. cit.*

110

only two pro-Boer seats that could have been expected to have withstood the onslaught.[46]

TABLE 7

PREVIOUS STRONGHOLDS OF LIBERALISM LOST BY PRO-BOERS

Constituency	1885	1886	1892	1895	1900
East Aberdeenshire	67·3	66·0	59·1	58·1	49·5
Sutherlandshire	61·7	71·5	70·5	64·6	38·06

Thus, the pro-Boer members were left with fifty-two seats in parliament. There was no single markedly characteristic feature of these seats. They ranged from urban constituencies such as Hull West and Northampton to large rural areas such as Ross and Cromarty and Denbighshire. But there are two significant facts which it is worth noting. In the first place the vast majority of these constituencies were strongholds of Liberalism in the purest sense and had been held by the party since 1885. Forty out of the fifty-two had remained Liberal without a break throughout the period and some, such as Morpeth, relatively unchanged by the redistribution of 1884, had been Liberal before that date. They were areas of staunch and traditional Liberalism. But more than this, they were areas which owed an allegiance to a particular brand of Liberalism: that associated with the name of Gladstone. Those members who had held their seats continuously since 1885 had, without exception, entered politics under the influence of Gladstone. Men such as F. A. Channing, who wrote in his biography that it was the influence of Gladstone's sympathy with 'nations struggling to be free that brought me in touch with the living forces and the supreme duties of political life';[47] and H. J. Wilson whose political philosophy has already been examined.[48]

[46] This very cursory analysis merely emphasizes the desperate need for detailed local studies. We cannot answer any of the real questions posed by these trends until such studies have been undertaken. We need to know, for example, how and why the changing economic and social factors of these constituencies affected the fortunes of the Liberal Party. Of course such analyses should cover the period 1880 to the 1920s and the apparent final demise of Liberalism as a viable alternative governing party.

[47] Francis Allison Channing, *Memories of Midland Politics 1885–1918* (London, 1918), p. 1.

[48] See Chapter I, p. 41.

In the second place, the one geographic-political feature common to the majority of these constituencies is that they were essentially small borough constituencies, usually with a significant local industry which provided the basis of the Liberal Party's working-class support. Only twelve can be identified as being urban.[49] The characteristic pro-Boer constituency consisted of a group of small market towns with some dominant traditional industry such as textile works, some form of engineering or mining. Thus, Thomas Burt's constituency of Morpeth consisted essentially of the mining towns of Morpeth, Bedlington and Blyth, the largest of which was Bedlington with a population of 7,440 where 49·2 per cent of the working male population were miners.[50] Similarly with Channing's constituency of East Northamptonshire, which encompassed the towns of Rushden, Wellingborough and part of Kettering. The largest town was Kettering and the boot-and-shoe industry was the dominant trade throughout the area: it comprised 45·2 per cent of the working male population of these towns.[51] It was these men who provided the solid core of his electoral support. He tells how the shoe hands at Finedon 'broke out into a tempest of cheers' when 'I spoke warmly and decisively my creed upon the war'.[52] J. E. Ellis's constituency of Rushcliffe, Nottinghamshire, contained hosiery and lace industries in the small towns of Arnold, Beeston and Carlton, and the mining town of Hucknall where 63 per cent of the men worked in the mines.[53] In the two main towns of C. P. Scott's constituency of Leigh, Lancashire, the cotton industry and coal mining together provided 54 per cent of the working population.[54] Mining was also the largest single occupation in the mid-Derbyshire and Houghton-le-Spring seats of J. Jacoby and R. Cameron and the

[49] They were: Aberdeen (2 seats), Battersea, Haggerston, Carnarvon Boroughs, Northampton, West Islington, North Manchester, Merthyr (2 seats), Hull West, Nottingham West.

[50] *Census of England and Wales*, 1901, County of Northumberland (*Accounts and Papers*, Vol. CXX), Cd. 1294 (1902), p. 72.

[51] *Ibid.*, County of Northamptonshire (*Accounts and Papers*, Vol. CXX), Cd. 1359 (1902), p. 60.

[52] Channing, *op. cit.*, p. 257.

[53] *Census, op. cit.*, County of Nottinghamshire (*Accounts and Papers*, Vol. CXX), Cd. 1292 (1902), p. 60.

[54] *Ibid.*, County of Lancashire (*Accounts and Papers*, Vol. CXIX), Cd. 1002 (1902), p. 178.

same was true of Sir William Harcourt's safe seat of West Monmouthshire whose main town was Tredegar where 58 per cent of the working men were miners.[55] J. E. Barlow's constituency of Frome, Somerset, included a variety of scattered industry; miners in Radstock, railway workers at Tiverton, mechanics and factory hands at Frome itself. His strength rested upon this working-class vote, and the work of the trade organizations in delivering it for him. It was reported that at Radstock every available vote was polled and most of them for Barlow.[56] Other, less notable, examples tell the same story. Grantham, a pro-Boer gain, had a fairly large agricultural machinery industry employing about 2,000 people and at whose works Priestley, the Liberal candidate, was cheered when he addressed them saying that he 'hoped that they would never again see such a terrible conflict between the British Empire and two small powers as the Dutch Republics'.[57] Loughborough had a considerable engineering interest. Holmfirth, in the West Riding, was in a sense the typical pro-Boer constituency. It was a mixed agricultural and mining constituency whose most important town was Penistone, where the most significant occupations were mining, woollens and agriculture and where these occupations provided 21 per cent, 11 per cent and 9·5 per cent respectively of the working male population.[58]

Thus, there is a general pattern which helps explain why these constituencies remained loyal to Liberalism in 1900. It does seem to have been a fact that the countryside was less affected by 'war fever' than the towns. The *Ashton Reporter* remarked:[59]

The war fever chiefly affected the towns. All the great demonstrations were in the larger cities and boroughs . . . bands of soldiers going off were enthusiastically greeted in the crowded streets. Another and another brilliant send off roused the national ardour of the populace. . . . People could think and talk of nothing but the war. . . . The country districts were but slightly affected by these influences.

[55] *Ibid.*, County of Monmouthshire (*Accounts and Papers*, Vol. CXX), Cd. 1361 (1902), p. 54; County of Durham (Vol. CXVIII), Cd. 1147, p. 76; County of Derbyshire (Vol. CXVIII), Cd. 1303, p. 64.
[56] *Somerset Standard*, 12 October 1900.
[57] *Census*, County of Lincolnshire (*Accounts and Papers*, Vol. CXIX), Cd. 1304 (1902), p. 102. See also H. Pelling, *Social Geography of British Elections 1885–1910* (London, 1967), p. 213; also *Grantham Times*, 29 September 1900.
[58] H. J. Wilson Papers, M.D. 2499, f. 9.
[59] Quoted in Pelling, *op. cit.*, p. 285.

It was noted in the Richmond division of the West Riding that, because of the agricultural question, 'the Khaki cry figures far less . . . than in any of the constituencies in the immediate neighbourhood'.[60] In the Warwickshire village of Tysoe this difference was also noticed: 'Jingoism is dead. In Tysoe it had never had vigour.'[61] The absence of 'war fever' in the country districts was explicable in simple terms of population concentration. There was far less opportunity for crowds to gather and less excuse, as peace meetings were mainly held in the towns.

But the primary explanation for the return of these pro-Boers is to be found in the support that they received from working men loyal to Liberalism. As the results indicated, there was no massive shift of Liberal voters to Conservatism. Those Liberals who disagreed with their candidate's stand on the war tended to abstain. This was illustrated in Hoxton where James Stuart was ejected. Although he had not been a pro-Boer in parliamentary terms the Conservative campaign was fought solely on this issue. In spite of the fact that he had devoted his life to social issues, this seems to have counted for little once the Conservatives successfully tagged him as a Little Englander. The total poll was about 400 votes down on that of 1895, the Conservative vote was about the same (2,866 to 2,862 in 1895) and the Liberal vote of 2,592 about 400 less than their vote of the previous general election (2,990), indicating that few actually changed sides but rather abstained. The same was true of Harcourt's majority in West Monmouthshire where the total poll was 822 down over that of 1895, Harcourt's vote down by 1,267 and the Conservative vote up by 445, which would again suggest that most Liberals who disliked Harcourt's anti-war stand were unattracted by the alternative of voting Conservative and that they abstained. In H. J. Wilson's constituency of Holmfirth, where his majority dropped by 770 votes, the *Penistone Express* of 5 October 1900, quoted Mr Fred Brown, a miner, as saying: 'There were some who had gone against Mr Wilson on the question of war, but they had not voted Tory; they wouldn't do that.'

And in general, in these constituencies which had a core of

---

[60] *Darlington and Stockton Times*, 8 October 1900.
[61] M. K. Ashby, *Joseph Ashby of Tysoe* (Cambridge, 1961), p. 197.

working-class support for Liberalism, the majority continued in their loyalty. This was the feature that all pro-Boers remarked upon when they came to write their biographies.[62] The newspaper reports of the time confirm the claim that the working-class vote was the crucial factor in their success. At Newbold, a mining town in J. Bayley's constituency of Chesterfield, it was reported that 400 or 500 miners were marshalled by the Secretary of the Derbyshire Miners Association and marched in procession to the polls to vote for Bayley.[63] Like many of his fellow pro-Boers Bayley's nomination was proposed by a Trade Unionist and seconded by a Nonconformist. Francis Channing provides another clear example of the pro-Boer dependence on working-class and Nonconformist support. The Secretary and President of the local Boot and Shoe Operatives Union urged their members to vote for Channing; the railway leader, Richard Bell, sent him a letter of support which he used to secure the railwaymen of Wellingborough. His working-class support was seen again and again at Liberal meetings. A shoe operative, Mr Wallis, at one of his meetings asked: 'Were they prepared to weigh South African policy against the social and economic reform their member had given 15 years of strenuous work to promote?'[64] Channing continually linked the war with social reform, claiming that 'but for the war they would have had £9 million surplus for old age pensions'.[65]

His organized Nonconformist support came from such bodies as the local temperance organizations. His attacks on the government's laxity with regard to Ritualism in the Church and its unconcern about the social evils of drink, illustrate his advocacy of issues designed to arouse the Nonconformist conscience. Thus, in his election manifesto, he made a point of condemning the government for a failure to 'prevent law breaking in the church by these sacerdotal village despots' and for refusing 'to pass a Sunday Closing Bill and prohibit the sale of liquor to children'.[66]

[62] E.g. see Aaron Watson, *A Great Labour Leader: The Life of Thomas Burt* (London, 1908), p. 195, where an anti-war meeting of miners who had been in the Transvaal is reported.
[63] *Derbyshire Courier*, 13 October 1900.   [64] Channing, *op. cit.*, p. 237.
[65] *Ibid.*, p. 238. See also a meeting reported in *Northampton Daily Chronicle*, 29 September 1900.
[66] *Rushden Echo and Free Press*, 28 September 1900.

The pro-Boer members of parliament were all ardent social reformers. It was this, of course, that provided the basis of their working-class support. And the conflict between the war and the problems of social reform were constantly emphasized by these men. It is important to realize, however, that virtually all the pro-Boers sat for constituencies where there was an important working-class vote, that this vote was the basis of their electoral strength, and that there is very little evidence that this strength was appreciably eroded in 1900.

There does not appear to have been any significant correlation between particular trades or occupations and anti-war sentiment among the working classes. Their loyalty was to Liberalism as a whole for traditional and social reasons and they were not markedly affected by the war to change this allegiance. Indeed, there were notable examples where it tended to strengthen their attachments to the Liberal Party. In Northampton, whose boot-and-shoe industry seems to have been adversely affected by the war, the Liberals regained the seat they had lost in 1895.[67] In spite of the fact that the other seat was held by Labouchere, the Conservatives, who had been rumoured to be seriously suggesting that Balfour or Chamberlain should contest the seat in order to oust Labouchere,[68] were unable to hold on to the second seat gained as a result of Liberal dissension in 1895. In Merthyr, the miners rejected the Liberal imperialist, Pritchard Morgan, and elected Keir Hardie and D. A. Thomas, both of whom were anti-war.[69]

A locally adverse economic situation tended to help the Liberals. This was partly because electors react against the government in such a situation, partly because the Liberals were associated more closely than the Conservatives with concern for social issues. An interesting illustration of this was provided by the 'mining divison' of Camborne in Cornwall where there were 3,000 unemployed tin miners.[70] This situation was partly due to the world-wide state of the tin market. In 1895 Strauss, the

[67] 41 per cent of Northampton's occupied males worked in the boot-and-shoe industry, see *Census*, County of Northamptonshire, *loc. cit.*

[68] *Northampton Daily Reporter*, 20 September 1900.

[69] For this contest and the part played by the anti-imperialism of the Welsh miners, see K. O. Fox, 'Labour and Merthyr's Khaki Election of 1900', *Welsh Historical Review*, II. No. 2 (1965).

[70] *Cornish Post and Mining News*, 27 September 1900.

successful Liberal Unionist candidate, had hinted that his position as a tin merchant would enable him to do something about this and that it would be in the interests of the constituency to elect him.[71] But this had not proved to be so, and in 1900 the area was even more depressed. The situation was aggravated by the fact that the area had provided a supply of miners for South African mines: men who earned £15 to £20 a month and who 'usually spent half the year at home in their Cornish villages'.[72] Every 'Friday morning from 1896–1900 the up-train from West Cornwall included special cars labelled "Southampton", the embarkation point for South Africa'.[73] In a good week it was not unusual for small villages such as St Just to receive £1,000 from those who had emigrated to South Africa.[74] The war stopped all this and many came home to be unemployed. The Conservative campaign was based upon an appeal to patriotism and imperialism and an attempt to smear Caine, the Liberal candidate and a pro-Boer, as a bad businessman.[75] The question of the war and its connection with the unemployment in the constituency dominated the election. Strauss promised that 'after the war there would be a larger demand for Cornish miners than ever before' and, appealing to patriotism, claimed that the war had been necessary because of grievances and that if the government was to blame at all for the depressed price of tin it was in being 'too lenient in securing English rights'.[76]

Caine based his appeal on social reform and anti-war sentiment. He seems to have been unsure just how far the latter would be an asset and at the beginning of his campaign his attitude tended to vacillate between outright condemnation and mere criticism of the diplomacy. But once it was evident that the war was not particularly popular among the miners, he lined himself up with Channing and Labouchere, blaming the war on the capitalists who wanted to drive out the expensive white

[71] John Newton, *W. S. Caine, M.P. A Biography* (London, 1907), p. 289. Herbert Thomas, *Cornish Mining Interviews* (Camborne, 1896), p. 322, where Strauss is described as one 'who has powerful connections in the financial world'.

[72] Henry W. Nevinson, *Changes and Chances* (London, 1923), p. 339.

[73] A. K. Jenkins, *The Cornish Miner* (London, 1947), p. 330.

[74] *Minutes of Evidence before the Royal Commission on Militia and Volunteers* (Reports, Vol. XXI), Cd. 2063 (1904), p. 291, question 21161.

[75] See *Cornish Post and Mining News*, 13 September 1900.

[76] *Ibid.*, 27 September 1900.

labour and substitute cheap black.[77] This campaign was note-worthy as being possibly the rowdiest in the country. Both sides suffered intense heckling, but Strauss especially was the target of much abuse. At some places towards the end of the campaign he could not obtain a hearing and on at least one occasion he was stoned out of a village.[78] Caine was elected by 108 votes and his victory was merely a reflection that the miners of the constituency were more attracted by the prospects of good money and a secure living than they were by the question of English rights.

However, there was no necessary correlation between the prosperity of trade in an area and the success of imperial candidates. Some towns which may have benefited from the war, such as Sheffield, tended to vote imperialist—although Maddison's defeat was as much prejudiced by internal squabbles within the Liberal Party as by any positive appeal by the Conservative candidate. But in Walsall, whose saddlery trade prospered as a result of the war, the Conservative was ejected and replaced by A. D. Hayter, a Liberal. Indeed the dominant issue of this campaign appeared to be that of social reform. Gedge, the Conservative, had alienated many of his supporters by voting against the Church Benefices Bill. The Tory news-paper in 1896 claimed that he 'no longer had the confidence of his party'. The aggressive campaign fought by Hayter against the financial wastage of the government's policy of extravagance and doles to the clergy and landlords forced Gedge into a defensive position. This was illustrated by the Conservative election address which was largely a defence of the govern-ment's inaction in the realm of social reform.[79] At Conservative meetings Gedge was forced to reply to accusations that he did not wish to see old-age pensions enacted and that he had broken his 1895 election promise to work for them.[80]

It would seem that, in general, where the war was seen to be adverse to working-class economic interests—e.g. Camborne and perhaps Northampton—then appeals to patriotism were in

[77] Ibid., 4 and 27 September 1900. This paper was the only one in the con-stituency. Strauss owned a part of it; thus, information on Caine is fairly sparse.
[78] Ibid., 11 October 1900. Significantly, it was mining students who disrupted Caine's meetings. Ibid., 1 October 1900.
[79] Walsall Free Press, 29 September 1900.
[80] Ibid., 22 September 1900.

vain. In areas where pro-Boers were standing and where they had a long-established record in the constituency there was no inclination to vote Conservative and the traditional alliance between the working classes and the reformist Liberals was emphasized to discourage this possibility. The degree to which imperialist candidates were successful in working-class constituencies appeared to depend upon the extent to which the Liberals could focus interest on social reform. Where they could do this and where they were opposed on a clear imperial platform, then social reform always emerged the winner.

This can be illustrated by the contest at Derby where, by a majority of nearly 1,400, the Liberals, Sir T. Roe and Richard Bell, won back the two seats lost to the Conservatives in 1895. Their opponents were Sir H. Bemrose and Geoffrey Drage, two very strong imperialist candidates. Drage was Chairman of the Imperial South African Association—the propagandist body for a 'British' South Africa. The choice of Bell as a candidate to run in harness with a sound local Liberal was wise.[81] The railwaymen were the dominant occupational group in the town and together with the engineering industry made up about one-fifth of the total number of male workers.[82] The local paper commented on how this election was essentially 'a working man's election'. Bell, whose candidacy was clearly designed to recapture the working men's vote, concentrated solely on social-reform issues, limiting himself in relation to the war to the claim:[83]

He was not one who disregarded the claims of Britishers in any . . . parts of the globe, but he did say there were grievances at home that required redressing before fighting for grievances that existed 7,000 miles away . . . there were far greater grievances in England than ever existed in the Transvaal.

His election address did not mention the war: it contained the whole battery of advanced Liberal social reforms, the eight-hour day, better housing, old-age pensions, reform of the House of Lords, nationalization of the railways and land and temperance

[81] Although not officially a Liberal, Bell's candidacy was organized by the Liberal Association, he took the Liberal whip, and persistently refused to support an Independent Labour group in parliament. He can, therefore, be treated as a Liberal.　　　　[82] *Census*, County of Derbyshire, *loc. cit.*

[83] *Derby Daily Telegraph*, 25 September 1900.

reform.[84] Bell fought a completely 'Labour' campaign; he left most of the speech-making about the war to Roe whose attitude was that typical of the 'centre' Liberals: that annexation was inevitable and that the Liberal Party 'have with the utmost loyalty tried to strengthen the hands of the Government'.[85] The Conservative campaign began as a straightforward appeal to the war issue. The Liberal Party's foreign-policy record was attacked, the war proclaimed as as 'great a task that had ever been undertaken by a nation' and the references to Majuba were frequent.[86] But there was a noticeable change in the Tory campaign as the effectiveness of the Liberal attack on the government's social record was felt. The Liberal newspaper had noticed before the campaign had really begun that the policy of the Liberals should be to 'counteract the Khaki mongers by pointing out that other issues, apart from the war, demanded attention'.[87] The Liberals refused to be shaken by the desire of the Conservatives to limit the contest to that of the war. Roe continually stressed the importance of other issues in his speeches and Bell talked nothing else but social reform. The success of these tactics was apparent by 27 September when a Conservative meeting concentrated solely on rebutting the charges made by the Liberals on the government's poor social-reform record. There were fewer references to the war, and Bemrose actually admitted Roe's theme that there were other election issues that needed discussion.[88] This became a common feature of Conservative meetings and it is evident that the aggressive campaign of the Liberals was having some effect. Thus, here was a clear case of an imperial appeal to a mainly working-class electorate which resulted in a resounding imperialist defeat. The local newspaper claimed that the result showed: 'The working class of this town appreciate to the full the valour of our soldiers but they had no patience with a government that sought to make capital out of it.'[89]

The working-class constituencies of London also illustrate the fact that this was as much a social-reform election as a war election for the working classes. But they do so in a different

---

[84] *Ibid.*, 22 September 1900. [85] *Ibid.*, 20 September 1900.
[86] *Ibid.*, 22 September 1900. [87] *Ibid.*, 18 September 1900.
[88] *Ibid.*, 28 September 1900. See also 29 September.
[89] *Ibid.*, 4 October 1900.

way. The issue in these seats was often not one of a conflict between imperial or social-reform candidates and where it was, the experience of Stuart's rejection by the Hoxton electorate is seen to be the exception rather than the rule.[90]

By 1900 all but eight of the London seats were held by the Conservatives. The local Liberal organization, like the national one, was in a parlous state, and after the election a committee was instituted to reorganize it. Local registers had not been attended to and only three constituencies had full-time agents. Thus, as Dr Paul Thompson has pointed out: 'The results were not a safe guide to opinions.'[91] Nevertheless, the issues involved in the election in the working-class districts are interesting, for they indicate that appeals to 'imperialism' and 'patriotism' were not sufficient to win seats neither were they considered sufficient by Conservative incumbents. There was, in general, no simple correlation in London between voting Liberal and Conservative and voting for social reform or imperialism. This was the mistake *Reynolds News* made when it commented on the results: 'Never was such a vast aggregation of ignorance and entire absence for better social life ever shown.'[92] Conservatives who wished to hold their working-class seats had to ensure that they looked after the interests of their constituents. This was illustrated by H. S. Samuel, Conservative candidate and retiring member for Limehouse, whose election address placed emphasis not on the war but on his work in looking after the interests of the rivermen—the most important social group within the constituency. It was paralleled in his speeches where he proclaimed several times that he did not want to fight a 'khaki' election but was seeking re-election on what he had done for the constituency. He had been responsible for a Bill which remedied the defective water supply to the area.[93]

A similar case was T. R. Dewar, Conservative candidate for

[90] Constituencies upon which this account is based are: Whitechapel, Limehouse, St George's-in-the-East, Poplar, Bow and Bromley, Bermondsey, Newington West, Rotherhithe, and Southwark West. All had electorates of over 60 per cent working class. See P. Thompson, 'Liberals, Radicals, and Labour in London 1880–1900', *Past and Present*, No. 27 (1964), p. 94.

[91] *Ibid.*

[92] *Reynolds News*, 7 October 1900.

[93] *East End News*, 21 September 1900. The same kind of thing was true of the Conservative member, J. Bailey, in Walworth who was a 'friend of the costers'. See *Southwark and Bermondsey Recorder*, 29 September 1900.

St George's-in-the-East. The smallest constituency in London, it comprised a small, well-knit, merchant class and a mainly Irish proletariat.[94] As with Samuel, his election address was not based solely upon an appeal to the war issue. It cleverly linked the war with the way in which it would most closely affect the working classes:

The war in which we are engaged has served a useful purpose in pointing to the necessity of a thorough reform and re-organisation of our Army system . . . the field hospital accommodation . . . [should be] made more satisfactory; the pay and chance of promotion . . . improved; and adequate state provision should be made for the widows and orphans.

But he also advocated 'such legislation as shall ensure for every working man and his family in the East of London decent and comfortable dwellings at fair rents'.[95]

The question of housing was very important. It was a serious problem accentuated by the large numbers of immigrants crowding into the East End; a problem which itself was to achieve wider prominence over the next few years as the demands for the regulation of immigration grew. Many of the immigrants, refugee Jews from Poland and Russia in the main, were destitute. It was calculated that over 700 had been relieved from the rates of the Whitechapel union in 1899 and the opinion was voiced that this question 'is more vital to East London than any change in the Imperial government could be'.[96] Dewar was praised because he was in favour of a check upon the unrestricted entry of alien immigrants:[97]

Possibly the greatest evil from which East London is suffering at the present moment, is the unrestricted immigration into this country of foreign paupers . . . to fight with Englishmen for their very houses. . . . There is only one candidate in the whole of East London who has dared to say straight out what we all think. That is Mr. T. R. Dewar.

The newspaper noted that 'there are now two issues in St George's: the war and alien immigration'.[98] And because

[94] Cornelius O'Leary, *The Elimination of Corrupt Practices at British Elections 1868–1911* (Oxford, 1961), p. 199.
[95] *East End News*, 25 September 1900.
[96] *East London Advertiser*, 13 October 1900.
[97] *Eastern Post and City Chronicle*, 29 September 1900.
[98] *Ibid.*

Strauss, the Liberal candidate, was opposed to restrictions being placed upon immigration, the issue became increasingly important in Dewar's campaign.

The problem was complicated everywhere in the East End by the Jewish vote. Whilst it was not true that Dewar was the only candidate who favoured a restrictionist policy,[99] it was true that this vote had to be courted. In St George's the Jewish voters formed 10 per cent of the electorate and were supposed to be the decisive factor in any election in this constituency. Whoever secured their allegiance was usually assured of election: 'The one uncertain element in the East London contests each year is the large Jewish vote. It is too large to be ignored, and too elusive to count upon. In no division is it more prominent than St George's-in-the-East.[100] Harry Marks, the previous Conservative member, had failed to secure this vote, with the result that in 1895 his majority in this usually safe Conservative seat had been only four. It was essential for Dewar to win their support. A meeting was held at which he satisfied the local community on Zionist questions and they promised to support him. He was returned with a majority of 296.

Conservatives who did not pay sufficient attention to local or national domestic issues tended to be worsted in the London elections. The desire of the electorate for a social-reform platform was evinced in various ways. In Bermondsey, Henry Cust, sometime editor of the *Pall Mall Gazette* and an ex-resident of the Transvaal, devoted most of his speeches to the war issue but was subjected to frequent interruptions from his audiences urging him to 'talk about a home policy'. The same was true of J. C. Macdona's campaign in Rotherhithe where the Liberal, Hart-Davies, made a strong appeal to the working-class interest on the basis of housing reform proposing that local authorities should be given more powers of purchase.[101] Both of these candidates suffered a drop in their majorities and a decreased share of the votes, although in both cases the total poll was lower than that of 1895.

[99] C. Kyd the Conservative candidate in Whitechapel also supported it but he failed to get elected. The issue here was almost certainly decided by the large Jewish vote which traditionally supported Samuel. See *East London Advertiser* 6 October 1900.
[100] *Ibid.*, 29 September 1900.
[101] *Southwark and Bermondsey Recorder*, 29 September 1900.

In the Lambeth, Clapham, Hackney and St Pancras constituencies it was the general rule for Conservative candidates to appeal on platforms composed of imperialism and social reform. H. Robertson, in Hackney South, devoted one-half of his election address to social reform, specifying an extension of the Workmen's Compensation Act, better housing, creation of old-age pensions and the extension of a Bill he had carried through parliament on allotments.[102] Similarly, Fred Horner's address in North Lambeth combined a strong assertion of the government's imperial policy with progressive domestic reform. Horner had been the originator of a scheme, which had influenced the 1899 Housing Act, to enable any occupier to buy his house. He showed himself more advanced than the Radicals on this issue for 'whereas my schemes made it compulsory for every local authority to put the Act into operation, the Radicals made it optional'. He declared himself in favour of the creation of old-age pensions, opposed to 'the unrestricted immigration of foreign paupers' and approved of the 'action of Conservatives in passing successive Acts legalising Trade Unionism'.[103]

In Clapham the local member was well liked and the Liberals only decided to challenge him in the last week of the contest. The independent local newspaper noted that 'none of us have the least reason to complain of Mr. Thornton. . . . His sympathies are with the people, as was evidenced by his action in the House on the question of the Latchmere Allotments at Battersea.'[104]

The St Pancras constituencies were, in general, more imperialistic. Perhaps this was because their electorates were between 16 and 40 per cent middle-class. Certainly, party divisions were more clearly on class lines here, it being noted in St Pancras North that 'there was no lack of faith in the poorer districts that Dickson [the Liberal] was to be the first man'. The attitude of most of the Conservative candidates was expressed by H. Graham, standing for St Pancras West: 'As soon as the South African question is settled the Government will continue to pass those Bills with which it is already identified for the benefit of the Working Classes.'[105] But even here the

[102] The *Mercury* (Hackney), 22 September 1900.
[103] *South London Chronicle*, 29 September 1900.
[104] *Clapham Observer*, 29 September 1900.
[105] *Camden and Kentish Towns, Hampstead, Highgate, Holloway and St. Pancras Gazette*, 29 September 1900.

Liberal Unionist candidate for St Pancras South, H. M. Jessell, devoted one-half of his address to social issues.[106]

In the constituencies held by the Liberals in London the same situation applied. Thus, in Southwark West, there was a direct conflict between a social-reform platform and imperialism in the persons of R. K. Causton, the Liberal, and Sir Alfred Newton, the Lord Mayor of London. Newton's platform was strongly imperialist, denouncing the 'insolent ultimatum' and the 'outrageous invasion of Natal'. Social reform, hardly mentioned in his address, was given pride of place in that of Causton. The constituency was one of the most overcrowded housing areas in London and his campaign was largely directed at emphasizing the need for municipal reform.[107] It was confidently expected that patriotic enthusiasm would influence the waverers 'who really hold the balance between the parties' in Newton's favour: 'If there is one person in the kingdom it will benefit, Sir Alfred Newton is he.'[108] In Newington West, the situation was paralleled almost exactly. Ricarde Seaver, the Conservative candidate, had been in South Africa and had had some connection with Rhodes. This was reflected in his campaign by the presence of a speaker from the Imperial South African Association and by the imperialism of his platform which deprecated the discussion of 'side issues'.[109] Seaver was put forward as an 'ideal man . . . at the present juncture' when the settlement was the most important question:[110]

For nearly 20 years he has been largely concerned with South African affairs. He has taken a [great] share in developing British industry in the Dark Continent . . . travelled over the whole of South Africa. . . . Probably a more reliable authority on the mining affairs of South Africa could not be found in England at the present day.

Captain C. W. Norton, the Liberal, who increased his majority by about 700, fought on a wider platform, including in his address the need for land law and registration reform.[111] In

[106] *Ibid.*
[107] *Southwark and Bermondsey Recorder, op. cit.*
[108] *South London Chronicle*, 22 September 1900.
[109] The Association was quite active in the election. One of its main speakers, and the one who attended this meeting, was Adrian Hofmeyr, a renegade Boer who later held an official position in the colonial administration of the Transvaal.
[110] *South London Chronicle*, 8 September 1900.
[111] *Southwark and Bermondsey Recorder, op. cit.*

Poplar, Sydney Buxton with the support of the local Labour Party—although they wished him to be more pronounced in his opposition to the war[112]—fought the campaign on a social-reform platform and increased his majority by 300.

Thus in London there was a very general pattern discernible which had two basic elements. In the first place where a candidate satisfied the electorate on the question of social reform—whether he was Conservative or Liberal—then he was returned, often with an increased share of the vote. Where a candidate did not do so and where he was opposed by a strong social-reform platform,[113] his share of the vote tended to decrease. This was apparent in Bow and Bromley where at the 1899 by-election, held just after the outbreak of the war and fought entirely on the war issue, the Liberal candidate, Harold Spender, obtained only 33 per cent of the vote. In 1900, George Lansbury, who stood under the banner of the SDF but who stressed unity with all left groups and in common with all other 'Labour' candidates, fought the election as a social-reform election, increased his share to 37 per cent.[114]

In the second place it was evident that imperial candidates stood little chance in Liberal constituencies if they concentrated solely on the war issue and if they were faced with a strong social-reform platform. Even Evans-Gordon and Claude Hay, who won Stepney and Hoxton from the left-wing Liberals Steadman and Stuart, deliberately fought widely based campaigns; and Evans-Gordon had judiciously indulged in the distribution of blankets and clothing during the previous winter.[115] This failure was best illustrated by Newton in Southwark West and Seaver in Newington West. It is probable that the social-reform platform of Dr T. J. Macnamara won him North Camberwell.[116] He was closely associated with the work-

---

[112] *East End News*, 2 October 1900.

[113] This is important. In those working-class constituencies such as St Pancras, Hackney, Clapham, quoted above, the Liberal campaign tended to be weak and disorganized. For this pattern to operate effectively it was essential that the Liberals fought an aggressive campaign. The Liberals who lost seats, such as Stuart and Steadman, fought defensive campaigns and allowed the Conservatives to gain the initiative.

[114] *East End News*, 21 September–5 October 1900.

[115] *Ibid.*, 21 September 1900; *Hackney Express*, 29 September 1900.

[116] See *South London Observer*, 22 September 1900.

ing men of the area[117] and was very clearly a social-reform and
not an imperialist candidate.

Tables 8 and 9 illustrate the connection that has been suggested between electoral support and a social-reform platform
in those London elections where social reform seems to have
been an important factor.[118]

TABLE 8

LONDON CONSTITUENCIES WHERE SOCIAL REFORM A FACTOR IN
ELECTORAL VICTORY

Constituency	Party	Winning candidate's share of vote per 100 votes cast	
		1895	1900
Camberwell North	L.	55·1	58·07
Limehouse	C.	59·9	55·7
Newington West	L.	53·7	59·6
Poplar	L.	55·8	58·4
Southwark West	L.	51·02	51·06
St George's-in-East	C.	50·01	55·08
Whitechapel	L.	50·3	51·0

TABLE 9

LONDON CONSTITUENCIES WHERE SUCCESSFUL CANDIDATE IGNORED
SOCIAL-REFORM ISSUES

Constituency	Party	Winning Candidate's share of vote per 100 votes cast	
		1895	1900
Bermondsey	C.	52·2	52·0
Rotherhithe	C.	64·5	62·6
Bow and Bromley	C.	57·7	63·3

[117] He was President of North Camberwell Radical Club.

[118] Other examples of government supporters assiduously cultivating working-
class votes by a favourable attitude to social reform exist. This was true in Bradford
Central where the Liberal Unionist, J. L. Wanklyn, earned the praise of the
Bradford Labour Echo on 15 July 1899 for his 'straightness'; 'Searchlight' wrote:
'I like a straight man, and Wanklyn appears to be built that way. If I lived in
Central I think I'd vote for him.' It was also true at the General Election where

Of course, the foregoing must not be taken to suggest that social reform as an issue was unusually important, or important for the first time in 1900. If present-day voting behaviour can serve as any guide to the past, it is probable that 1900 illustrated traditional voting patterns rather than any unique concern with issues. That is, people voted the way they did for reasons of tradition, status desires and the plethora of reasons that psephologists, sociologists and political scientists now consider important. Part of that pattern, however, was a traditional working-class attachment to the Liberals as the party of social reform. It is irrelevant whether that was just to the Conservatives or not. Where Conservatives did sit for working-class constituencies, they too had to take note of this concern with social reform. The London working-class constituencies illustrate this very well. Where there was a larger proportion of non-working-class voters, such as in the St Pancras constituencies, the Conservative members did not talk much about social reform. Their appeals were more imperialistic and patriotic. But in the working-class constituencies of London which returned Conservative members, the reverse was true.

It has often been forgotten that Conservative candidates did not necessarily appeal for electoral support solely on the basis of their party's association with patriotism. To have done so in working-class constituencies would have been prejudicial to their chances, as certain of the 1900 contests illustrate. Why working-class voters were so attached to their Conservative MPs, especially in the East End of London, is not clear. The answer cannot, however, lie solely in the 'jingoism' of the working class. There was, as has been shown, very little correlation between imperial appeal and electoral success. All kinds of extraneous and 'irrational' influences could have a bearing on the attraction of Conservatives for working-class constituents. If a candidate, for example, was thought to be wealthy enough

---

his replies to the test questions of the Trades Council were more favourable than those of Anderton, the Liberal. Thus he supported railway nationalization, Anderton did not; he supported legislation for a minimum wage in the sweated trades, Anderton was equivocal. See *Bradford Daily Argus*, 1 October 1900.

In Ashton-under-Lyme, the Conservative member intervened on the men's side in a tram strike and claimed the credit for getting the men reinstated whilst their grievances were examined. See *Ashton-under-Lyme Herald*, 29 September-6 October 1900.

to spend money in the constituency or to bring employment to the area this tended to work in his favour. Thus, Dewar's support in St George's rested upon the solid conservative pillars of the tradesmen and the publicans, but he also had 'a large following of the working-class voters, who appreciate the fact that he is a large employer of labour'.[119] The election of Lowles for Haggerston in 1895 was probably influenced by the fact that he had arranged for the distribution of 500 food cards, worth 6d per head, to the most needy in the winter of 1894–5.[120] Similarly, the election of A. Strauss for the Camborne division in 1895 was partly due to a feeling that his influence as a tin merchant would rebound to the benefit of the constituency. This could, of course, work for the Liberals as well. Causton was a 'large employer of labour in the district' and a man of 'generous and philanthropic disposition'.[121] In Newington, Norton's personal acquaintance with the electors, whom he visited annually, and the Catholicism of Seaver, were considered to have favoured the Liberal incumbent.[122]

It is, perhaps, evident that the 1900 election was not a simple and straightforward appeal to Khaki. As far as the working classes were concerned more subtle considerations were at work. There is no doubt that those members who represented London working-class constituencies had a very special relationship with their constituents based not on such ephemera as imperial issues but upon a system of mutual benefit and reward which deserves to be investigated further. There were many elements to this relationship. Deference was probably one:[123]

Go into the slums . . . of any community, usually the stronghold of conservatism, for these people have been compelled and taught to live on charity and patronage, but if you find in this desert—a dwelling with white curtains, a bright door knocker and flowers in the window —you have found a Radical who has not lost hope and wants to get on. . . . Men on railways, the goods side and drivers and firemen not brought into touch with the public are Radicals, but passenger guards

---

[119] *East London Advertiser*, 6 October 1900.
[120] O'Leary, *op. cit.*, pp. 198–9.
[121] *South London Chronicle*, 22 September 1900.
[122] *Ibid.*, 6 October 1900.
[123] F. Gray, *Confessions of a Candidate* (London, 1925), pp. 9–10.

and porters also underpaid but with funds augmented by tips and the patronage of the rich, are conservatives.

Within the context of a Conservative East End, the absence of patriotic symbols and consciousness was puzzling:[124]

The Union Jack is never seen in East London, except on the river, it does not float over the schools; the children are not taught to reverence the flag of their country as the symbol of their liberties and their responsibilities; alone among the cities of the world, East London never teaches her children the meaning of patriotism, the history of their liberties, the pride and privilege of citizenship in a mighty Empire.

It was not understood that this no more implied anti-imperialism than voting Conservative implied an acceptance of imperialism. Both merely illustrated how unimportant such concepts as flag and Empire were to working-class life. The course of the 'Khaki' Election in these working-class constituencies indicates how they were not much affected by the issue. Conservatives such as Dewar and Samuel would be supported because they brought some tangible benefit to the community. Dewar was an employer of labour and Samuel's Water Bill ensured a constant and clean supply of drinking water to the constituency. This could be contrasted with the failure of a man like Sir Alfred Newton who had nothing to offer but his jingo patriotism.[125] As W. M. Thompson's reaction to the London results illustrated, Radicals failed to realize that not all social benefits came from Liberal legislation.[126] The typical Radical programme that Thompson had been trying to propagate had very little relevance to the prejudices or desires of working-class voters living in overcrowded tenements in Whitechapel or Newington. They were interested in immediate and material benefit and if a Conservative promised to bring this by his influence and wealth they were happy to vote for him. Some, such as Frederick Rogers, realized the irrelevance of many of the Radical shibboleths:[127]

[124] Walter Besant, *East London* (London, 1901), p. 14.
[125] See a letter he wrote to L. Courtney, 21 July 1901, blaming Courtney for the deaths of 20,000 'gallant Englishmen' noting that 'your action has been purely perverse—the basis of anti-patriotism, probably'. Courtney Papers, Vol. 8, ff. 80–2.
[126] *Reynolds News, op. cit.*
[127] Frederick Rogers, *Life, Labour, and Literature* (London, 1908), p. 115.

I had long seen through the fallacy of popular Radicalism. . . . I proclaimed from many a club platform that if Throne, Church, and Peerage were swept away at once the working classes would benefit as little by the change as they did by the destruction of the monasteries at the Reformation.

Nevertheless, it is significant that so many ideally 'imperial' candidates were rejected by working-class constituencies. This tended to be the case when imperialism was countered with a strong social-reform electoral appeal. The example of Derby and various London constituencies has been noted, but others exist. At Crewe, with its powerful railway and engineering interest,[128] the attempt to exploit war feeling in favour of the Conservative candidate failed in the face of opposition from a Liberal who totally ignored the war and concentrated entirely on social issues.[129] The traditionally Conservative town of Stockport was won by a Liberal whose platform was an indictment of the government's social-reform record and who was opposed by an imperialist candidate who seems to have been selected largely because he had spent thirteen years in South Africa.[130]

It is, thus, apparent that the working class do not seem to have voted for imperialist candidates just because they were imperialists. Where they did support Conservatives their support was dictated by more intricate reasons than imperialism. Undoubtedly, further investigation would reveal the solid foundations of this support. It has been the purpose of this chapter to illustrate how imperialism as an electoral issue was of very little force in working-class constituencies; and how their support of pro-Boer or imperialist candidates was dictated by considerations of more immediate importance than the war.

[128] 48 per cent of occupied males engaged in these industries.

[129] J. Tomkinson, the Liberal, talked exclusively of social reform, old-age pensions and housing, leaving the war issue to his wife and Lord Crewe. The Conservatives imported Imperial South African Association speakers. See *Crewe Guardian*, 3 October, 1900.

[130] See *Stockport Borough Express*, 27 September 1900.

IV

The Jingo Crowd

T H E South African War is today remembered largely because it was instrumental in adding a new word to the English Language; a word that was a product of the 'New Imperialism' and which, appropriately enough, was to be little used after 1914. That word was 'mafficking'. The situation from which it grew was remarkable to an age that was unaccustomed to such spontaneous victory celebrations. On the night of 18 May 1900, news travelled like wildfire. At 9.20 p.m. the Lord Mayor of London announced from the Mansion House that the besieged garrison of Mafeking had been relieved. In retrospect it is incredible that the imagination of the country should have been caught by this dusty little town on the South African veldt. But thanks to the dubious military ability and tactics of its commander and the fulsome praise of a press desperately anxious to secure incontrovertible evidence of British pluck and valour, everyone's eyes had been centred on Mafeking. It did not seem to matter that Baden-Powell—who after the war was kicked upstairs—had come perilously near to disobeying orders in allowing himself to be entrapped; nor did it detract from the glamour of the occasion that valuable troops had to be diverted to rescue him. Seldom has one man ever built such a successful career on incompetence. Indeed, the events of Mafeking Night are less difficult to understand than the reason why Mafeking itself was thought to be so important.

Within a few minutes of the relief announcement, the route from the Mansion House, along Ludgate Hill, Fleet Street,

Strand, Pall Mall to the War Office (where the 'No News' bulletin remained posted) was filled with 'people giving vociferous demonstrations of their delight'.[1] Similar scenes were repeated the length and breadth of the country, from Aberdeen and Ayr to Plymouth and St Ives. In the words of one lady who was then a young girl, 'We went wild'. There was surprisingly little damage done to property or person: in Middlesbrough, a woman was shot and killed by a drunken husband, and in a very few places damage was done to the property of those suspected of pro-Boer sympathies.[2] But overall, on Mafeking Night itself the crowds and their behaviour were characteristically non-violent and non-retributory.

This is important. It must be recognized that Mafeking Night —and the other, similar, occasions such as the celebrations over the relief of Ladysmith—did not exhibit features that were to characterize the jingo crowd of this era. The Mafeking Night events were a celebratory occasion. The crowds were celebratory crowds as were those of Armistice Night and VE Night. It was a time for rejoicing; England had regained her honour. And this is what the crowds were about. That is why there was so little damage to person or property on the night of 18 May. Thus, Mafeking Night is important *only* as a counterpoise to events of a more harmful nature: it was not an instance of the jingo crowd.

The crowd with which we are primarily concerned is the organic crowd where there are present at least the elements of a common vengeful or retributory purpose.[3] It is, therefore, extremely important to draw a clear distinction between the riots that grew out of Mafeking Night and other celebratory occasions, and the purposive disruption of peace meetings. As will be illustrated, even the riots that emerged from the disruption of a peace meeting were often nearer in type to the mafficking situations. It is historically inaccurate and of little value to label indiscriminately every crowd disturbance even remotely connected with the war, as being indicative of the jingo mood. A

[1] *The Times*, 19 May 1900, p. 11.

[2] *Ibid.*

[3] Following the definitions of L. L. Bernard in *Encyclopedia of Social Science* (New York, 1933), where the mob is defined as 'a direct contact group . . . highly excited form of crowd'. And an organic crowd as a crowd 'which has a principle or sentiment which has some physical embodiment. It is purposive if not truly rational.'

mob can gather for many reasons and its actions are usually a result of its inherent dynamic. The crowd that concerns us is that whose purpose was clear, whose aims were fixed and whose targets were peace meetings and their promoters.

The mafficking mob, however, frightened some contemporary observers, and acceptance of their strictures on it has determined that it is now seen as the characteristic popular response to the war. It was viewed by serious middle-class reformers as a horrifying demonstration of the results of the passions of war upon the uncivilized people of the 'abyss'. C. F. G. Masterman wrote how[4]

three times at least . . . the . . . richest city in the world was in the hollow of their hands. . . . Hitherto it has failed to realise its power. . . . It has been wheedled into amiability and smoothed with honeyed words. Through the action of a benevolent autocratic Government it has now been invited to contemplate its strength. It has crept into daylight . . . it is straightening itself and learning to gambol with heavy and grotesque antics in the sunshine. . . . How long, before, in a fit of ill-temper, it suddenly realises its tremendous unconquerable might?

It was these kinds of insultingly inaccurate images that created the picture of the jingo crowd that we possess today. The mob of the Boer War is by implication a working-class mob aroused by the base materialistic aggressiveness of imperialism, manipulated by imperialists,[5] potentially threatening civilized society; it was so dangerous that its least threatening aspect was that it could be used by selfish interest groups against their enemies. Thus, *New Age*, the quintessence of middle-class Radicalism, wrote:[6]

At Tunbridge Wells the mob . . . was deliberately instigated to its devilish work by certain local publicans anxious to be revenged for Mr. Dodd's work for Temperance. At Scarborough, the young men of fashion organised the patriotic attack on the property of the Rowntrees because the latter have strenuously contended against drunkenness and prostitution in the town. And in other towns jerry-builders and sweaters have employed the mob to wreak vengeance on social reformers who happen to be opposed to . . . the war.

[4] [C. F. G. Masterman], *From the Abyss* (London, 1902), pp. 2 and 7.
[5] This idea is one of the most important themes in J. A. Hobson, *The Psychology of Jingoism* (London, 1901).   [6] Editorial, *New Age*, 21 June 1900, p. 392.

But such shocked impressionistic accounts leave much to be desired. The jingo crowd deserves more serious study than it has received in the half century that has elapsed between Hobson and Rudé. Irrational bureaucratic difficulties continue to make some of the source material inaccessible to the student of the period; yet there is enough information provided by contemporary newspaper accounts of rowdyism at peace meetings and the various riots that occurred during the war, to enable us to fill the gap created by the paucity of official documentation.[7]

The events of Mafeking Night were, on the whole, harmless. There were isolated cases of violence and destruction, but these resulted more often from the celebratory nature of the occasion than from any clear patriotic purpose.[8] It was during the nights following Mafeking Night, over the weekend, that the crowd turned its attention to supposed pro-Boers. The features and characteristics of this aspect of the jingo crowd, that which emerged from the celebrations of Mafeking Night and which was, in essence, a continuation of the celebratory crowd of that night, are easy to distinguish. They fit very closely the kind of characteristics which Elias Canetti has associated with the aggressive, 'baiting crowd'.[9] Such a crowd, having exhausted its good nature in the 'most wonderful and harmless saturnalia of the century',[10] turns its attention to those who refuse to join it, those whom it nominates as its enemies. In the context of the Boer War, and Mafeking Night, when many people did refuse on principle to join in celebrating imperialism, those enemies are 'traitors within the walls'.[11] The attacks on the premises of reputed pro-Boers fits into this pattern. Canetti's description of

[7] There were at least two reports written by the Chief Constables of Scarborough and Aberdeen to the Director of Public Prosecutions or the Treasury Solicitor who performed this function during this period. Both of them are in a Public Records Office category which is closed for 100 years. It is, however, unlikely that they contain any startling revelations. They were both concerned with the possibility of prosecutions under the Riot Act of 1886, but no prosecutions of this nature were attempted and it is, therefore, probable that their evidence value is only marginal.

[8] Exceptions to the good nature of the Mafeking Night crowds were the attacks made on Stead's house in Wimbledon and that on a house believed to be owned by Rev. Silas Hocking.

[9] E. Canetti, *Crowds and Power* (London, 1962), pp. 15–29.

[10] 'The Seer', *Club Life*, 23 May 1900, p. 152.

[11] Canetti, *op. cit.*, p. 23.

the baiting crowd is an exact description of the mood and dynamic of the post-Mafeking Night mob: 'This crowd is out for killing and it knows whom it wants to kill. . . . The proclaiming of the goal, the spreading about of who it is that is to perish, is enough to make the crowd form.'[12] The point about the crowd was its assertive nature; its aim was to establish its patriotism and to confront those considered, by rumour, to be unpatriotic.

There are three notable occasions which can be used to illustrate this type of crowd and which will help to explain why this crowd is not considered to be significantly different enough to be justly regarded as part of the 'jingo crowd'. Two of the three occasions occurred immediately following Mafeking Night, and the third during the celebrations for the relief of Ladysmith when the same kind of conditions were present.

In Dover, on the night of 19 May 1900, the shop of a Mr J. F. Brown, a local tradesman, was attacked. Brown was a member of the local Chamber of Commerce and was suspected of pro-Boer sympathies because of a speech in which he had urged a re-examination of Britain's attitude to the rest of the world.[13] At the end of a torchlight procession on the Saturday night following the relief of Mafeking it was rumoured that Brown had hung a Transvaal flag from his shop. This was untrue and later attributed to a 'sudden false alarm circulated by some mischievous youngster or irresponsible persons'.[14] But it is illustrative that even when it was seen to be false the fact that he was supposed to be pro-Boer was sufficient justification for the £140-worth of damage done to his shop. Quiet was not restored until a squad of soldiers marched down from the castle.

At Tottenham on the following Sunday night the events followed a similar pattern. Henry Bish, a hairdresser, was supposed to have spoken disparagingly to his customers of British troops and to have expressed a wish that they should all be killed.[15] He was also unfortunate enough to have a blue advertising flag hung over his shop which was mistaken for a black Boer flag.[16] Some individuals demanded that he take it down, a crowd assembled, taunted him with being a German

---

[12] *Ibid.*, p. 49.   [13] Interview with Brown, *Dover Express*, 26 May 1900.
[14] *Dover Observer*, 26 May 1900.
[15] *Tottenham and Stamford Hill Times and Stoke Newington Chronicle*, 25 May 1900.   [16] *The Times*, 22 May 1900, p. 16.

and a pro-Boer and, after attempts were made to set the shop on fire, the crowd was dispersed by the police.

The Margate riots of 13, 14 and 15 March 1900, paralleled the previous examples in that the immediate cause for the crowd's fury were the pro-Boer, anti-royalist sympathies of a furniture dealer, W. J. Powell, who like Bish and Brown was accused of displaying a Transvaal flag and of inverting a picture of the Queen. It was the time of the relief of Ladysmith and it is noticeable that on the first night—of the day when the news had first been received—the crowd which gathered outside his shop acted in a boisterous but not destructive manner and restricted its patriotic activities to hooting. On the following nights, however, the rumours that had swept the town during the day encouraged the gathering of a larger crowd which behaved more aggressively and broke some of the windows of the store. The local newspaper claimed that the 'gathering was a very good-tempered one, and seemed actuated by a spirit of mischief rather than anything else'. It wondered whether 'the actors in the riot or the very respectable-looking onlookers enjoyed the fun most, for the loud cheering . . . whenever there was a smash of glass, came from the spectators chiefly'.[17]

It was common practice for the newspapers to comment on the 'good nature' of the crowds during these events. Doubtless this was in part due to a desire to play down the demonstrations but it must be admitted that in no instance, either during these occasions or during the riots that grew out of peace meetings, was the Riot Act read. When, as in the incident at Dover, soldiers were marched through the town, they were well received. This contrasted with the crowd's attitude to the police who were often as much a target for the rocks and stones as were the pro-Boer premises. Thus, of those arrested after the Margate disturbances, three of the five accused were charged with assaulting the police in the execution of their duty;[18] and in Scarborough when a riot occurred directed against a private peace meeting sponsored by the Rowntrees, the Mounted Police were attacked when they rode to disperse the crowd.[19]

Looting, too, tended to be absent. Thus, during the Scarborough riot on the night of 12 March 1900, the glass front of

---

[17] *Keble's Margate and Ramsgate Gazette*, 17 March, 24 March 1900.
[18] *Ibid.*, 24 March 1900.   [19] *Scarborough Evening News*, 13 March 1900.

one of the Rowntree shops was totally destroyed. It was estimated that the damage amounted to about £150 but there was no reported looting of the goods in the window. The *Scarborough Post* doubted if 'a single act of petty theft was committed'.

The problem of whether the crowds on Mafeking Night were in a state of riot occasioned some discussion when compensatory claims for damaged property were made to the police. The point was that under the Riot Act of 1886 compensation would only be paid if it was established that the crowd had been 'riotously and tumultuously' assembled. The Receiver of Police asked the Home Office for advice as to whether this had been the case and whether 'provocation had been offered to the persons assembled' by the claimants. He explained that 'the crowds assembled in various parts of the Metropolis did damage generally to but a small extent, to the homes of those whom they considered were sympathisers with the Boers'. He outlined the various claims that had been received and which included the Tottenham affair, the attack on Stead's house, and the attack on the house in Highgate which was believed to be that of Silas Hocking. It was written on the cover of the file that

in the Tottenham case it seems clear that damage done within the Act was committed. In the Highgate case it is not clear that there were persons 'riotously or tumultuously assembled together,' but as the fact of somewhat disorderly crowds having been about on the night of the 20th is notorious, perhaps no further proof is required.

And one of the law officers minuted that the damage of property by assembled crowds should be considered evidence of their being 'riotously and tumultuously assembled together and therefore damage is liable to compensation'.[20]

The Home Office replied to the Receiver that 'the claims in question may be accepted without regard to provocation unless it should appear that direct provocation was offered at the time by some overt act to the persons assembled'.[21] It is clear that the legal advisers felt that in most of the cases compensation was justified. There was some doubt about the Wimbledon case because it was found that the damage was committed by boys.

[20] Receiver of Police to Secretary of State, 11 June 1900, P.R.O., H.O. 45/B 30667/20.
[21] Home Office to Receiver, 15 June, P.R.O., Mepol. 5. 31/296/28.

Even though the Riot Act was not read the crowds were sufficiently tumultuous to warrant compensation.

The most significant feature about Mafeking Night had been the spontaneity of the demonstrations. The news had spread within minutes by word of mouth: 'Drivers of trolleys and vans shouted out the tidings as they drove down Ludgate Hill. . . . The cabmen on the ranks sent up hurrahs . . . total strangers shook each other heartily by the hand.'[22] The disturbances that coincided with a known peace meeting were usually not so spontaneous. This is not to imply that they were the result of organized conspiracy, although in several cases there was the suspicion of this. A correspondent in Scarborough, for example, during the riots of 12 March noted 'an invitation . . . by one who was too well-dressed to indulge in the throwing of bricks to four youths to "get round into York Place where there were a lot of big windows" '. A letter printed in the *Scarborough Mercury* regretted[23]

that in addition to the gang of roughs who did most of the stone throwing, there should have been a number of local Unionists amongst the crowd who by their presence and manner . . . excited the crowd to further rowdyism. One could not help thinking . . . that it was not so much a question as [*sic*] the principles of peace as against those of war, that concerned the rioters. It appeared to be a remnant of that bitter feeling that has been shown against the victims of the disturbance from time to time [i.e. the Rowntree family] by a section of their political opponents, who consider they have old scars to wipe out.

It was commonly believed that the excitement caused by events of the war were used by certain individuals to incite crowds to attack political or social enemies. This was true, for example, of the Pretoria Night disturbances in Tunbridge Wells where a group of young men paraded outside the home of Councillor Lawson Dodds sparking off the worst disturbance the town had experienced since the Webber riots of the 1860s. On the following two nights, 6 and 7 June, larger crowds gathered, reaching some 5,000 on Wednesday, 7 June. But it was on the first night, when some of the windows of his house had been smashed, that most damage had been done. *New Age* referred to these demonstrations as having been inspired by the publicans

[22] *The Times*, 19 May 1900, p. 12.
[23] *Scarborough Mercury*, 23 March 1900.

of the town.[24] Dodds was an influential man locally, he was anti-war and a temperance advocate. In 1901 he failed in an attempt to establish a Temperance Working Men's Club in the town.[25] It is thus possible that he had some powerful enemies who deliberately incited elements of the crowd against him on Pretoria Night. There was the suspicion of this against Alderman Luturidge, a major in the Volunteers, who was an organizer of the victory procession out of which the demonstration had originated. At a Council meeting the following week he denied any connivance in the disturbance, claiming that 'a number of young fellows had come to his house between eleven and twelve' but that he had advised them to go home quietly and had been completely unaware of any demonstration. A letter in the local newspaper asserted that the rowdy element in the crowd had been influenced by drink, and this was not unlikely in view of the fact that the disturbance grew out of a victory procession:[26]

I mixed with the crowd for the purpose of analysing it. I had ample evidence that drink and drunkenness was the productive factor of the disturbance. I should think that three-fourths of the people were law-abiding citizens. . . . But it was painfully evident that the unruly . . . were primed with drink and ready for any devilment—and these were not all of the loafer element, but many respectable young men.

There was general agreement, however, that 'youth' was the prime cause of the rowdyism. The local paper referred to the 'few noisy youths who were the originators of the disturbance'. And it divided the crowd into 'three-parts sightseers, and one-part youths, with whom the patriotic rejoicing afforded the excuse for a little discreditable horse play'.[27]

But it was upon the newspapers that the prime responsibility for inciting the riots was placed. Their wide and often provocative advertisement of what were usually private meetings was certainly a common feature.[28] Thus, a Gateshead newspaper rebuked the local Stop-the-War Committee for acting with 'a remarkable reticence as to their intentions . . . the preparations

[24] *New Age*, 21 June 1900, *loc. cit.*
[25] *Club Life*, 2 February 1901, p. 12.
[26] *Tunbridge Wells Gazette*, 6 June, 13 June 1900.
[27] *Ibid.*, 13 June 1900.
[28] For an example in Sheffield of the deliberate publicizing of a private meeting see S. C. Cronwright-Schreiner, *The Land of Free Speech* (London, 1906), p. 160.

for holding the meeting have been so quietly completed that un-
charitable persons might suspect those concerned . . . of a desire
to do something on the sly . . . afterwards representing the thing
done as the work of the public'. They urged all to attend:[29]

Their organisation of the meeting is an invitation to all interested in
the subject set for discussion; and we hope the request will be largely
responded to . . . since speaking there must be, let the voice heard be
that of the people, and not that of a mere coterie, and let there be no
uncertainty in its utterances.

A Tory paper in Scarborough, the day of the peace meeting of 12 March 1900, carried an editorial on the Stop-the-War
party, and a long article about Cronwright-Schreiner headlined:
'Pleading for the Boer right to oppress the English' which carefully catalogued all the occasions upon which he had failed to
secure a hearing. The editorial noted that 'they really cannot
expect the average man in the street to give a patient hearing to
such rubbish as this'.[30]

When the Young Scots' Society organized a meeting to be
addressed by J. X. Merriman, the *Edinburgh Evening Despatch*
in seven successive editorials referred unfavourably to the meeting. It regretted the decision of the Town Council to let the
Waverley Market to 'men who have earned notoriety by
advocating the cause of the enemies of their own country'. It
stigmatized the Young Scots' Society as 'the pro-Boer movement in Edinburgh', and it lamented the fact that such a meeting
could be freely held in England. After the meeting the paper was
given the excuse to condemn the 'ruffianism of the stewards' by
the publication of a letter from the Secretary of the Edinburgh
Independent Labour Party which mentioned that 'some miners
from Cobbinshaw have expressed a readiness to come in for a
fight'. What was not added was the fact that the Secretary
advised against the importation of the miners and that the
stewards who successfully kept order were all members of the
Young Scot's Society or of the Independent Labour Party.[31]

On the occasion of Lloyd George's celebrated foray into
Birmingham to hold an anti-war meeting in December 1901,

[29] *Gateshead Daily Chronicle*, 9 March 1900.
[30] *Scarborough Post*, 12 March 1900.
[31] *Edinburgh Evening Despatch*, 13–26 April 1900; *Edinburgh Evening News*,
25 April 1900.

there was a lengthy build-up evident in the local Conservative newspaper. It reminded its readers how 'this most virulent anti-Briton', had insulted Chamberlain, had 'made out our soldiers and our ministers to be wholesale inhuman butchers' and asserted that 'to invite such a man . . . to speak in the Town Hall is an insult to the city and to every loyal inhabitant'.[32] An article in the paper countenanced the forging of entrance tickets by implying that it merely showed how concerned the citizens were for the good patriotic name of their town. It started a rumour that 'two hundred Irish roughs have been engaged to eject intruders', piously hoped that 'the person who has hired the Irishmen for tomorrow's meeting will re-consider his decision; otherwise a riot of very serious dimensions may be provoked'.[33] Approval was expressed of a huge attendance which enquiry had foreshadowed in Victoria Square: 'The University students are credited with the intention of joining the throng and altogether there is promised a very noisy, though, one hopes, a harmless expression of the disgust with which the city regards the gathering.'[34]

Once the expected disturbance had taken place the pro-Boers were always to blame: 'The Birmingham Liberal Association deliberately defied the warnings given and courted the disaster they experienced.'[35] The *Scarborough Post* thought that 'the pro-moters of these meetings . . . have incurred grave responsibility considering the present feeling of public temper', commenting that the hostility to Schreiner was 'not only understandable, it is honourable and commendable'.[36]

In London it was usual to accuse various elements in the City of having engineered the disturbances. The City and specifically the Stock Exchange were certainly very patriotic. The Stock Exchange greeted the news of the relief of Ladysmith with[37]

cheer upon cheer . . . all the members uncovered and sung 'God Save the Queen' . . . many brokers gave their clerks a holiday, and those clerks who were not given it took it. . . . Members . . . considered that

[32] *Birmingham Daily Mail,* 16 December 1901.
[33] Previously it had printed the story as a 'rumour' but it very soon attained a ring of truth and was used as such.
[34] *Birmingham Daily Mail,* 17 December 1901.
[35] *Ibid.,* 19 December 1901.
[36] Editorials, *Scarborough Post,* 12 March, 13 March 1900.
[37] *Financial News,* 2 March 1900.

it was not a day on which to take seriously anything but football and the singing of patriotic choruses.

There is very little evidence, however, that conspiracies to incite rioting were hatched there. The *Morning Leader* accused the *Financial News* of plotting to disrupt a meeting held in the Queen's Hall on 18 June 1901, at which Merriman and Sauer were scheduled to speak. The paper was virulently opposed to the meeting and there was some justification for the complaint of *New Age* that 'a day or two before the date of the meeting . . . in the Jingo press appeared the most open incitements to riot'.[38] Letters were printed in the City newspaper which urged 'as many Englishmen as possible to make an effort to attend and uphold the honour of our Empire'. The editorial asserted, in spite of a disclaimer by Victor Fisher, that Dr Leyds would be present and would address the meeting. This particularly inflammatory editorial is an extreme example of the type of writing that characterized the jingo press. That it was a City newspaper was only more significant. It began by referring to Fisher as 'Fischer' and continued:[39]

If it be true that this meeting 'has been organised and will be addressed only by British subjects,' it is a more shameful gathering than we have even ventured to imagine. 'British subjects' who countenance Messrs. Merriman and Sauer, who meet to pass resolutions in favour of Messrs. Kruger and Leyds, at a time when those persons are at war with the British Empire, and British soldiers are falling fast in the quarrel, and British widows and orphans being rapidly multiplied as a result of it, cannot be adequately described in any language that we could put into print. The meeting is a disgrace to civilisation—an infamy indescribable.

It is quite possible that such reports as those carried by the *Financial News* and the *Daily Mail*, that Dr Leyds would attend the meeting, encouraged people to demonstrate outside the hall. The *Morning Leader* certainly believed that this was so and in an interesting editorial used this as an indication of the gullibility of the crowd:[40]

It is pitiable that a crowd could be found to believe such lies. It is lies like these . . . which brought the war about. . . . The crowd which

[38] *New Age*, 27 June 1901, p. 411.
[39] Editorial, *Financial News*, 19 June 1901.
[40] *Morning Leader*, 20 June 1901.

believed Dr. Leyds was in the Queen's Hall also believed that the Boers were oppressing the Uitlander as the Turks oppressed the Armenians. They went to storm the Queen's Hall moved by a perfectly natural indignation. . . . Their motives . . . were quite honest and respectable. They sincerely believed that the Boers were brutal tyrants. . . . The hostile part of the crowd had not the faintest conception of what is really happening in South Africa. It was a warm hearted, almost sentimental crowd.

A similar point about crowd gullibility was made by a correspondent of the *Glasgow Evening News* after he had been attacked by a crowd outside an anti-war meeting because he was wearing a soft hat: [41]

I am a war not a peace man, but . . . I have a partiality for soft felt hats . . . no sooner did I make my appearance in South Albion Street . . . than I was assailed with a yell—'Here's a Boer; lets go for him.' The crowd—flabby well-groomed medical students and dirty corner boys mostly—hurled the most fervent imprecations at me. . . . Everyone seemed animated by the single desire to do me some violence. . . . It is certain I was known to no-one, nor could my politics have been a matter of public knowledge, much less of public concern. I am driven back on the hat theory. . . . How small a matter, then, suffices . . . as a pretext for violence, abuse, and rowdyism. I am satisfied that extremely few of the . . . people who bawled and sang and shouted . . . knew what they were bawling for . . . I should analyse the animating motives and sentiments of my mob as this—six-tenths inborn love of violence and rows; three-tenths fondness for amusement of the horse play sort; one-tenth patriotism.

The situations and events described above are interesting because whether they emanated from a celebratory occasion, or whether they were a result of a nearby peace meeting, they confirm characteristics that are common to all excited crowd forms. They closely resemble the 'mob' situation, they are an excuse for excesses of spirit or revenge against certain individuals that always occur during such riot, or near-riot, situations. They reveal nothing new about this particular crowd, nothing that would make it different from other crowds. For our purposes another aspect of the jingo crowd is of greater interest: that of the crowd involved in the 'rational' and purposeful disturbance of peace meetings.

[41] *Glasgow Evening News*, 9 March 1900.

Two dominant characteristics of the jingo crowd can be discerned from a study of the rowdyism that accompanied the holding of anti-war meetings. The first and the most obvious is the youth of those who tended to be to the fore both in the actual disruption of the peace meetings, and in the riots that accompanied them. Complete details of those who were arrested as a result of the disturbances are seldom given in the local papers but all the written reports emphasize this feature of the rowdies. The riot at Birmingham, however, during Lloyd George's visit to the town, resulted in twenty-seven casualties, and one young man died as a result of the baton charge made by the police. Because of accusations that were made of police brutality there was considerable interest in those injured and a full report of their cases and ages was given.

There were some twenty-seven males admitted for treatment to the hospital, most of them with such injuries as cut hands or bruised arms. Of these only four were aged thirty or over. The youngest person admitted was a child aged seven and there were two who were twelve and fourteen respectively. The average age in all was twenty-seven. Similarly, of the ten people arrested on this particular occasion and charged with either behaving in a riotous and disorderly manner or with assaulting the police, the average age was 22·5; the oldest being a basket maker of forty-six, the youngest a clerk of sixteen.[42] In the case of the Scarborough riots the ages of those arrested were not recorded, but at least nine of the twenty-three charged were referred to in the court as 'boys' and the *Scarborough Mercury* commented: 'To pounce upon newspaper boys and telegraph messengers was a childish exhibition of authority when others more guilty were allowed to go scot free.'[43] The same was true of those arrested after the meeting at the Queen's Hall on 19 June 1901, where the average age was 25·9 years.[44]

It was this age group which all observers agreed were the rowdy element in the crowds. A letter to the *Midland Free Press* concerning a meeting at Leicester on 20 February 1900, commented that 'the noisy party was mainly composed of youths from 16 to 17 to 20 years of age' and the newspaper report described them as 'young bloods' who were out for some 'fun'.

[42] *Birmingham Daily Mail, op. cit.*
[43] *Scarborough Mercury*, 27 April 1900.   [44] *Morning Leader, op. cit.*

This was corroborated by the fact that there were attempts by supporters of the war to gain a hearing for the pro-Boers. A Mr Wicke 'endeavoured to read a letter from Sir John Rolleston urging a fair hearing' but was unable to do so.[45] It is clear that in this instance 'fun' rather than patriotism was the dominant consideration.

Similarly, at the Young Scots' meeting in Edinburgh on 26 April 1901, it was noted that 'the portion not in sympathy [with the meeting] were young men gathered at the back of the hall'. In the crowd outside the hall were 'groups of youths with Union Jacks', there were 'several young men arrested'.[46] A Liverpool meeting held early in 1902 at which Leonard Courtney spoke, was confronted with 'the approach of a gang of youths . . . well-booted and batoned. . . . They came marching up Mount Pleasant . . . booing and cheering.'[47] At a Liskeard meeting addressed by Lloyd George and Emily Hobhouse the latter claimed that 'it seemed a strange thing that the people of Liskeard should allow a few thoughtless and ill-mannered boys to spoil a meeting'. As Lloyd George rose to speak 'a hundred or more youths . . . surged on to the platform . . . making all manner of noises'.[48]

If youths were the prime offenders in the actual rowdyism that disturbed meetings and attacked pro-Boer premises, it should also be recognized that the rowdies were comparatively few in number. As the *Morning Leader* remarked of the crowd at the Queen's Hall meeting already mentioned, 'the rather considerable crowd . . . were obviously for the most part good-humoured spectators waiting to see what might happen . . . the few fire-brands who sought to incite violence . . . were quietly conducted to strong lodgings for the night'.[49] This was corroborated by letters written to the newspaper by members of the crowd: 'There were patches of Jingoes with little flags, but the great majority of the people were working men and women who arrived to attend the meeting and stood waiting patiently for admission to the hall;' and another 'having failed to get in before the door was shut I myself formed part of the said crowd,

[45] *Midland Free Press*, 24 February 1900.
[46] *Edinburgh Evening News*, 27 April 1901.
[47] *Liverpool Daily Post*, 11 January 1902.
[48] *Liskeard Weekly Mercury*, 7 July 1900; *Western Morning News*, 6 July 1900.
[49] *Morning Leader, op. cit.*

and I can testify that more than one-half of it was perfectly silent and apathetic'.[50] The report of the *Herald of Peace* was more explicit: 'The ringleaders, inciters to violence, and those who mainly inflicted injury were for the most part well-dressed young men, apparently clerks.'[51]

The place of the clerk was at times an important one, especially at demonstrations in London. It was also symptomatic of the most significant and interesting characteristic of the jingo crowd. The essence of the successful disturbance of a meeting is the existence of small groups of individuals with common purpose who can be termed 'leaders'. In the jingo crowd these 'leaders' tended to belong exclusively to the middle-class. They clearly attended the meetings with the intention of disrupting them and seldom was there any evidence of sophisticated organization in their efforts. In some instances, however, it was clear that leading Conservatives had deliberately organized them to prevent meetings from being held. One such example was at Northampton on 7 February 1900.

At the end of January a local Peace Committee had been formed to work in co-operation with the national South African Conciliation Committee, although it seems to have been nearer to the Stop-the-War Committee in attitude. A committee was elected which included J. Gribble and E. Paulton of the Trades Council, members of the Bradlaugh Radical Association and the Social Democratic Federation both of which affiliated to the Peace Committee. The Liberal Party in the town was under the influence of its Chairman F. Tonsley, who was later to resign over the re-adoption of Labouchere as candidate, and did not affiliate as a body. But several of its leading members joined and one of them, Councillor Johnson, took the chair at the meeting in question.[52] The all-party nature of the Committee was reflected in the speakers it secured for the 7 February meeting. They included Labouchere, J. M. Robertson and Hyndman.

The local Conservatives had suffered in the past from Radical rowdyism. They now saw a situation which could be exploited to their advantage.[53] Various ruses were used to ensure that the

[50] *Ibid.*   [51] *Herald of Peace*, 1 July 1901, p. 90.

[52] *Northampton Daily Reporter*, 1 February 1900; *Northampton Mercury*, 2 September 1900.

[53] The *Northampton Daily Chronicle*, 8 February 1900, a Tory paper makes this very point.

hall would be packed with opponents of the meeting.[54] It was announced that Mr A. J. Darnell would speak 'for Britain and her soldiers'. Darnell was a solicitor and the leader of the local Conservative Party. It became apparent during the meeting that he intended to use it as a party platform upon which to confront Labouchere with the ignominy of losing a resolution before an audience of his constituents. Thus, claiming that he had obtained the permission of the Chairman to speak last of all:

he refused to be placed upon absolutely different terms to Mr. Labouchere who was speaking in front. He did not think they were going to put any time on Mr. Robertson so he told them that it was their meeting, they could do what they liked, and if they did not fall in with his suggestion they must take the responsibility.

The threat was quite explicit and when requested to quiet the meeting he refused because 'the promoters had declined to give him fair play by . . . not [allowing] . . . him to speak until the other speakers had finished'.[55] The meeting had to be abandoned, Labouchere and Hyndman were escorted away by the police and A. J. Darnell was left to address the meeting rejoicing that 'Northampton had vigorously followed up York's answer to the critics of the Government'.[56]

In Brighton a similar pattern was revealed at a meeting of the League of Liberals Against Aggression and Militarism on 22 November 1901, which was addressed by R. C. Lehman. This meeting, held in opposition to the wishes of the local Liberal Association, was subjected to a series of disruptions led by a Mr Ballard and a 'pale, handsome, dashing young fellow' whose name was Turner. Ballard was an ex-Conservative councillor and a prominent solicitor. Although admission to the meeting was by ticket, many hostile to the gathering entered the Athenaeum Hall by the back entrance. These included Turner who, on being refused entry at the main door, 'protested that he had come to make a speech on his own views, that he had been out with the Yeomanry . . . and had been invalided home

[54] A circular was sent out advertising the meeting for 7.15 when it was really due to start at 7.45. The circular announced that Darnell would speak.
[55] *Northampton Daily Chronicle, op. cit.*
[56] *The Times*, 8 February 1900, p. 10, described this meeting as having been disrupted by 'organised opposition'.

with enteric'. Ballard was the recognized 'leader' as the report in the *Brighton Herald*—an independent paper but one which supported imperialism—indicates: there were

many interruptions—many of them merely silly—from Mr. Ballard, cheers for Mr. Ballard, whistling and all kinds of noises . . . then Mr. Ballard hauled out from somewhere . . . a large Union Jack, furled round a staff, which he cuddled in his arm. Then out stepped from the same noisy corner the young Brighton Yeoman . . . [who] climbed up on the platform, and took a seat there. . . . There he sat, while the hostile element, which now had the meeting in their power, sang 'Sons of the Sea,' and other patriotic songs.[57]

The Chief Constable requested that the meeting be abandoned and the promoters melted away. Some violence took place—again stimulated by several of the 'excited young men' who set upon an 'old gentleman'. The Yeoman, Turner, 'who had taken a lively part in the various tussles and who was in a very excited state . . . delivered a little speech. . . . He said it was a great disgrace for English people to allow these meetings.'[58]

A meeting at Derby in January 1902 paralleled Northampton in that local Conservatives were again prominent and were clearly acting in concert. The opposition was led by Mr H. Maiden and Mr A. Goodhall, who was a local footballer. Both were young men and both members of the Tory Party. The meeting had been convened by the Derby Peace Society and Joshua Rowntree was scheduled to speak on 'Christianity and War'.[59] Immediately he rose the applause was drowned by counter-cheers and he stood for twenty minutes trying to gain a hearing. Goodhall and Maiden refused to quieten the audience and led in the singing of patriotic songs. The meeting had to be abandoned to the control of the Conservative Party. Mr T. H. Wells, the Conservative sub-agent, who had 'mounted the platform with the other interrupters, said he should like to propose a resolution of confidence in the Government' and this was seconded by Mr H. Moe 'another prominent Conservative'. There seems little doubt that 'the disturbance was in fact engineered by the young bloods of Toryism'.[60]

---

[57] *Brighton Herald*, 23 November 1901.   [58] *Ibid.*
[59] Also the title of a Quaker pamphlet by Rowntree.
[60] *Derby Daily Telegraph*, 10 January 1902.

Individual initiative, often by those connected with the Conservative Party, then, was an important factor in the characteristics of the jingo crowd. But group initiative was possibly a more common factor in causing the break-up of anti-war meetings. The groups were composed essentially of young men and in Scotland the moving spirits were the university students. This can be illustrated most clearly by the experience of the Scottish towns visited by Cronwright-Schreiner during his speaking tour in the early months of 1900.

He began his tour at Glasgow on 6 March, addressing a meeting at which even the local Conservative newspaper admitted 'the majority of the audience . . . were friendly'.[61] There was some rowdyism but it was adequately contained by Keir Hardie and his stewards. The rowdy element was 'composed of people who consider themselves as belonging to a higher stratum of society'.[62] On this occasion, as on many others, the staging of a peace meeting sparked off a series of disturbances in the streets. A band of students wrecked the front of the office of the *Labour Leader*.[63] And on the following night, in Edinburgh, what was to become a common pattern of the tour was established.

The size of the crowd prevented Schreiner from reaching the hall. He was manhandled in the street by a group 'which was composed mainly of respectably dressed young men whom I took to be students'.[64] The hall itself was packed with opponents of the meeting: 'Quite three-fourths of the audience was made up of students, buoyant of mood, robust of lung.' Not that this was very surprising for 'from the moment that it was known that Mr. Cronwright-Schreiner . . . was to speak in Edinburgh, threats to wreck the meeting were uttered in University student circles'.[65] Keir Hardie was the only one who could obtain a hearing. Most of the abuse was directed against Theodore Napier, Chairman of the local Stop-the-War Committee, who was assaulted when the platform was stormed by about 150

---

[61] *Glasgow Evening News*, 7 March 1900.

[62] Cronwright-Schreiner, *op. cit.*, p. 66.

[63] *Ibid.*, p. 74.

[64] *Ibid.*, p. 79.

[65] *Ibid.*, p. 98; *Scotsman*, 8 March 1900. Note that the Trades Council sent a delegation to this meeting.

students. The efforts of the crowd outside to rush the hall were led by the students who were joined by a[66]

number of Yeomanry sharpshooters . . . whose determined efforts to oust the constables threatened at any minute destruction to the door of the hall, and their weight added to that of . . . members of the University fifteen who were in front proved such an assistance . . . it was well for the police that they received reinforcements.

Five people were arrested, three of whom were students, and the other two were described as an 'army student' and a 'law clerk' aged seventeen and twenty-one respectively. They were all charged with disorderly conduct and creating a disturbance. Although not necessarily the 'leaders' of the disturbance—one of the students clearly was and was charged with assaulting Napier—the arrests illustrate the composition of the crowd both outside and inside the hall.[67] A letter from J. H. Smith to Campbell-Bannerman confirms this: 'These non-ticket holders and the disturbers of the peace who had obtained tickets were all well-dressed rowdies of the middle classes—students, lawyers, men of the clubs. . . . The working men present were quiet and orderly.'[68]

At Dundee, too, on 8 March it was the students and the young gentlemen of the city who composed the rowdy element. The *Dundee Advertiser* carried several letters after the meeting specifically accusing the students; one complained of 'the young men of educated and cultured appearance who wrecked last night's meeting'. Another, writing under the title of 'Students and Rowdyism', hoped that 'the day is not coming when these two terms shall each be suggestive of the other. . . . The frequency of scenes in which students are reported to take a conspicuous part is significant.'[69] The students themselves denied these charges. The college magazine wrote: 'It wasn't even a student who ultimately proposed the motion in favour of the war, but a young fellow in business in our city.'[70] They also denied any part in the attack on the house of Reverend Walter Walsh which took place after the meeting had been abandoned, confusedly claiming that 'they endeavoured to prevent it', that

[66] *Scotsman, op. cit.*   [67] *Edinburgh Evening News*, 8, 16, 23 March 1900.
[68] Quoted in Cronwright-Schreiner, *op. cit.*, p. 118. It should perhaps be treated with some caution as no such letter can be found in Campbell-Bannerman's papers.
[69] *Dundee Advertiser*, 12 March 1900.   [70] *Ibid.*, 14 March 1900.

they did 'remarkably little, not nearly enough in fact . . . their conduct was characterised by nothing worse than an exuberance of patriotism, not by any means in excess of the demand'.[71]

At Aberdeen, however, on 20 May, the evidence for student rowdyism is clearer. Organized by the SDF-inspired local Stop-the-War Committee and coming just after Mafeking Night, the meeting was fairly successful. There was a group of rowdy students who had obtained admission by attending a religious service which had been held before the meeting in the same hall. The situation outside the hall and the riotous aftermath, however, were serious enough to warrant the chief magistrate's request that fifty soldiers march through the town in case the Riot Act had to be read. Once again the local newspapers, even the Conservative ones, agreed that it was the students who were the ringleaders. There also occurred that same night the attack on the dispensary of a Dr Gordon Beveridge who wrote to the *Evening Express*: 'I am not a party man on this war question and I have no connection direct or indirect with to-night's war meeting. Yet some miscreants have attacked my house and smashed my windows.'[72] The following morning some students again visited the dispensary and repeated the performance until the police arrived. According to the police, the most noticeable feature of the crowd on the Sunday night, i.e. the night of the meeting, was 'that the rowdy element of the community was conspicuous by its absence'. 'Rowdy' in this context referred to 'hooligan' or 'criminal' for it goes on to say: 'It consisted largely of respectable citizens, among those present being many prominent church members and workers, as well as representative business people.' The presence of a German lecturer at the university prompted the students to attack him on the following Monday afternoon. He was pelted with eggs and peasemeal and had to be rescued by the proctors.[73] The students themselves were proud of the part they had played in these events as a letter from three residents of Marischall College testifies:[74]

Our attacks . . . on the residences of Dr. Beveridge and Dr. Ferdinands were to demonstrate to the public in general that we intend to stamp out all those specimens (very uncommon, by the way) called pro-

[71] *Ibid.*, 17 March 1900.
[72] Cronwright-Schreiner, *op. cit.*, p. 376; *Evening Express*, 21 May 1900.
[73] *Evening Express, op. cit.*   [74] *Ibid.*, 23 May 1900.

Boers. We have seen that Dr. Beveridge now defends himself by saying that his views . . . were not the views of Mr. Schreiner, but what meant his war-like attitude before the Sunday crowd, his attending a socialist meeting, and his weakness of not proving himself to the satisfaction of everybody that he is still on the side of Brittania [*sic*]?

The same sort of evidence is rarer for the rest of the country. It has already been noted how the students at Birmingham were 'credited with the intention of joining the throng',[75] and there is little reason to doubt that they did attend. In London the Stock Exchange element was sometimes prominent. This may have been true at the Trafalgar Square demonstration of 24 September 1899. *Club Life* reported how 'it was noticed by reporters that the noise and disturbance was created by young clerks, medical students and beardless youths'.[76] The *Star* commented on 'the band of boys in straw hats and high collars . . . [who] are probably too young to remember some earlier scenes in Trafalgar Square'.[77] But of the six arrested on this occasion none was a clerk as far as is known—two were not listed as having any occupation in the newspaper report and the other four were all young manual workers.

This, however, was not always the pattern at the London meetings. The aforementioned Merriman and Sauer meeting showed a very different result. It has already been noted how the Stock Exchange was accused of 'plotting' to disturb this meeting. The *Morning Leader* asserted that the rowdies were 'the Stock Exchange gangs who were present in response to orders'.[78] Of the seven arrested for causing a disturbance outside the Queen's Hall on this occasion three were clerks, two of whom were from the Stock Exchange. Of the four others arrested, two were working-class—a porter and a whip-maker; and two were middle-class—a medical student and the son of the proprietor of the *People* and the *Globe*.[79]

One final example of middle-class group 'leaders' as characteristic of the jingo crowd can be examined. W. T. Stead, at the beginning of the war, as a part of his War Against War crusade, addressed several meetings including one at Norwich on 5 November 1899. It was an unsuccessful gathering, broken

[75] See p. 142.
[76] *Club Life*, 7 October 1899, p. 8.
[77] *Star*, 27 September 1899.
[78] *Morning Leader*, 20 June 1901.
[79] *Ibid.*, 21 June 1901.

up by rowdyism created and led by 'half-a-dozen scions of successful traders or professional men'. These young men were known as the 'young lions' of Norwich. They were a well-known set and comprised the sons of leading solicitors in the town including Edward Bullard, the son of the junior member of parliament for the city. A reporter was

struck by the strength of representation which the legal profession had. Foremost in the fray was Mr. Gilbert Kennett, and in the busiest parts of the building I noticed Mr. Emerson Jr., Mr. Cooper Jr., Mr. Orams Jr., and a Mr. Martin, who I believe, is associated in some way with Messrs. Cozens-Hardy and Jewison an important law firm in the town.

Stead was greeted with an outburst of yells from the 'young lions' when he rose to speak. A show of hands to hear him was claimed to be 'about four to one in favour' but when he tried again, 'howling, yelling, cat-calls, abuse, and noisy demonstrations from some squeaking instrument . . . rendered it impossible to hear a word'. Led by Bullard, the 'young lions' then stormed the platform and captured the meeting.[80] This demonstration was successful, but it is interesting to contrast this with the anti-war meetings of a Workmen's Committee formed at Norwich in May 1900. It centred around a nucleus of the Social Democratic Federation, the Independent Labour Party and the Radical Club. It held fortnightly meetings and during the summer of 1900 they seem to have been very successful. One particular meeting[81]

took place at Heigham Radical Club and there the attendance was so large that it had to be held in the open air. Mr. Fred Henderson delivered an able and strongly worded address, but not withstanding that fact, the 'Young Lions of Norwich' found no representatives willing or able to closure free speech.

The resolution that this meeting passed illustrated the amalgam of Socialist and Radical elements within the committee. It condemned the war as a capitalist's war 'in which . . . the independence of the Dutch Republic [has been] threatened, for the financial gain of the same class against which the English work-

[80] *Daylight*, 11 November 1899, p. 4.
[81] *Ibid.*, 12 May 1900, p. 4; 23 June 1900, p. 2.

ing men have to fight in matters of social reform and industrial questions at home'.[82]

Official reaction to the disturbances does not seem to have varied much. The Home Office was far more sympathetic to the victims of rowdyism than the local authorities. A debate in parliament on 15 May 1900, centred around the issue of whether government leaders—and in particular Balfour—had given encouragement to rowdyism by a statement that he had made excusing the rioters as being possessed with an excess of patriotism, and whether the government had been less than eager to punish miscreants. But, as government spokesmen pointed out, the preservation of law and order was a local responsibility and however much they may deplore damage to property or danger to life they could only intervene if requested or if a prosecution was brought under the 1886 Riot Act.[83] At the local level, there was some suspicion that certain members of Town Councils had connived at the rioting and that the police were less than active in protecting victims from the fury of the crowds. Cronwright-Schreiner claimed that his manhandling in Edinburgh was witnessed by two policemen who 'saw all that occurred, and . . . never stirred a finger to help'.[84] And noted that at this meeting 'the police were most remiss in their duty'.[85] Even the *Scotsman* thought 'it rather remarkable that the force of policemen on duty . . . was . . . so meagre—certainly during the earlier part of the proceedings'.[86] The same accusation was levelled at an Exeter Hall meeting in the same month where, after the first attempt of the crowd to storm the building had failed, the police were sent for but took half-an-hour to arrive in spite of the fact that they were within five minutes of Bow Street police station.[87] Whatever the attitude of the police, that of the Town Councils was much clearer. In Scarborough, following the riot of 12 March 1900, the Chief Constable desired to send a report to the Public Prosecutor. At the Watch Committee meeting of 23 March two Liberal councillors proposed that the report be sent to the Home Office. The Conservatives, perhaps to prevent 'their friends being exposed',[88]

---

[82] *Ibid.*, 23 June 1900.   [83] *Hansard*, 4th Series, LXXX, 940–82.
[84] Cronwright-Schreiner, *op. cit.*, pp. 80–3.
[85] *Ibid.*, p. 112.   [86] *Scotsman, op. cit.*
[87] *The Times*, 3 March 1900, p. 9.
[88] *Scarborough Mercury*, 30 March 1900.

moved and carried an amendment which stated that 'the Committee do not send any communication to the Public Prosecutor, but that the Police be instructed to give every facility to private persons in any proceedings which they might institute against known offenders'.[89] This amendment would have ensured an end to the affair, for Rowntree had already intimated that he had no intention of prosecuting. But the attempt of the Conservatives to draw a veil over the episode failed, due to the intervention of the Town Clerk. His advice, that the Chief Constable was obliged to send the report, was being disregarded, and he warned them at the following meeting that the amendment was illegal and the committee out of order. The Conservatives were still reluctant to accede and tried to persuade the Liberals to withdraw their resolution. Only when the Liberal members of the committee began to walk out, placing the remaining Conservatives in an impossible procedural position, was it decided to rescind the amendment.[90]

In Edinburgh the Conservative majority on the Town Council prevented an attempt to secure a public enquiry into the events of 7 March 1900. The connection between the jingo crowd and the Conservatives was certainly one of sympathy. The Liberals claimed that 'the question involved was the right of public meeting', but the Lord Provost was more interested in linking the originators of the meeting with the Boers, claiming that 'one of the other gentlemen was a friend of the Queen's enemies'.[91]

In Dover, the magistrates were accused of being openly biased against Brown and the bail for one of the accused having been at first refused was granted upon a protest from a local councillor who offered to stand it.[92] In Tottenham, where two men were charged with riotous behaviour and wilful damage to the property of Henry Bish, the magistrate, a Mr Fordham, said that 'a man has a perfect right to hang a Boer flag—if he is foolish enough to do so', and was not satisfied that the prisoners did the damage and discharged them. It is interesting to note, however, that although the magistrate dismissed the charge of riotous assembly, the Home Office, when the case was reviewed

---

[89] *Ibid.*, 6 April 1900. [90] *Ibid.*

[91] *Edinburgh Evening Despatch*, 15 March 1900. The resolution was defeated by 24 to 18.

[92] *Dover Observer, op. cit.*

for compensation, was satisfied that the crowd had been a riotous one.[93]

The essence to the successful break-up of a meeting lay in the fact that a small number of individuals or a group of determined people could sustain a barrage of noise against the speakers. It needed only a few to initiate a disturbance which, once started, tended to create its own cumulative dynamism. The secret of holding a peaceable meeting, therefore, lay either in excluding these opposers, which usually proved impossible even at meetings open to ticket-holders only, or removing them by the use of a large number of stewards. The promoters of anti-war meetings very soon developed this technique and where they were able to ensure a sufficient number of stewards they were usually able to ensure a successful meeting. The stewards at the Young Scot's meeting in Edinburgh were accused of unnecessarily brutal behaviour when ejecting 'well-dressed youths [who] were seized by organized bands of ruffians . . . and haled with blows and kicks'.[94] These two hundred youths 'were an organised body whose sole object was to break up the meeting' and had formed a compact mass in the hall by pre-arrangement.[95] The concentration of disturbers in one part of the hall was an essential feature to the successful disruption of a meeting and was also noticed at Brighton, but with care in the placing of the stewards rowdyism could be prevented. At Glasgow on 6 March 1900, despite the presence of a group of patriots, Keir Hardie avoided rowdyism by ensuring that the stewards were gathered an hour before the meeting opened and were dispersed at strategic points throughout the hall.[96]

In spite of the generally universal rowdyism that characterized most attempts to hold anti-war meetings during this period, there were those that escaped the usual disturbances. A meeting held under the auspices of the Social Democratic Federation at Plaistow and chaired by Percy Alden, vigorously denounced the war but was not the occasion for any rowdyism. Similarly, a Hyndman meeting at Mile End Vestry Hall was held successfully in spite of an attempt 'on the part of several hundreds of

[93] For this case see *The Times*, 22 May 1900, p. 16; 26 May 1900, p. 16. *Tottenham and Stamford Hill Times and Stoke Newington Chronicle*, 1 June 1900.
[94] *Scotsman*, 27 April 1901. [95] *Edinburgh Evening News*, 29 April 1901.
[96] *Glasgow Evening News*, 7 March 1900.

jingoes, brought to the meeting by the means of specially issued posters' to prevent it.[97] The local paper complained that this meeting had been unfairly reported in the London press as having been broken up whereas, in fact, the entrance of Hyndman 'brought the greatest part of the audience . . . to their feet cheering uproariously' and that 'after the first twenty minutes or so the meeting was almost as quiet as a Sunday school except for the marks of appreciation by the audience'. A pro-war amendment received only twenty votes, the main resolution was carried by an overwhelming majority.[98] Likewise, a publicly advertised Cronwright-Schreiner meeting at Canning Town was held successfully in Mansfield House. Cronwright-Schreiner's remarks on this meeting may be worth quoting:[99]

Before the mobs were worked up by the Imperialist press and the agents of the war party to wreck meetings . . . it was possible to hold a well-advertised meeting against the war in a densely populated part of London, without any mob gathering, without any rowdyism. . . . The orderly behaviour of the meeting, I feel certain, in the light of my subsequent experiences was also in a measure due to the fact that Canning Town is a working man's part of the Metropolis, and that there are no 'gentry' there.

While it may be true that rowdyism was cumulative and that one incident encouraged another, there was one part of London which was definitely largely working-class and which Cronwright-Schreiner subsequently described as 'the only place in Great Britain where it was possible for me to address without organised rowdyism an open, well-advertised public meeting'.[100] That place was Battersea. This was, in part, due to the strength of the Battersea Stop-the-War Committee, formed in February 1900 around a nucleus of the local SDF branch. The committee was the familiar amalgam of the left. Affiliated to it were: Battersea Labour League, Battersea Ethical Society, the Liberal and Radical Association, Battersea Spiritualist Society, Clapham Labour League, the local branch of the Municipal Employees Union, and the Amalgamated Society of House Painters and Decorators.[101] It would appear that the Socialists were the driving force behind the committee: 'Most of the work has been

[97] *West Ham Citizen*, 17 February 1900.
[98] *Ibid.*   [99] Cronwright-Schreiner, *op. cit.*, p. 18.
[100] *Ibid.*, p. 280.   [101] *Ibid.*, p. 281.

done by the Battersea branch of the Social Democratic Federation and the Battersea Labour League.'[102] Their efforts, however, were separate from those of Battersea's member of parliament, John Burns.

When the committee had first been formed he had been asked to join but failed to reply to the letter of invitation. He then consented to speak at a meeting but cancelled his acceptance when he learned that Cronwright-Schreiner was also to appear on the platform. It is not clear why he had no wish to co-operate with the committee, for throughout May to August 1900 he held anti-war meetings every Sunday in Battersea Park. It may have been that its Socialist flavour discouraged him.[103] This was the explanation given by Cronwright-Schreiner and also by the committee itself. At a meeting in August 1901 the Chairman, Councillor Lethbridge, referred sorrowfully to 'some who professed to be in sympathy with the Stop-the-War Committee in principle but who kept away from the meetings— possibly through jealousy of its promoters'.[104] Essentially a 'loner' as far as party organization was concerned, he considered himself strong enough to stand alone. As there were considerable stresses in the Labour League-Socialist alliance— which formed the basis of his support in Battersea and was the essence of the Progressive majority on the Vestry—it may have been that he considered it politic to remain aloof. Many of his most active supporters, however, were willing to co-operate with the anti-war committee. Thus W. Matthews, a Labour League man who was Chairman of the Vestry and also of the Stop-the-War Committee, chaired Burns's summer park meetings.

There were, then, two sets of meetings proceeding concurrently in Battersea, none of which was subjected to rowdyism. This was partly due to the effects of superior organization. At the meeting of 6 May 1900 attended by Cronwright-Schreiner, G. B. Clark and George Lansbury, there were five hundred stewards, 'all youngish men who knew their work and meant to do it'. Disrupters were efficiently dealt with: 'If any

[102] C. Parsons to Cronwright-Schreiner, *ibid.*, p. 286.
[103] *Mid-Surrey Gazette*, 7 April 1900, for an anti-war meeting which ended with the singing of the Marseillaise at which Hyndman was the principal speaker.
[104] *South Western Star*, 16 August 1901.

man made the least disturbance he was quietly touched on the shoulder and warned.' If this did not suffice, stronger measures were taken: 'As soon as Dr Clark rose, a few Imperialists began to interrupt proceedings. . . . As they wouldn't stop, they were seized by the stewards . . . and passed out from hand to hand like rockets and shot out into the street.'[105] This meeting was entirely free, tickets were only issued for the platform seats. It was reported that 'the audience were almost breathless in their eagerness to hear the speakers putting the anti-jingo side of the great question. . . . The hundreds of warm faces showing unrestrained excitement.'[106] Similarly with the meetings Burns held in Battersea Park, which were not just an attack on the war but on the whole trend of foreign policy and which attracted audiences of up to 5,000. It was noted that the audiences had been attentive throughout and that 'although on the third Sunday one or two well-dressed youths made themselves prominent there has been great good feeling and some enthusiasm at all the meetings'. Burns, in a typical diary entry, wrote that at one of the meetings he spoke 'for 90 minutes against the war to 4,000 people. Spoke well, people kind, attentive, interested and unanimous. A ground swell of opposition from the friends of the publicans but tackled them and they collapsed.'[107]

Perhaps as a result of SDF influence, the Battersea Stop-the-War Committee, at times, took a more extreme position than the national organization. At a meeting in the Queen's Hall in June 1901 the official resolution limited itself to protesting against the continuance of the war and demanded the 'immediate offer of such terms of peace to the burghers of the two republics as a brave and freedom loving people can honourably accept'. An amendment was moved by two Battersea men, J. P. Dixon and C. Parsons. The latter was a Socialist, Organizing Secretary of the meeting and Secretary of the Battersea branch of the Stop-the-War Committee. Their amendment proposed the deletion of the words after 'terms' and the substitution of the following: 'As shall include the complete independence of the two Republics.' It was 'received with acclamation and car-

[105] Cronwright-Schreiner, *op. cit.*, pp. 287–8.
[106] *Mid-Surrey Gazette*, 12 May 1900.
[107] *Ibid.*, 2 June 1900; Burns Diary, 20 May 1900, Add. MSS. 46318.

ried'.[108] Similarly, at a Battersea meeting the following August which was attended by Keir Hardie and Stead, there was an attempt to make the official resolution stronger. The promoters had drawn up a resolution vaguely demanding peace and the restoration of the authority of the Boer Republics. An amendment was moved to the effect that the meeting should send a resolution to Kruger encouraging him to persevere with the war. But, 'even a democratic platform at Battersea would not accept that and . . . the meeting decided by a shout that the original resolution was strong enough'. Stead's speech which followed restored unanimity to the meeting by pouring out a 'torrent of invective as nearly swept away even a Battersea audience'. The resolution was carried with only four dissentients.[109]

The local Stop-the-War Committee believed that the greatest triumph of Battersea was that it was virtually the only place in England where Cronwright-Schreiner could obtain a complete public hearing.[110] Equally impressive and perhaps an even greater achievement was the reception given to the Afrikaaner delegates, J. X. Merriman and J. W. Sauer. This meeting was one of the few graced by the presence of John Burns, perhaps because it was not officially organized by the Stop-the-War Committee: the Merriman-Sauer tour was organized by a separate committee of well-wishers which co-operated with the anti-war organizations in arranging meetings. The meeting was highly successful. Scheduled to begin at 6.30 p.m., the crowd was so dense by 6 p.m. that it was difficult to get near the door of the Town Hall. This crowd was unique, however, because it was not hostile. The local 'imperialist' newspaper, the *South Western Star*, which for long had tried to maintain that Battersea was as patriotic as anywhere else in England, was forced to admit despairingly that[111]

only in Battersea could there be held such a meeting. . . . The people generally have refused them [i.e. Merriman and Sauer] a hearing. On Sunday evening it was demonstrated that Battersea in patriotism, as in everything else, is unique . . . in the interests of free speech and equal rights 200 stewards . . . were got together . . . there was no

108 *The Times*, 20 June 1901, p. 6.   109 *South Western Star, loc. cit.*
110 *Ibid.*, 22 February 1901. Stop-the-War Committee Annual Meeting.
111 *Ibid.*, 7 June 1901.

need for the stewards. A more orderly and a more enthusiastic meeting has never been held in Battersea.

Over 1,400 people attended and the platform included Dr G. B. Clark, Mrs Gray of the SDF, F. A. Channing, W. P. Byles and Harold Rylett, who represented the Stop-the-War Committee. Merriman 'had a tremendous reception. It seemed that the masses of people would never stop shouting and stamping and waving their hats.' There was no attempt to disturb the meeting: 'No opposing sound was heard, no antagonistic gesture seen.'[112]

Battersea was not only unique, however, in being able to hold successful anti-war meetings. It was also the only place in England where an imperialist meeting could be captured. The only similar incident discovered of this kind of pro-Boer rowdyism was in the Warwickshire village of Tysoe on Mafeking Night when a bonfire planned by the local supporters of the war was destroyed by 'the sons and younger workmen of the pro-Boers'.[113] The Battersea meeting was held under the auspices of the Imperial South African Association and was chaired by one of its leading officers, a man named Hancock. The lecturer, A. H. Sytner, was continually heckled:[114]

It is doubtful if there were half-a-dozen present who agreed with what he said. Almost the whole of those in the building were Labour Leaguers or supporters of the Stop-the-War Committee. The meeting totally failed in its objects. It was called for the Imperialistic side of the controversy to be heard; instead of that it was turned into a pro-Boer meeting with a collection for the wives and children of the burghers.

Lantern slides of the war leaders were shown; all the British generals, with the exception of Buller, were hooted; cheers were given for the Boer leaders.[115] When the Chairman refused to

112 *Ibid.*

113 M. K. Ashby, *Joseph Ashby of Tysoe 1854–1919* (Cambridge, 1961), p. 196.

114 *South Western Star*, 8 March 1901.

115 Buller was always a favourite amongst the working class, probably because he was always associated with a care for the comforts of the ordinary soldier. He refused to move into Natal until the catering arrangements had been completed to his satisfaction. See J. Symons, *Buller's Campaign* (London, 1963), p. 140.

The Battersea Liberal and Radical Association at their quarterly meeting in October 1901 passed a resolution of sympathy when he was suspended from active service. And in December 1901 there was a demonstration in Hyde Park 'of 100,000 British working men for Buller against the £100,000 given to Roberts

allow a resolution the meeting was taken over by Messrs Sanders and Matthews and other leading Stop-the-War men and a resolution moved and carried 'that the meeting agreed with that passed by the Borough Council opposing the war'.[116]

The ability of Battersea to hold successful anti-war meetings was not solely due to the strength of the local Peace Committee. Unlike most other towns in the country the local Vestry and later the Borough Council were solidly against the war and were not afraid to use the local Council as a platform for their views. The ease with which they were allowed to do this is indicative of the hold that radical politics had in Battersea. So strong was their opposition to the war that the Finance Committee recommended against giving a maintenance allowance to the families of men with the Reservists on the grounds that the war was a capitalist's war being waged against liberty and that such a body as the Battersea Vestry ought to lend no assistance even to those who were engaged in it against their will. The extreme Progressives, however, were placated by an amendment which recognized the duty of the state to pay such allowance as was necessary, yet directed that in its absence the money should be paid from the Vestry funds.[117] This question arose once again, though in a slightly different form, when a deputation from the Widow's and Orphan's Fund requested the use of the Vestry horses to take part in what was supposed to be a purely charity procession to raise money for the soldiers' families. The attitude of many Progressives was typified by that of Mr J. Brown who claimed that 'this country's brought down to a very low level when it's obliged to appeal to public charity to support the families of men who are fighting the cause of the moneymongers in South Africa'. Similar sentiments were echoed by Mr Lethbridge who believed that 'all these side shows are got up to make it [war] more popular'. Twenty-four Progressives voted against the request but most felt that although the war was deplorable it was their duty to assist those who suffered by it and the resolution was carried by a majority of sixteen votes.[118]

---

for political services to his friends'. See *Club Life*, 2 November 1901, p. 6, and 7 December 1901, p. 6.

[116] *South Western Star, loc. cit.*   [117] *Ibid.*, 24 November 1899.
[118] *Ibid.*, 11 May 1900.

The war dominated many of the Vestry meetings. Relatively innocuous issues were used both by the Municipal Alliance (i.e. the Moderates) and the Progressives as a platform from which to proclaim their loyalties. Thus, a decision to let the Latchmere Baths to a Stop-the-War meeting at one-half the normal charge of thirty shillings was the occasion for a prolonged discussion on the war. The Moderates accused the Progressives of being 'engaged in a political conspiracy. They were guilty almost of a veiled form of treason in supporting the enemies of the country.' The Progressives claimed that Chamberlain was the enemy of the country and the Boers the friends of justice. Mr Stone, a Progressive, denounced the war in 'unmeasured terms. The friends of peace . . . were not the enemies of the country . . . her enemies . . . [were] "the rascally crew who were prepared to do anything . . . if they could increase their fame and fill their purses." ' He lamented the fact that 'there was no prophet in the land—no Gladstone who could have prevented this war'.[119] On this occasion it had been the Moderates who had raised the question but the Progressives were equally capable of using local Council issues for the same purpose. Thus in May 1901 a list of recommended new street names included those of Joubert and Methuen with a distinct preference for the former. After some discussion Mr Haythornthwaite, Moderate, moved that the proposal be sent back for a suggestion other than that of Joubert, at which several councillors called out 'Botha' and 'De Wet'. Mr Lane illuminated on the reasons why Joubert was preferred to Methuen:[120]

Without any hesitation they had decided on Joubert. . . . He was the man who stopped the destruction of the whole of the British forces after Spion Kop. Methuen, on the other hand, was known in the army as 'Mad Jack.' He had led his troops to destruction. Joubert was the man who had done the most to save the British troops in South Africa.

The name Joubert Street was adopted.

On another occasion, the Moderates urged that the Union Jack be raised over municipal buildings at public events in a move that was clearly calculated to illustrate the lack of patriotism of the Progressive vestrymen. It was blocked by an amendment which declared:[121]

[119] *Ibid.*, 13 April 1900.   [120] *Ibid.*, 10 May 1901.
[121] *Ibid.*, 29 June 1900.

Seeing that the Union Jack has become of late years the symbol of a grasping commercialism, this Vestry declines to place a Flag-staff on the Town Hall, believing that the true interest of an industrial population lies, not in the display of bunting, but in a steadfast adherence to the principles of social and economic freedom.

The amendment was carried by a large majority.

The fiercest debates, however, occurred in January and February 1901 when the Borough Council, as it had become after the 1900 municipal elections, passed a resolution condemning the methods of the British military authorities and demanding independence for the Boer states. The episode is interesting for it illustrates the distaste felt for a resolution which cast an implied slur on the British soldier—a feature also noted in the similar resolution of Aberdeen Trades Council. It also—and it is not clear whether this was a result of the nature of the resolution—illuminated evidence of a split in the Progressive alliance; a split that, later in the year, was to cause a loosening of Progressive control of local government.

The resolution, which claimed violation of the Hague agreements on warfare with regard to the confiscation and the pillaging of private property, was moved by Mr Fred Knee. He emphasized that its purpose was to provide a counter-weight to 'municipalities all over the country tumbling over each other in their eagerness to welcome back an unsuccessful general', and to condemn annexation and the demand for unconditional surrender. This prompted a Municipal Alliance councillor, H. J. Smith, to propose an amendment condemning the resolution as an unpatriotic action and expressing confidence in the government. He launched into a tirade against pro-Boers in general, offering to hang 'them on the electric light standards' and Mr Knee in particular, doubting whether he 'was an Englishman'. The amendment received the full support of the Moderates plus the vote of one Progressive.[122]

At the following meeting the extent of the Progressive split was revealed. It was not generally believed that Knee's extreme motion would be carried, for another Progressive, Mr A. Brown, had proposed that:[123]

This Council, while believing that the British military authorities in South Africa are on the whole actuated by humane considerations in

[122] *Ibid.*, 25 January 1901.   [123] *Ibid.*, 15 February 1901.

the conduct of the campaign, are of the opinion that the principles laid down at the Hague Conference should be strictly adhered to; further, that the earliest possible opportunity should be taken by His Majesty's Government to bring about peace, on a basis honourable alike to the Boers and the British.

In the course of his speech he argued that the Boers had made more departures from civilized warfare than the British and instanced the use of the white flag and the expanding bullet.[124] He was supported by Mr Livsey and Mr Howarth Barnes, both Progressives. The latter objected to the Council considering imperial issues and attempted to get the motion ruled out of order on these grounds. The Mayor prevented this by asserting that as the Council contributed to the costs of supporting Reservists' families this entitled them to consider such matters. The main point of difference between the two factions was the attitude to the military conduct of the campaign and the desire of the original resolution that independence be restored to the Boer states. Brown claimed that this was absurd because they had never had any independence. He failed to carry his amendment by 23 votes; and the original motion was then passed by 27 votes to 19.

Both these meetings were punctuated with Stop-the-War rowdyism. The one Progressive who had voted for Smith's amendment did so as a protest against the 'hissing and howling' of the gallery during the proceedings. After the meeting people from the gallery assembled in front of the buildings and 'reviled the leading Moderates. Several . . . were followed by a mob, who jeered continuously.' At the second meeting, the chamber had been showered with anti-war leaflets and Brown's speech was greeted with rowdy opposition from his own party and from the gallery. The Municipal Alliance leader, Haythornthwaite,

---

[124] The controversy about the use of the white flag and the expanding bullet was a common one during the war. Both probably had some foundation, and were used by anti- and pro-war groups to illustrate the wickedness of their opponents. The imperialists always denied that expanding bullets were used by the British, but D. Reitz in *Commando* (London, 1929), p. 136, claims that they were found on dead British soldiers. It is certain that British soldiers had them. Captain Lafone, of the 2nd Battalion, Devonshire Regiment, wrote home to his parents: 'I have discarded all of those man-stopper bullets Father bought me as they say if you are captured with them on you, the Boers shoot you as they are expansive bullets.' 10 December 1899, letters of Captain Lafone, Add. MSS. 39558, f. 26.

tried to use the presence of the disturbers to secure an adjournment in an attempt to prevent the resolution going through. But the Mayor, who was sympathetic to the pro-Boer motion, refused to allow the question to be put and the meeting broke up in considerable disorder.[125]

The split that was exhibited amongst the Progressives over this issue became extant in March during the Guardians' election.[126] Essentially a split between the Labour League and the Socialists, it was foreshadowed by the earlier split in that Fred Knee was a Socialist. The massive Progressive majority depended upon this alliance. Whether it was really a middle-class working-class alliance as Paul Thompson seems to suggest is not clear. The Labour League was largely working class in its officers—W. Matthews was a stonemason by trade—but it is probable that there were middle-class elements within it.[127] It is probably more accurate, however, to see the split as a working-class Liberal-Socialist split. The vast majority of Progressive councillors were certainly working class,[128] and the SDF branch had been very strong in Battersea, but seems to have closed in 1899, although its individual members such as C. Parsons, W. S. Sanders and Mrs Gray remained very active in local politics. The alliance held firm throughout the municipal elections in 1900 in spite of the attempts of the Municipal Alliance candidates to use the pro-Boer antics of the Vestry to arouse the antipathy of the electors. Indeed, this tactic rebounded upon them; instead of the pro-Boers suffering, the Alliance candidates had been refused hearings. A meeting at the Town Hall addressed by the Municipal Alliance leaders had ended in the uproar that so frequently characterized pro-Boer meetings,[129] and the Progressives were returned with a majority of forty-three.

But the alliance between the Labour League and the Social Democrats had never been an easy one. They had been encouraged by the unifying issue of the war to remain at peace but

[125] *South Western Star*, 25 January, 15 February 1900.
[126] P. Thompson, *Socialists, Liberals, and Labour* (London, 1967), p. 185. The split was at least nine months older than he seems to believe.
[127] It is impossible to discover the social occupations of the councillors, the Trade and Street Directories only list occupation if the man was a self-employed tradesman.   [128] Thompson, *loc. cit.*
[129] *South Western Star*, 14 September 1900.

with the preparations for the election of the Guardians, 'the Progressives secretly resolved upon the extinction of the Socialist candidates. . . . They [i.e. Socialists] waited all night for terms from the Progressive leaders, but none arrived.'[130] The Socialists, therefore, decided to run their own candidates in Winstanley and Church wards against the Progressive and Municipal Alliance candidates. A meeting was held to try to come to some arrangement. Burns considered it important enough for his attention but he received a very poor reception from the Socialists. He noted in his diary that the result of the election was 'as I expected but such conflicts must be avoided in the future'.[131] The outcome was the loss of the wards to the Municipal Alliance and a weakening of Socialism: none of their candidates were returned and the local paper commented that 'the ascendancy of the Labour League has been maintained . . . but at the expense of its principles'.[132] The same sort of conflict caused the loss of Latchmere Ward in the by-election of December necessitated by the death of W. Matthews. The low poll, a result of the apathy among Progressive voters, caused this seat, previously a 'stronghold of Progressivism', to fall to the Municipal Alliance candidate.

It may be instructive to round off this examination of Radical Battersea with an illustrative example of a typical form of 'patriotism' which will show how the external manifestations of patriotic pride, which so often became jingoistic, were essentially a middle-class phenomenon. This was the Patriotic Carnival of 23 May 1900, designed to celebrate the relief of Mafeking and to raise funds for the *Daily Telegraph* Reservist Fund, and whose efforts to obtain the use of the Vestry horses have already been noted.

Some Progressives had objected to the Vestry giving the organizers any assistance because they believed that the purpose of the Carnival was to stimulate support for the war. And although the organizing committee claimed that 'they had nothing whatsoever to do with the politics of the war. Their object was to assist those in need',[133] there was some truth in the accusation. The idea of a Carnival had originated with the

<hr>

[130] *Ibid.*, 29 March 1901.
[131] Burns diary, 25 March 1901, Add. MSS. 46319.
[132] *South Western Star, loc. cit.*   [133] *Ibid.*, 11 May 1900.

Bolingbroke Ratepayer's Association—a middle-class body centred in the well-to-do area of Battersea which bordered on Clapham Common and containing several who were associated with local conservatism. The organizing committee included at least two Municipal Alliance vestrymen in J. Calder Cameron and H. J. Miseldine as well as the Conservative candidate for the constituency, G. W. Garton. Local tradesmen provided the vast majority of the floats, the railwaymen contributed a team from their ambulance club and the Vestry grudgingly equipped 'a beggarly array of unadorned water vans and dust carts which added nothing either to the interest or the brightness of a patriotic carnival'.[134] The enthusiastic reception the Carnival received was most manifest from the small-villa residents of Broomwood Road and neighbourhood: 'Assembled at their windows . . . they cheered the cars with great heartiness and made a liberal display of coloured lights.'[135] The routes of the procession are also interesting, for on the two days that it paraded not once did it venture into the really working-class stronghold of Shaftesbury estate, or into the poorest area of Battersea by the river. On both occasions its assembling point was Bolingbroke Grove, in the heart of the wealthiest district of the area. Its route on the first night was almost entirely limited to the 'well-to-do' and 'fairly comfortable' regions.[136] On the following night only seven of the twenty-nine streets along its route were areas of 'poverty and comfort'—that being the lowest classification of road travelled by the procession. It would not, of course, be possible to draw any *positive* conclusions from this; it is an interesting comment, however, that three-quarters of the forty-nine streets paraded were streets which can be classified with a reasonable degree of certitude as middle-class.[137] This is not to assert that the procession did not go into the working-class suburbs because of the fear of the reception it would receive. It is not known why this particular route was chosen. Certainly, a carnival is always well received in working-class society; it provides colour, music and excitement. But it

---

[134] *Ibid.*, 25 May 1900. [135] *Ibid.*

[136] These classifications are, of course, from Booth, *Life and Labour in London* (2nd ed., London, 1902-3), 3rd Series, V, p. 196. The route of the Carnival was traced by using newspaper reports of roads traversed and then following them on Booth's map of Battersea to obtain social classification.

[137] I.e. everything from Booth's classification of 'Fairly Comfortable'.

should be noted that it was only St John's Road—a 'well-to-do' street—that was decorated with[138]

flags stretching from side to side of the road . . . houses were as gay as a wealth of bunting could make them. Window sills and all other projects were loosely draped with the tricolour, festoons hung from house to house and numerous patriotic devices appeared on the walls.

What was distinctive about Battersea that it could be so free of the kind of pro-war rowdyism that existed elsewhere in the country? It was not, of course, free from 'mafficking' nor was it anti-patriotic. On Mafeking Night Burns noted in his diary: 'On arrival home found thousands of people outside and passing my home, singing "God save the Queen" etc. ad lib. ad nauseam, continued this nonsense till 3.30 a.m.' And on the following night: 'Streets crowded with wildly excited people . . . never have I seen such a wild delirium over so small a victory . . . well organised gang of political opponents . . . managed to break three of the french windows.'[139] Indeed, the Battersea experience illustrates very well the distinction that is drawn between the Mafeking crowd—the victory-celebration crowd— and the selective, sometimes organized, 'rational' rowdyism that distinguished the behaviour of the jingo crowd at peace meetings. The former existed in Battersea, as indeed it could be expected to do, but the latter did not. It is true that this can in part be explained by the absence of a markedly jingoistic social group such as university students living in the area; but the existence of this sort of group was not essential to rowdyism as the Brighton episode illustrated. What Battersea did have and what most other places lacked was a strong tradition of radicalism, a member of parliament who was a widely respected opponent of the war and an ex-working man, and a strong, dynamic anti-war organization initiated and sustained by the considerable experience of its Socialist members in organization and agitation. Indeed, it is probable that the closure of the Social Democratic Federation branch in 1899 had a stimulating effect on the anti-war agitation, freeing individuals from routine branch work for the anti-war movement. It also possessed an almost solid anti-war local government. This was especially unusual because of the shameless way in which the war was allowed to dominate

[138] *South Western Star, loc. cit.*
[139] Burns diary, 18, 19 May 1900, Add. MSS. 46318.

local-government issues. It would be interesting to know how far the initiative for this came from the Socialist wing of the Progressive majority. W. S. Sanders suggests in his memoirs that the credit for Battersea's dynamism in every respect should go to the influence of the local SDF branch:

As the political complexion of the parish was, on the whole, Liberal and Radical, *our pressure* resulted in the establishment of a number of municipal institutions including free public libraries, baths and wash-houses, and a town hall, long before Labour and Socialism became the ruling influence in the district. (Italics added.)

He dates this progress from 1894 when the system of electing the Vestry was reformed and a Socialist-Trade Union-Progressive combination was formed returning eighty out of the 120 vestrymen: 'From that day the local authority of the district, inspired by the socialist faith of those early days, has been in the forefront of municipal progress.'[140]

It is probable that Sanders overestimated their influence. Certainly, as the Guardians' election showed, the Socialists were helpless without Progressive support. But they were essential to the secure Progressive control of the local government, and they certainly seem to have been the most active and dynamic element in the anti-war movement. Although they provided the dynamism, they were aided and abetted by the Radical members of the Labour League such as Matthews and W. Davis. In the final analysis, however, none of this would have mattered if the working men of Battersea had not wanted it to. This is the most distinctive feature of all: the solidly working-class character of the area. Two-thirds of the population were working class.[141] They were the electors who returned local councillors who were vehemently opposed to the war in the municipal elections of 1900. Conservative attempts to turn the war to their advantage backfired, just as they did during the General Election of the same month. Thus, the point of this study of Battersea has been to illustrate that jingoistic patriotism and the working classes did not necessarily go together. The marked absence of a group of jingoists deliberately indulging in mob antics is remarkable in this mainly working-class suburb. It leads to the conclusion that this was not an intrinsic feature of working-class behaviour

---

[140] W. S. Sanders, *Early Socialist Days* (London, 1927), pp. 71–3.
[141] See Appendix IV.

or attitudes. Taken in conjunction with the earlier examples it leads one to suspect that such behaviour and attitudes were more a feature of middle-class groups and of groups which wished to have a middle-class status in society.

It is important to appreciate that this is not intended to imply that members of the working class did not take part in this type of jingo rowdyism. The occupations of those arraigned on five notable occasions illustrate that they did:

Trafalgar Square, 24 September 1899	Cabinet-maker, carman, stoker
Harlesden, Mafeking Night	Labourer, navvy, painter, engine-driver
Scarborough Riots, March 1900	2 barmen, 3 sea captains, 2 telegraph messengers, 3 labourers, laundryman, bottler, bricklayer, newsvendor
Birmingham Riots, December 1901	Carpenter, silversmith, painter, basket-maker, brass-polisher, art-metal worker, machinist, railway shunter
Margate Riots, March 1900	2 boatmen, labourer

It is important to realize, however, that in four of those cases the riots occurring must not be confused with rowdyism at an actual peace meeting. Although in the instances of Scarborough and Birmingham the riots may have emanated from a peace meeting, only in the case of Trafalgar Square were the arrests made while a meeting was in progress. This distinction should not be made too fine; it is merely intended to illuminate the very real difference between attending a meeting with intent to disrupt and being a part of a riotous or boisterous crowd. Such occasions have a dynamic and meaning all of their own; a dynamic which is usually unrelated to any rational or purposive objective. They are an excuse to get drunk,[142] to indulge in the

[142] This was especially true in Margate where two of the accused were charged with being drunk. In Scarborough only one was so charged.

well-known working-class sport of police-baiting,[143] or even to commit an act of revenge against an individual under the cover of crowd anonymity. These disturbances do not involve—indeed they usually preclude—any 'rational' decision by the constituents. The excitement of the crowd, the ease with which an individual subsumes himself in the crowd identity, can be amply documented from the evidence at our disposal.[144] But the decision to interrupt and prevent a peace meeting is different; it involves a rational decision in favour of one set of attitudes as opposed to those being expressed. Once the disturbance reaches a critical point then the 'riot mentality' may take over and the situation may become a riot situation—as perhaps in the Scarborough case—where individuals who would not have dreamed of interruption previously join in the disturbance with vigour and ease. The interesting fact as far as this study is concerned is that those who took the rational decision to interrupt and prevent a peace meeting from being held do not seem to have been members of the working classes. The recurrent feature of a small group of middle-class men and youths deliberately disturbing the anti-war speakers is inescapable. This small group, or even individuals, were all that was needed to bring a meeting to a state of 'near-riot'. This can be said to occur when the crowd mentality takes over and the individual loses his identity to that of the crowd and is prepared to shout slogans and to commit acts which in his saner moments he would not do.[145] In the jingo crowd those who were consciously aiming at creating this state of affairs were not members of the working class.

Furthermore, such behaviour was not necessarily typical of the working-class crowd. There was no necessary connection between the working-class character of the crowd and any kind of rowdyism. Writing of the Northumberland pit-men, Robert Spence Watson claimed:[146]

[143] In the case of Birmingham, four of the nine accused were charged with assaulting the police. In Margate three were charged with this—one with inciting the mob to attack the police. In Scarborough three of those arrested were arraigned on this charge. In Harlesden one of the four was charged with assaulting a constable.

[144] Thus, at Dover during the attack on Brown's premises one of those accused of breaking one of the windows claimed he had committed the act on impulse: 'I was on my way home and someone shouted GO ON.' Dover Observer, 26 May 1900.

[145] This is one characteristic of crowd behaviour upon which all observers from Le Bon and Hobson to Canetti seem to agree.

[146] R. S. Watson, Joseph Skipsey: A Memoir (London, 1909), p. 52.

I have known several cases where there have been meetings held upon labour difficulties which were fiercely acute at a time when men and the officials of their union did not agree. This is perhaps the severest test to which men can be put, but, although there was some turbulence and some disorder, the meetings ended in patient listening to that which had to be said in defence of conduct of which they did not approve, or in votes of thanks to those who addressed them.

A Dr J. Johnson, visiting Joseph Lister, the Bradford landowner and Socialist, wrote of a Labour demonstration:[147]

A striking feature . . . was the quiet seriousness and enthusiasm which pervaded it and the entire absence of anything like horseplay or even frivolity—it evidently meant business and had come with a serious purpose underlying that of enjoying an afternoon in . . . Lister's park.

These testimonials are very different from those of men such as C. F. G. Masterman, whose *From the Abyss* painted such an unflattering, though not wholly unsympathetic, picture of the working-class crowd. This book is, in fact, typical of writings on the characteristics of working-class crowd and collective behaviour at this period. They all tend to over-emphasize its 'primitive' nature and to see it as a reflection of the working man's unsophisticated mind and intellect. A few, such as Stephen Reynolds, treated working-class society with respect and with a seriousness that its character and customs deserved. But this was the exception. A description of a Toynbee Hall audience will illustrate the more typical attitude to crowds of working men.[148]

He [i.e. the speaker] finds the working man suspicious, given to attributing bad motives, a thorough believer in the corrupt and fallen nature of man, and unable to grasp the value and meaning of intellectual activity. . . . They fasten upon the obvious and shallow. . . . The very mention of the British Empire excites laughter as a subject to which no sincere man would dream of alluding.

The same point was made, each in their different ways, by,

[147] Mattison Collection, Brotherton Library, University of Leeds.
[148] Anon., *Toynbee Record*, June 1908, p. 50.

among many others, Canon Barnett and Lady F. Bell.[149] Partly it was a reflection of their middle-class patronizing bias; and partly it was a failure to understand working-class society, imposing on it, in the manner of most reforming Victorian philanthropists, their faith in absolutes of cultural behaviour. It was this same failure which underlay the writings on the jingo crowd and the equation of jingoism with working-class patriotism. Both imperialists and anti-imperialists drew the same conclusions from the same events. The imperialists, however, did not need to explain or deplore. For them it merely confirmed the correctness and popularity of their own opinions. But observers like Hobson and Masterman were so influenced and horrified by Mafeking Night that they failed to realize what 'The Seer' of Mildmay Club realized,[150] that this was essentially a celebratory crowd. They were appalled by the absence of any mass opposition to the war into believing that Mafeking Night was symptomatic of the adoption of the immoral imperial code of the war by the working class. Indeed, it was their reaction, rather than that of the crowds, that was hysterical. The Independent Labour Party, also, was not unaffected. Its *News* piously remarked that on Mafeking Night[151]

in many instances the towns were abandoned by the police to the unrestrained riot and licence of the mob. Positive violence and indecency were not infrequent accompaniments of the celebrations. . . . Restraint and respectability . . . on the part of any person or household were taken as unmistakable signs of pro-Boer sympathies.

In fact, the amount of damage done on Mafeking Night was quite small. Only at the weekend, as has been shown, did the crowds turn their attention to the pro-Boers. What is more, the distinction between the celebratory crowd and that which disturbed peace meetings was not recognized. It was the instigators of the latter crowd who were consciously counterpoising one set of attitudes to another.

The analysis of jingoism conducted by Hobson was a reflection of this basic misunderstanding. His book, *The Psychology of Jingoism*, was a moralistic comment coloured by a failure to

[149] For Barnett see *Religion and Politics* (London, 1911), pp. 121–30; for Lady F. Bell, see F. Bell, *At the Works* (London, 1907), pp. 126–42.
[150] He described it as 'the most wonderful and harmless saturnalia of the century'. *Club Life*, 26 May 1900, p. 15.   [151] *ILP News*, May 1900, p. 4.

observe society at any deeper level than that of events like Mafeking Night. Furthermore, his analysis revealed nothing new or significant. His belief that jingoism was transmitted through the media of the public house and the music hall, conveying 'by song . . . crude notions upon morals and politics appealing by coarse humour . . . to the animal lusts of an audience stimulated by alcohol into appreciative hilarity',[152] was not only not true but what it did describe was nothing peculiar to the imperialist age. It merely revealed Hobson's low opinion of the 'brutal' and 'credulous' working class. Hobson, like most other writers on this subject, was duped by the seeming mass excitement caused by the war into believing that this was a new feature peculiar to the age. They assumed that something was very rotten in British society. In fact, the mafficking crowd, vulgar though it may have been, was not a 'mob', was not generally in a legal state of riot, neither, as one historian has suggested, was Mafeking Night itself an 'orgy of rowdyism'.[153]

The truly jingo crowd was that which disturbed peace meetings, for it represented a body of attitudes completely opposed to those symbolized by the meeting. Furthermore, this crowd was not a working-class phenomenon. It was the typical patriotic reaction of middle-class youth. It was characteristic of middle-class patriotism. Some observers realized that this type of jingo patriotism appealed mainly to the higher-status groups and to those with a status-anxiety problem. Significantly, these observers were those who were in close contact with the working class. Writing of the Trafalgar Square demonstration, a clubman commented:[154]

The war party had it all their own way on Sunday week . . . composed of the clerk element and some of the shop-keeping class the din made by the Imperialists rendered all speaking abortive. The 'respectable classes,' who, strange to say, are always in favour of rowdyism, fancied they made a great victory.

Thus, emphasis on such occasions as Mafeking Night and other 'near-riot' situations detracts from a true appreciation of the nature of the jingo crowd. For a true grasp of the significance

[152] Hobson, *op. cit.*, p. 3.
[153] E. Halévy, *Imperialism and the Rise of Labour 1895–1905* (London, 1961), pp. 94–5. [154] *Club Life*, 24 May 1900, p. 328.

of the crowd events of those years the distinction must be drawn between 'irrational' actions induced by a crowd mentality and the essentially 'rational' disturbance of peace meetings by non-working-class groups.

V

⋄⋄

The Pattern of Recruitment
for the Boer War

⋄⋄

VOLUNTEERING for the Boer War is an interesting phenomenon which will be examined in this chapter in the light of
contemporary assumptions about its relationship to social class
and patriotism. Where it has been possible to procure statistical
facts they have been used but they are, on the whole, frag-
mentary for this period. The *Annual Report of the British Army*
failed to appear in the years 1899, 1900, 1901 because of the
'pressure of war'. It was explained that 'units engaged in active
service could not supply the information required, nor, considering the manner [in] which . . . they were divided up, would the
information have been accurate'.[1] As an illustration of the dis-
location caused by this 'frontier war', this is interesting, but to
the social historian it means the frustration of not being able to
conduct any survey, limited or detailed, into the regular army
at a time when such a survey would be of much value. Fortunately, the *Reports of the Inspector-General of Recruiting* to
some extent fill the gap but it does mean that detailed analysis
is impossible. Regular-army records, then, are virtually non-
existent for this period.

The same is less true of the Volunteer movement. The
Attestation Forms of the Imperial Yeomanry are still preserved
at the Public Records Office and they have been used in this
chapter; some records of the City Imperial Volunteers also survive. But, in general, these are the exceptions. Thus, no detailed

---

[1] *General Annual Report of the British Army for Year 1902* (Accounts and Papers,
Vol. XXXVIII), Cd. 1946 (1903), preface.

records exist of the nature and composition of the active-service companies that were raised from each volunteer battalion and reliance has to be placed upon descriptions given in secondary sources.

The Volunteer movement, however, is more relevant for the purpose of this work than the regular army. This is not only for the reason of convenience attached to the relative superiority of volunteer evidence. In the first place, the volunteer companies raised or formed for the specific purpose of the war were regarded by contemporaries as being illustrative of the classless nature of the patriotic response to England in need. Thus, an Imperial Yeoman wrote:[2]

Who does not remember with pride the great outburst of patriotism which, like a volcanic eruption, swept every obstacle before it, . . . welding the British race in one gigantic whole, ready to do and die for the honour of the Old Flag, and in defence of the Empire which has been built up by the blood and brains of its noblest sons. The call for volunteers for Active Service was answered in a manner which left no doubt as to the issue.

And it is useful to test this against the pattern of recruitment in its relation to social class. In the second place, the response to the need for volunteers tended to react adversely on the regular army. Not only did volunteers tend to be better paid than the ordinary soldier, but they also attracted men of a 'better class'.[3] The result was that regular army recruitment for the infantry tended to decrease throughout the war. As the *Report of the Inspector-General of Recruiting for Year 1900* noted: 'In spite of the impetus given to recruiting by the war, the actual number of recruits enlisted for the Infantry is 241 less than in 1899;'[4] and in 1901 the story was repeated: 'The enlistment of large numbers of men for the South African Constabulary, and the Imperial Yeomanry, with their high rates of pay, has to a certain extent injured recruiting for the Infantry.'[5] In the third place,

[2] P. T. Ross, *A Yeoman's Letters* (London, 1901), p. vii.

[3] The pay for an Imperial Yeoman was five shillings per week. 'The men are of a better class than the regulars.' See [R. Rankin], *A Subaltern's Letters to His Wife* (London, 1901), p. 75.

[4] *Annual Report of the Inspector-General of Recruiting for Year 1900* (Reports, Vol. IX), Cd. 519 (1901), p. 7.

[5] *Annual Report of the Inspector-General of Recruiting for Year 1901* (Reports, Vol. X), Cd. 962 (1902), p. 8.

there was a clear difference between volunteering for the period of one year, or for the duration of a supposedly short war as those who joined the volunteer units agreed to do, and volunteering for a period of three years which was the minimum amount of time allowed with the regular-army colours. Volunteering was, thus, quite specifically related to the South African conflict.

To prevent confusion, it is necessary to explain the differences between the various units mentioned in this chapter, and to distinguish them from the reservists and militia. There were three main groups of units formed specifically for service in South Africa all of which were composed of volunteers from both inside and outside the established Volunteer movement. First, there were the active-service companies which were units of about 110 men raised from each volunteer battalion in early 1900. These companies were composed entirely of recruits from the volunteer regiments and were attached to their county battalions of the line. They were designed as back-up strength for the regular army and their duties were primarily related to ordnance and guarding the lines of communication. In the second place, there were the City Imperial Volunteers. This unit was the most celebrated of those which served in South Africa. Unlike the other units drawn from the Volunteers, it was formed into an integrated fighting force, included a mounted-infantry section and a battery of artillery reputed to be of the most advanced design. Its strength was over 1,000 men, who were drawn from the London volunteer regiments and from those of the Home Counties.[6] The third of the volunteer units, the Imperial Yeomanry, was the largest and most significant. It was a mounted-infantry regiment drawn from the existing yeomanry and volunteer regiments and from men who had never been associated with the movement but whose riding and shooting ability qualified them to join. Indeed, such men formed 71 per cent of the strength of the force.[7] Within the Imperial Yeomanry were some of the most glamorous of the units that fought in South Africa. These were the units raised and financed by individuals such as Lord Lovat who raised Lovat's Horse from

[6] The Unit contained Volunteers from the Surrey, Middlesex and Essex regiments.
[7] Computed from Imperial Yeomanry, Attestation Forms, P.R.O., W.O. 128/1–165.

his estates in Inverness, and Lord Paget who raised Paget's Horse, and Lumsden's Horse, a company of 250 Anglo-Indian tea, coffee and indigo planters.[8] Such companies as these represented most clearly why the Boer War has sometimes been called the 'last gentleman's war'. A member of Paget's Horse wrote:[9]

We are a gentleman's corps; there can be no doubt of that. The long line of hansoms at Chelsea barracks . . . every variety of gloves from dogskin to reindeer suggested—nay, proved—that we were gentlemen . . . who could doubt it hearing the click, click, of the spurs, and marking the polish of jack-boots, and the easy carriage of the practised horseman?

But these three groups must be distinguished from the Militia and the Reservists. The Militia was the age-old 'Constitutional Force' established by statute which since the 1880s could be raised by ballot if sufficient volunteers were not forthcoming. It was the only part of the armed forces where there was the hint of conscription and perhaps because of this it had been largely ignored. It was intended primarily for home defence and for filling garrisons vacated by the Regular Army. The Reservists were militiamen who had signed on the reserve-army list and who could be mobilized at any time for service at home or abroad. Both these groups were partially mobilized in the autumn of 1899, the Reservists going to South Africa and thirty-five of the militia battalions being used to fill vacancies in the home garrisons.[10] The Militia was of little consequence during the war, it was constantly under strength, under-equipped and its members were poorly trained. It was, in general, rural-based and, in contrast to the Volunteers, composed mainly of agricultural labourers.[11]

Both the Reservists and the Militia will be ignored in the following analysis. They were a part of the regularly constituted armed forces in the sense that their members were obliged to report for service if embodied. There was no such compulsion on the other units mentioned and all the men in the

[8] Henry H. S. Pearse, *The History of Lumsden's Horse* (London, 1903), pp. 427–36.

[9] C. Rose-Innes, *With Paget's Horse to the Front* (London, 1901), p. 3.

[10] *Volunteer Record and Shooting News*, 11 November 1899, p. 263.

[11] See *Minutes of Evidence before Royal Commission on Militia and Volunteers* (Reports, Vol. XXXI), Cd. 2064 (1904), p. 171, questions 17665–8.

active-service companies, the City Imperial Volunteers and the Imperial Yeomanry, were those who freely volunteered their services.

The decision to request volunteers for service in South Africa was taken suddenly and with some reluctance in December 1899. The War Office, like the nation in general, had made the mistake of believing that little effort would be required to subdue the Boers. There was much justice in the claim made by a regular-army officer, who wrote a book detailing the shortcomings of the War Office and army organization, that this was an 'absent minded war'.[12] Many inadequacies were exposed during the war ranging from the ineffective water filter issued to the troops, to the poor medical and hospital facilities that were provided. The whole affair seems to have been entered into with extreme casualness; the manner in which the expeditionary force was dispatched illustrates this. Its details were arranged by a committee of military heads of departments of the War Office to whose meetings Buller, the designated Commander-in-Chief, was not invited. The first troops from England did not arrive in South Africa until over a week after war had broken out and Natal had been invaded.[13] Indeed, many of Buller's subsequent difficulties in the first three months of the war can be attributed to the hasty and ill-prepared arrangements which had characterized the whole enterprise.

From the very start of the crisis there were demands that the Volunteers be allowed to go to South Africa. One of the first voices raised in support of this demand was that of Colonel Eustace Balfour, who commanded the London Scottish Rifle Volunteers and who, in August, had offered to select a full company of his own regiment for use in South Africa.[14] This was rejected by the War Office and regarded as 'inopportune' by the *Volunteer Record and Shooting News* which claimed that 'the occasion was not of such a grave nature to warrant such a display'.[15]

[12] W. E. Cairns, *An Absent Minded War* (London, 1901).

[13] Sir Redvers Buller to Tremayne Buller, 3 November 1899, Buller Papers, P.R.O., W.O. 132/6.

[14] Guy Harden Guilliam Scott and G. L. McDonnell, *Record of the Mounted Infantry of C.I.V.* (London, 1902), p. 1.

[15] *Volunteer Record and Shooting News*, 16 September 1899, p. 139.

With the outbreak of war these demands became more insistent. One of the most active protagonists for the use of the Volunteer movement was Sir Howard Vincent, MP for the Central Division of Sheffield. A proposal that he made to the War Office in October can be seen as the genesis of the City Imperial Volunteers. As Commanding Officer of the Queen's Westminster Volunteers, he wanted to form a self-sufficient regiment from the London companies.[16] In a letter to the *Volunteer Service Gazette* he argued that 'a Royal Warrant may authorise the engagement of soldiers of any rank under special conditions. . . . There is no reason why specially enrolled officers, non-commissioned officers, and soldiers should not be formed into one corps.'[17] Similar offers came from Lord Lovat and from A. M. Brookfield, member of parliament for Rye, Sussex. Lovat offered to raise 150 stalkers and gillies from his own properties and take them out for use as scouts—the purpose for which his unit was eventually used.[18] Brookfield made a similar proposal urging Sir Evelyn Wood that he be given permission to raise 1,000 men from the Sussex units. The War Office, however, failed to view any of these schemes with much enthusiasm, especially as both Vincent and Brookfield had strongly implied that they would expect to command the units. To the gallant member for Rye, Wood replied:[19]

I cannot believe in any possibility of our accepting a Volunteer Battalion for they would cost as much to transport as a line Battalion, and could not possibly be as efficient.

And George Wyndham, Secretary of State for War, replied rather brusquely to Vincent's proposal:[20]

It would be a great mistake to issue regulations for the special enlistment of Volunteers until there is some prospect of their being required.

Now in as much as the Volunteers are intended primarily for home defence it is not intended to invite them to enter the Regular Battalions abroad until the Militia Reserve of such Battalions have been

[16] Samuel Henry Jeyes and F. D. How, *Life of Sir Howard Vincent* (London, 1912), p. 309.

[17] *Volunteer Service Gazette*, 3 November 1899, p. 9.

[18] Sir F. Lindley, *Lord Lovat 1871–1933* (London, n.d.), pp. 76–7.

[19] A. M. Brookfield, *Annals of a Chequered Life* (London, 1930), pp. 247–8. When the Imperial Yeomanry was formed, Brookfield was given command of the 14th company.

[20] Letter printed in *Volunteer Service Gazette*, 1 December 1899, p. 70.

exhausted. There is at present no probability of this, and therefore, no immediate prospect of our being able to avail ourselves of the patriotic offers of the Volunteers.

Within two weeks of this letter to Vincent, however, the worsening situation in South Africa had induced a change of mind in the War Office. The offer of the Lord Mayor of London to raise a corps of 1,000 volunteers from the city had been accepted,[21] and plans had been formulated to create the active-service companies and the Imperial Yeomanry.

The reluctance of the War Office to employ the Volunteers was not solely due to the fact that they did not believe that the situation warranted it. Apart from the fact that there were doubts about the military capabilities of the movement and its officers, there was the problem mentioned in Wyndham's letter to Vincent of the constitution of the force. The original circular from General Peel to the Lords-Lieutenant granting permission to form volunteer corps in 1859 (the time of a French-invasion scare) had stated quite explicitly that 'it be liable to be called out in case of actual invasion or appearance of an enemy in force on the coast or in case of rebellion arising out of either of those emergencies'.[22] This limitation to home service was empha-sized further by the oath which committed each volunteer to serve 'Her Majesty in Great Britain for the defence of the same against all her enemies'.[23]

The Volunteer movement had always been very aware of this restriction but at times of crisis it was not unknown for en-thusiasts to urge that the Volunteers be used in colonial wars. Thus, there were schemes in 1882 for the formation of a mounted-infantry corps for service in Egypt when it seemed that the subjugation of that country would be a major task.[24] And indeed, there was a minor precedent in that a detachment of the 24th Middlesex Rifle Volunteers (the Post Office Bat-talion) had been sent to Egypt to administer postal duties.[25]

In the last session of the Liberal government of 1894–5, there was some debate as to whether the working of the original Act

[21] Ibid., 22 December 1899, p. 120.
[22] M. Hale, Volunteer Soldiers (London, 1900), p. 17.
[23] Ibid., p. 28.
[24] Volunteer Service Review, 1 September 1882, p. 259.
[25] Ibid., 15 January 1883, p. 68.

should be changed to allow the Volunteers to be called out 'in case of National or Imperial emergency'—words that were to be used in the Imminent National Danger Act of 1900. A select committee was set up to look into the whole matter but the problem seems to have been viewed solely in terms of the timing of the embodiment of the force. Thus, the committee agreed with certain volunteer officers that[26]

the national security might be seriously imperilled under conceivable circumstances falling short of actual or apprehended invasion and that it may be expedient that certain exposed forts . . . be manned by Volunteer artillery and that corps enrolled for submarine and other coast defences should be called out at a much earlier stage than the language of the act would seem to authorise.

But there was in all this no thought or suggestion that a change in the wording of the Act implied that Volunteers could be used for service overseas. And a Bill to effect this change in wording was dropped on the advice of the Institute of Volunteer Commanding Officers (acting as an advisory board to the War Office) who believed that the original phrasing of 'actual or apprehended' invasion was wide enough to allow the government to embody the Volunteers 'at any moment when we engage in hostilities with any civilised power'.[27]

Thus, when proposals from volunteer officers like Balfour and Vincent—who seem to have been over-eager to prove their military prowess—were made to use the force in South Africa, the movement as a whole was acutely embarrassed. The *Volunteer Service Gazette*, the 'official organ' of the volunteer services, devoted a long editorial explaining why the use of the Volunteers was not feasible:[28]

The services of the Volunteers cannot be employed abroad, having regard to the present constitution of the Force. Others have volunteered to do garrison duty at home . . . but what of those who have remained silent? It must not be thought that they are wanting in patriotism, but they are doubtless of the opinion . . . that Volunteering for active service is not consistent with the constitution of the Force. They are prepared when called upon to fulfil their part of the voluntary

[26] *Volunteer Service Magazine*, July 1894, p. 84; September 1894, pp. 184–5.
[27] The *Volunteer*, 19 November 1898, p. 30.
[28] *Volunteer Service Gazette*, 13 October 1899, p. 806. Also for same argument see editorial in the *Volunteer*, 23 September 1899, p. 305.

contract in faithfully serving 'Her Majesty in Great Britain for the defence of the same against all Her enemies and oppressors whomsoever'; and should any change occur in rendering it possible, they would doubtless be prepared to defend British rights abroad as well as at home.

The constitution of the force was not the only reason why service abroad was considered inappropriate. There was also the fear, held by both the War Office and many volunteer officers, that the volunteers would be more of a hindrance than a help. This fear was expressed by a letter signed 'Colour Sergeant' and written to the *Volunteer Record and Shooting News*:[29]

Volunteers . . . would be more or less an encumbrance to the military authorities at the base of active operations, let alone at the front, if they were by any chance ever sent there, for although their training has been fairly carried out, their knowledge . . . could not be utilised without a sound course of field training being imparted. . . . Let Volunteers then, by all means, be taught to carry out their . . . obligations to the nation, but do not impress them with the idea of foreign service, for which they were never intended, and, what is more, totally unfitted, and let those in power refrain from giving men the idea of overrating their abilities as citizen soldiers.

Thus, there were two very powerful motives operating on the War Office to refuse volunteer help. But once the decision to use them had been taken the legal position had to be regularized. This was accomplished in the short term by accepting Volunteers as regular soldiers who enlisted under special conditions and who were not liable for the minimum three years' service if the war ended within that time. Their officers were given temporary commissions in the regular army. This solution was clearly unsatisfactory as a long-term answer to the problem, and early in 1900 a Bill was drafted which was designed to effect the wish of the Secretary of State 'that the Volunteer may be put in the same position as the Reserves or the Militia in regard to being called out for service'.[30] This seemingly innocuous measure was, in fact, a momentous landmark in the development of the Volunteer movement and presaged the creation of the Territorial Force under Haldane. For the intention behind the change was that 'the Volunteers should be made more easily

[29] *Volunteer Record and Shooting News*, 14 October 1899, p. 183.
[30] Imminent National Danger Act 1900, P.R.O., W.O. 32/214.

available and that the requirement of a proclamation announcing "actual or apprehended invasion" should be replaced by one merely declaring "great emergency" '. This wording was far wider than that which had been contemplated in 1894–5. The draft of the Bill proposed that the volunteer should choose to make himself liable for one of two possibilities, one of which was the option to serve in any part of the world, within or without the Empire. An unsigned memorandum of 4 May 1900 explained the two objects of the Bill: [31]

To assimilate the condition under which the Volunteers may be called out to those under which the Reserve forces may be called out and the Militia embodied . . . to enable the Volunteers, if they think fit, to enter agreements by which they will be liable to serve (a) at anytime, whether an emergency has been declared or not, and (b) outside as well as inside the United Kingdom.

This Act, arising out of the needs of the army in South Africa, not only corrected the legal difficulty presented by the prospect of volunteer service overseas but threatened to revolutionize completely the purpose and function of the movement.

The Bill regularized a situation which, since the end of 1899, had been administratively clumsy, but it also threatened an extension of the volunteer force far beyond its original purpose. The clause which gave the Volunteers the option to be ready to serve anywhere in the world was defended by Lansdowne in the Lords, when introducing the Bill, as a measure of precautionary efficiency: 'We think we should know beforehand what number of men we can count on.'[32] Throughout the debates in the Commons Wyndham, anxious to play down this section of the Bill, emphasized that it would increase the efficiency of volunteer mobilization by abolishing the Proclamation necessary for their embodiment.[33]

The general line of attack by the Liberals concentrated on this second clause which allowed the Volunteers to offer to serve abroad because it 'will completely destroy the principle on which the Volunteer force is based',[34] and because 'it placed men at the disposal of the Government for any action they might wish to take abroad'.[35] Doubts about this aspect of the Bill were

[31] *Ibid.* [32] Hansard, 4th Series, LXXXIII (1900), 532–6.
[33] *Ibid.*, LXXXVI (1900), 353. [34] *Ibid.*, 362. Captain Norton.
[35] *Ibid.*, 378. Captain Sinclair.

widespread on both sides of the House and during the second reading Wyndham—describing the clause as 'not so much of importance as of method and convenience'—agreed that he would not press the offending section, merely retaining that which made the Volunteers liable to be called out for service at any time.[36]

Even this failed to satisfy the Liberals, who saw in certain clauses of the Bill ominous hints of conscription. Among the Liberals only C. P. Scott and John Burns seemed fully to realize that the abandonment of the clause specifying that Volunteers could be used anywhere in the world was no guarantee that they would not be used for military service overseas. Scott pointed out that the clause allowing the force to be called out when a national emergency was imminent or apprehended could have applied to the situation after the defeat at Colenso. In spite of Wyndham's assurance that this clause would only apply to the United Kingdom, Scott asserted: 'The effect of this change will be that instead of depending on the definite words of the Act we shall depend upon the good-will of the Government.'[37] Burns attacked the Bill on the grounds that it threatened to lead to militarism and conscription—issues that were to arise during the next few years. He felt that it was an attempt to convert the Volunteers into 'something like a conscript force under conscript conditions'. He spotted what was, perhaps, the obvious ploy of the government in abandoning the offending section of the Bill:[38]

The Volunteers, under the phrase 'imminent national danger or great emergency,' could be called upon to strengthen the depleted garrisons of the Regular Army, and they could be called out for purposes which under the present law could not be legal. . . . You will damage the Volunteers as part of our national defence and will convert that force into a more or less compulsory force probably for service abroad.

This complete reversal of volunteer policy by the government went virtually unnoticed in the country. Burns was undoubtedly right when he commented that 'I do not believe that there is one Volunteer in a thousand who knows of the existence of this measure or who has considered its terms with his comrades'.[39]

---

[36] *Ibid.*, 382. Arnold-Foster opposed it because it was merely an emergency measure and was not part of any general scheme of reorganization.

[37] *Ibid.*, 937. [38] *Ibid.*, 946–7. [39] *Ibid.*, 949.

The actual process of decision-making which caused the government to reverse its previous attitude and call for Volunteers is unclear.[40] But it is probable that it was dictated by events in South Africa rather than by the pressure of men such as Sir Howard Vincent at home. It is certain that very soon after Wyndham had dismissed Vincent's proposal as unnecessary the need for more troops forced a reappraisal. Buller had written home soon after his arrival in South Africa that he needed more mounted infantry,[41] and Wyndham was writing to Charles Boyd just four days after his letter to Vincent: 'It may be well to have some mounted Infantry regiments as separate corps instead of, as now, companies drawn from line battalions.'[42] Here was the genesis of the Imperial Yeomanry; but the failure of Buller to relieve Ladysmith and the disasters of Magersfontein, Stormberg and Tugela which all fell between 9 and 15 December, earning the week the title 'Black Week', dictated that the net be cast wider than merely mounted infantry. It is clear that the decision to use the Volunteers was taken some time during this week, for Wyndham wrote to his mother on 16 December:[43]

We propose—this is private until confirmed by the Cabinet now sitting—
1. To take up all the fastest ships.
2. To send out the 7th and 8th Divisions; 8 Battalions of Militia; special corps of Volunteers and Yeomanry.

This decision came into force with Army Order 1 of 1900 which authorized the formation of the active-service companies, Imperial Yeomanry and the City Imperial Volunteers.

There was, of course, a danger of the enthusiasm defeating its own ends. There were immediate complaints that the planned numbers of Volunteers for the active-service companies was too small. The point was that the active-service companies were attached to the regular army county regiment—one company per regiment. Thus, if in a county there were four battalions of Volunteers, each supplied about thirty men to make up the company. In Lancashire, the 7,000 strong Manchester Brigade

---

[40] This appears to be due to the weeding of the War Office records at P.R.O.
[41] Julian Symons, *Buller's Campaign* (London, 1963), p. 141.
[42] Wyndham to Boyd, 28 November 1899, printed in: Guy Wyndham, *Letters of George Wyndham* (Edinburgh, 1915), I, p. 476.
[43] Wyndham to Mother, 16 December 1899, *ibid.*, p. 482.

was required to supply only 100 men when, it was claimed, 'there are more than a hundred anxious to go from each individual corps'. An article in the *Volunteer Service Gazette* fulminated:[44]

Here in Lancashire, where we have some 30,000 Volunteers the proportion strikes everyone as being utterly inadequate. It means . . . that with all the hundreds ready to enrol themselves less than 20 men will be accepted from such battalions as the 1st, 2nd, 4th, or 5th, V.B. Manchester, each of them not less than 1200 strong. The Salford Fusiliers . . . with a splendid contingent of 120 stalwart men ready for service will be called upon only for something like 30.

And it went on to demand a County of Lancashire Imperial Yeomanry organized and raised like the City Imperial Volunteers.

The War Office was, indeed, overwhelmed by the response of the Volunteers to the call for their services. This was, significantly, most noticeable amongst the 'gentlemen's' companies such as the Queen's Westminster which had 200 members ready to leave their jobs and embark immediately if their services were required. Two-thirds of the Inns of Court Rifle Company had volunteered for foreign service or garrison duty.[45] This was truly the last gentleman's war, not in the sense of the methods of warfare—where it ranks perhaps with Weyler's Cuban campaign—but in the sense that it was possible for individual initiative from wealthy gentlemen to play such a large part in the war effort. The phenomenon of such men as Lord Lovat, Lord Paget, Sir Alfred Newton, H. Seton-Karr, MP, raising semi-autonomous units often commanded by their patrons, betrayed a whole set of attitudes surrounding the spirit with which the war was entered into. There was a strong belief in the traditional British virtues of 'amateurism'; a belief that good breeding, blood, sound horsemanship and excellence on the grouse moors fitted a gentleman for war.

The *Volunteer Service Gazette* reported a scheme which illustrated the sporting and adventure attitudes which were part of the middle-and upper-class ethos of this campaign. The idea was to raise a corps of 'gentlemen' to serve as an integral part of the Imperial Yeomanry. The point about it was that enrol-

[44] *Volunteer Service Gazette*, 5 January 1900, p. 146.
[45] *Ibid.*, 22 December 1894, p. 114. The Queen's Westminster was a middle-class company, 53 per cent of its rank and file were clerks.

ment 'is so arranged that groups of friends have an opportunity of serving in the same corps'.[46] It was the specialist corps that tended to be raised by individuals and composed of gentlemen. Paget's Horse and Lovat's Scouts both performed scouting duties for the Imperial Yeomanry, and the Sharpshooters raised by Seton-Karr were a crack rifle-shot corps. They were, to a large extent, privately financed. The government gave the usual yeomanry capitation grant of £65 but the organizing committee of amateurs had a free hand in the selection of recruits, subject to the necessary medical, horseriding, and rifle-shooting standards laid down by army regulations.[47] The most famous of all such units and one composed solely of recruits drawn from the Volunteer regiments was CIV.

The City Imperial Volunteers were raised on the initiative of Sir Alfred Newton, the Lord Mayor, and grew out of Vincent's proposal made earlier in the autumn for a volunteer battalion. The idea was that the City should raise and equip a force of 1,000 men. An interview with the Commander-in-Chief on 15 December extracted an unofficial invitation to form the corps and the following day the Secretary of State accepted 'your generous and patriotic offer on behalf of the City of London to raise a corps . . . for service in South Africa'. The Common Council of the City met on 19 and 20 December and voted £25,000 towards the cost, the Lord Mayor announced that contributions would be forthcoming from the merchant and livery companies and that C. H. Wilson, the Hull shipowner, had undertaken to provide a fully equipped transport ship.[48] Friction soon arose, however, when the City appeared to go back on its obligations and tried to persuade the War Office to provide regimental transport in South Africa. Newton wrote on 5 January 1900 requesting the provision of the necessary transport, and received this reply:[49]

I am directed to point out that your Lordship's offer dated 20th December addressed to Field Marshal Lord Wolseley . . . was to 'equip and transport to the seat of war . . . a regiment of Volunteer marksmen' . . . with transport and all details complete.

[46] *Volunteer Service Gazette*, 5 January 1900, p. 147.
[47] H. Seton-Karr, *The Call to Arms* (London, 1902), p. 16.
[48] *Volunteer Service Gazette*, 22 December 1899, p. 120; *Reports of C.I.V.* (London, 1900), p. 1.
[49] Transport File, CIV Collection, MS. 10197.

Having in view the terms of the above letter and the strain which is felt by the Military Authorities in maintaining the supplies of transport . . . Lord Lansdowne felt it expedient to recommend for the acceptance of . . . your offer. . . . Under the circumstances no steps have been taken by this department to provide the transport waggons and articles of camp equipment enumerated in your letter . . . and Lord Lansdowne consequently regrets that he is not in a position to have them supplied from Government stores.

Friction also arose over the designation of a regular-army officer to command the regiment. There was a universal assumption that volunteer officers would command. Vincent had hoped that he would be given command of his proposed regiment and would have commanded the infantry division of CIV if he had passed the medical examination.[50] Indeed, Vincent refused to be discouraged. He insisted on going out to South Africa and 'begged Lord Roberts to let me do something', and later in 1900 renewed his offer to raise a corps of 1,000 mounted infantry with himself in command.[51] But this kind of desire and the disagreements that inevitably arose from it were nothing new. They appear to have been endemic to the Volunteer movement and centred around the demands of volunteer officers to have autonomous control over their regiments. From the very beginning of the Volunteer movement the desire of volunteer officers to have absolute autonomy conflicted with the desire of the War Office to impose its own standards of efficiency on the movement. In 1862, the *Volunteer Times* urged that the War Office cease meddling in volunteer affairs and allow the movement to hold its own field days under its own officers.[52] The desire of the volunteer officers to retain control of their units was expressed most clearly by Sir J. H. A. MacDonald who wrote that in 1888 when given command of a Scottish Infantry Brigade he[53]

soon found . . . that it was not intended that the Brigadier of a Volunteer Brigade was to have any real authoritative oversight of the battalion allocated to him. He had no right to issue any orders for instruction, nor to inspect any of his battalion. . . . Still worse was it

[50] *Volunteer Service Gazette*, 5 January 1900, p. 146.
[51] Jeyes and How, *op. cit.*, p. 319.
[52] The *Volunteer Times*, 26 July 1862, p. 234.
[53] Sir J. H. A. MacDonald, *Fifty Years of It. The Struggles and Experiences of a Volunteer of 1859* (London, 1909), pp. 373–4.

that, if I urged upon them training in any particular direction, the officer commanding the Regimental District could come to hold an inspection and tell the battalion the exact opposite of what I had endeavoured to instill into them.

The war and the use of the Volunteers obviously heightened this desire and to a certain extent illustrated the gentleman's-war mentality pervading the whole of the volunteer force. In CIV Colonel Eustace Balfour was the foremost protagonist in this controversy. His interest was probably not uninfluenced by personal motives; on 23 December 1899, he wrote to Colonel Boxall:[54]

I had hoped to have heard from someone today as to my appointment to command a wing (dismounted) of the City of London Imperial Volunteers. After having volunteered it does not look well to withdraw—and I am ready to go on. . . . But I must know at once. . . . All my action is paralysed. The W.O. [sic] does not know and never will learn that Volunteers have private affairs to arrange.

Opposition to War Office control came into the open at a meeting of commanding officers of the London regiments on 22 December 1899, where it became obvious that there was considerable resistance to a regular-army officer commanding the regiment. The Lord Mayor warned the committee in his opening remarks: 'We have worked the broad lines and the Committee, I say it very respectfully, must not alter them.'[55] Balfour soon raised the very issue the Lord Mayor wished to avoid, seeming at one stage to make it a condition of his remaining on the committee.[56] The committee disliked the fact that a regular-army officer had been appointed without their prior consultation. Their hurt pride was aggravated by the fact that it was known to Balfour, who made it known to the rest, that the Commander-in-Chief had appointed a Regular because of the acrimony a volunteer appointment would have caused among other volunteer officers. Balfour and some others seem to have determined to force a showdown. In this they were partly successful, for it was clear that the work of the committee would be stultified if they

[54] Meeting of Commanding Officers, 22 December 1899, CIV Collection, MS. 10199.   [55] Ibid.
[56] Ibid., 'I will not go further unless we understand that a Volunteer is to command.'

were not appeased. At some time during the meeting 'some fresh information' reached Balfour and was revealed by Boxall:[57]

The Corps will now assume larger proportions and it will not be limited to 1,000 men. There will be a Colonel Commandant and two Lieutenant-Colonels. The Colonel Commandant will be a Regular and well known to all here and the Lieutenant-Colonels will be Volunteer officers (cheers), but please do limit discussion to the subject of committees.

This satisfied Balfour's demands and the organizational work of the Committee proceeded. Colonel Mackinnon was the regular-army officer appointed Commandant and Cholmondeley and Boxall were the two volunteer appointees.

Like the City Imperial Volunteers, the Imperial Yeomanry was a result of the patriotic initiative of independent gentlemen. Wyndham claimed the credit for its creation, writing to his father: 'The Imperial Yeomanry is my child.'[58] And there seems little doubt that the civilians of the War Office were its most enthusiastic supporters. Certainly Wolseley, who complained that he had not been consulted, was opposed to the experiment of using the 'imperfectly drilled and disciplined Yeomanry'.[59] But, as Lansdowne pointed out, Buller wanted mounted infantry and they were the only source from which it could be provided.[60] It was not, however, Wyndham who originated the idea to use the yeomanry. An Army Board meeting of 18 December 1899, noted the offer of Lord Chesham and the Earl of Lonsdale to raise, equip and transport a force of 2,300 men to South Africa at their own expense. The Board recommended acceptance of this 'patriotic offer' and suggested that the force should be regarded[61]

as distinctively the contribution of the Yeomanry of the kingdom to the present war, preference being given to members of the Yeomanry to enlist in it . . . and that the War Office having decided the general organisation of the force, the complete working out of the scheme should be left in the hands of the proposers.

Thus, it seems likely that the idea of an Imperial Yeomanry, originating with Chesham and Lonsdale and following the

[57] *Ibid.*

[58] Wyndham to Father, 20 December 1899, Wyndham, *op. cit.*, p. 484.

[59] Raising of the Imperial Yeomanry and Division into Units, P.R.O., W.O. 32/079/499, f. 6.   [60] *Ibid.*, f. 8.

[61] Formation of the Mounted Infantry, W.O. 32/079/683.

pattern set by Paget, Lovat and Newton, was taken over by Wyndham and Lansdowne who, supported by Evelyn Wood, overcame Wolseley's objections. Contrary to what actually happened, Wyndham regarded the figure of 2,300 as an accurate estimate. He wrote to Lansdowne on 26 December 1899: 'I doubt if they will secure more than 2,500 recruits from the existing Yeomanry' and suggested that the balance of 8,000 required by Buller would have to be made up from civilians and Volunteers.[62] Thus, the Imperial Yeomanry became Wyndham's 'baby' but it is noteworthy that both Chesham and Lonsdale were seated on the committee set up to administer the project and that Chesham commanded one of its units in South Africa.

The terms for raising the Imperial Yeomanry were communicated to the press on 24 December and the response must have surprised Wyndham. In Northumberland and Durham, a Mr H. H. Scott donated £1,000 to the creation of the two counties' yeomanry contingent. By the evening of the same day over £10,000 had been subscribed.[63] In Nottingham the following notice was posted:

In accordance with a communication issued by the War Office, offers of service to form a Nottinghamshire contingent of the Imperial Yeomanry are invited from the Sherwood Rangers, the South Notts. Hussars, and also from the Nottinghamshire Volunteers and Civilians who may possess the necessary qualifications, as given below, and who will be specially enrolled for the purpose.

Possession of a horse was not a necessary requirement. This committee, like all local Imperial Yeomanry committees, were prepared to purchase the number of mounts needed to horse the qualified men. Within twenty-four hours of the posting of the notice, 160 men had volunteered.[64]

Thus, by January 1900, when recruiting started in earnest, the pattern had been established. Decisions which seem to have been taken under the pressure of necessity and which were, in large part, the result of 'patriotic' individual initiative, were to produce a total volunteer contingent of about 54,000 men who

[62] W.O. 32/079/499, f. 4.
[63] K. B. Spurgin, *On Active Service with the Northumberland and Durham Yeomanry* (Newcastle, 1902), p. 1.
[64] R. L. Birkin, *History of 3rd Regiment Imperial Yeomanry* (Nottingham, 1902), p. 7.

served in South Africa. The way in which they had been raised and the obvious lack of preparation on the part of the War Office did give some justification for Wyndham's claim that the Volunteer Bill of 1900 would prevent this kind of thing recurring. As to their value in South Africa, there was considerable disagreement. The Boers had a very low opinion of CIV who stayed at the front for only a year, and the professional soldiers were scornful of the Imperial Yeomanry.[65] Nevertheless, the total was impressive and it is worth closer examination to throw light on the assumptions current at the time as to the operative factors in motivating men to volunteer.

In spite of the fears later expressed through a Royal Commission on the general state of health in the country, it was possible to dispatch over 50,000 able-bodied men to South Africa during the three years of the war.[66] Of this number, as shown in Table 10, the Imperial Yeomanry provided well over 60 per cent—an indication of the significance of mounted infantry in this war.

TABLE 10

TOTALS OF VOLUNTEERS FOR THE SOUTH AFRICAN WAR[67]

	1900	1901	1902	Total
Imperial Yeomanry				
1st contingent 1900	10,242			10,242
Draft of 1901		16,597		16,597
Draft re-enlisted men		655		655
Draft of 1902			7,239	7,239
TOTAL				34,733
Volunteers				
Infantry draft 1900	10,568			10,568
Infantry draft 1901		4,530		4,530
Infantry draft 1902			2,449	2,449
Cyclist draft 1901		218		218
CIV draft 1900	1,949			1,949
TOTAL				19,714

[65] See Captain Lafone to Father, 9 May 1901, Letters of Captain Lafone, Add. MSS. 39558, f. 141.

[66] The Inspector-General of Recruiting noted in his report for 1900 that of 20,292 who volunteered for active-service companies only 14,068 were fit.

[67] Table adapted from *Annual Report of the Inspector-General of Recruiting for Year 1902* (*Reports*, Vol. XI), Cd. 1417 (1903), p. 31.

These totals alone tell us very little, although they do suggest some interesting trends to be examined later on. A fact about volunteering that needs to be stressed at this point is that it was essentially an activity of youth. This is perhaps not very surprising. Every kind of volunteering was an activity which would especially attract only the young. The largest single age group recruited into the regular army was that between the ages of eighteen and nineteen. The Volunteer movement, on the other hand, was probably most attractive to men in their early twenties. Tables 11 and 12 illustrate this.

TABLE 11

NUMBER OF REGULAR-ARMY RECRUITS AGED 18–19 YEARS
PER 100 RECRUITED, 1893–1902[68]

Year	Percentage
1893	40
1894	42
1895	44
1896	44
1897	46
1898	43
1899	no figures
1900	no figures
1901	no figures
1902	41

If an analysis is made of those who volunteered for the Imperial Yeomanry or a volunteer regiment throughout the war years and who, therefore, probably joined with the purpose of going to South Africa, the predominantly youthful composition of the unit is illustrated.

TABLE 12

NUMBER OF VOLUNTEER AND IMPERIAL YEOMANRY RECRUITS AGED
BETWEEN 17–25 YEARS PER 100 RECRUITED, 1900–2[69]

Year	Volunteers	Imperial Yeomanry
1900	62	61
1901	63	85
1902	62	88

[68] Table calculated from *General Annual Report of British Army, op. cit.*, p. 24.
[69] Table compiled from *Annual Returns of Volunteer Corps of Great Britain*, 1899–1902. Imperial Yeomanry, Attestation Forms, P.R.O., W.O. 128/1–165.

The connection between volunteering and youth is not too significant. There was quite clearly a statutory and a physical age limit above which volunteering, at least for the rank and file, was impracticable. For the City Imperial Volunteers the age of thirty was the limit for the ordinary private. The officers were exempt and Sir Howard Vincent, who had suffered a heart attack in October 1899, fully expected to go out in command of the infantry division of the CIV.[70] Of greater interest, and a key to the volunteering response to the Boer War, is the variation in the rough educational index taken by the recruiting officer and incorporated in the report of the Inspector-General of Recruiting. Although no qualitative standard was laid down, the figures are revealing.

TABLE 13

EDUCATIONAL ABILITY PER 1,000 RECRUITS FOUND FIT, 1896–1902[71]

Ability	1896	1897	1898	1899	1900	1901	1902
Well educated	69	46	49	71	83	98	55
Able to read and write	899	923	922	899	889	879	925
Able to read only	11	14	11	13	15	13	9
Unable to read	21	17	18	17	13	10	11

Table 13 shows the trend of an increase during the war years in the proportion of those who were well educated. It is suggested from these figures that they responded with enthusiasm to the opportunity to volunteer for service in South Africa. This was in marked contrast to those of a lesser educational standard. Their proportions remained fairly stationary with a slight tendency to decline throughout the war period. It rose sharply to a peak the year the war ended and when the proportion of those 'well educated' began to fall back to its more natural position. Although these figures are of little value by themselves and although the trend they suggest does not correspond in all its details to that which we shall find in the Imperial Yeomanry, it is interesting in relation to the proud claim of commentators at the time that the response to the need for

[70] Jeyes and How, *op. cit.*, p. 311; *Volunteer Service Gazette, loc. cit.*
[71] Table compiled from *Reports of Inspector-General of Recruiting*, 1900–2.

volunteers was classless. Writing of the Imperial Yeomanry, T. F. Dewar claimed: [72]

I fancy that never since 'Britain first, at Heaven's command, arose, etc.'; has there been such a turning upside down and topsy-turvey of ranks and classes. In the row in which I lay [in a troopship] were a groom and a commercial traveller, an Oxford man and a country doctor, two grandsons of peers, and a Volunteer subaltern, turned private for the nonce. The man cleaning saucers in the corner . . . is a full private, now hospital orderly, but also the son of a famous British Ambassador; and yonder tall fellow, newly promoted to the rank of Lance-corporal, is the grandson of an eminent bishop, and has given up a west-end practice in order, as he puts it, to 'see the show through.'

It is thus necessary, in order to correct and modify this enthusiastic picture, to examine the social composition of those units for which figures are readily available—the CIV and the Imperial Yeomanry—and to relate these to the pattern of recruitment as spread over the three years. This will help us to understand what in actual practice was the working-class response to this war. It will also suggest the connection between different social classes, patriotism and volunteering.

A breakdown of the social composition of the City Imperial Volunteers with the purpose of isolating the working-class occupations illustrates that the force was dominated by those who were almost certainly *not* working class in status or attitude. [73] Out of a total strength in January 1900 of 1,949, just over 1,000 (51·6 per cent) were men whose occupations placed them outside the working class. Furthermore, the clerks formed the largest single occupational group, making up about 30 per cent of the total force and 60 per cent of the non-working-class members. Clerks thus formed the backbone of the City Imperial Volunteers and this was probably only a reflection of their important role in the London volunteer regiments. None of the working-class occupations came near to equalling the number of clerks in the unit. The largest single working-class occupational group—the labourers—numbered only eighty-seven, comprising about 4·2 per cent of the total strength.

[72] T. F. Dewar, *With the Scottish Yeomanry* (Arbroath, 1901), p. 14.
[73] See Introduction for discussion of problems of defining 'working class'. See Appendix V for detailed social composition of CIV.

If we make the same kind of distinction between working-class and non-working-class occupations for the Imperial Yeomanry, we find that the bulk of the membership (58 per cent) was working class in occupation.[74] Like the City Imperial Volunteers, however, there was the same strong representation of clerks and also of those who were closely associated with the landed and upper classes—such as grooms—and who could be expected to share attitudes typical of those they worked for. Indeed, the 58 per cent working-class membership is almost certainly below the average level of working-class participation in Her Majesty's Forces.

The large number of grooms, farmers, and 'Yeomen' is explained by the fact that the Yeomanry was traditionally country-based. The committee appointed in 1900 to report on the organization of the force remarked that[75]

the men who have . . . sustained the Yeomanry force, come from classes connected with the land. The country gentlemen, yeomen, farmers, and certain tradesmen have for a century formed the backbone of this force, and should the present wave of enthusiasm be in time diminished, they would be found continuing to give the same service as before. To many it is a hereditary duty to give . . . service to the Yeomanry. . . . Being horsemen from boyhood, and having, as a rule, a horse at hand for their own use, they could, and would, upon the order to mobilise, present themselves at the place of assembly the same day or the next. They are the employers of labour.

And the main recommendation of the committee was that men who did not own horses should be supplied with them on a permanent basis. This was aimed at 'obtaining recruits for the Yeomanry from other classes than those referred to above',[76] the object being to retain those who had volunteered during the war but who would not normally have done so. This purpose was probably achieved. The records of the Dorset Yeomanry show how the war led to a considerable expansion of that force. From averaging a yearly strength of 218 over the six years 1894–9 it rose to a yearly average of 287 between 1900 and

[74] See Appendix VI for detailed breakdown of social composition of IY.
[75] *Report of Committee on Organisation, Arms, and Equipment of the Yeomanry Force* (Accounts and Papers, Vol. XL), Cd. 466 (1901), p. 3.
[76] *Ibid.*, p. 11.

1904. It would appear that those who joined during the war were retained. Table 14 illustrates this and Table 15 illustrates the six largest occupational groups of the Imperial Yeomanry.

TABLE 14

STRENGTH OF DORSET YEOMANRY, 1894–1905[77]

Year	Number
1894	223
1895	219
1896	218
1897	219
1898	212
1899	215
1900	234
1901	264
1902	315
1903	306
1904	318
1905	332

TABLE 15

LARGEST OCCUPATIONAL GROUPS PER 100 OF THE IMPERIAL YEOMANRY[78]

Occupation	Percentage
Commercial, i.e. clerk, etc.	11·4
Skilled craftsman	8·9
Groom and servant	8·5
Farmer	8·0
Labourer	7·1
Gentleman	6·0

A more significant and important breakdown, however, is to determine the pattern of recruitment for both working-class and non-working-class groups by month and by year. Figure 1

[77] Table compiled from M. F. Gage, *Records of Dorset Yeomanry* (Sherborne, 1906), p. 178.
[78] Table compiled from Imperial Yeomanry Attestation Forms.

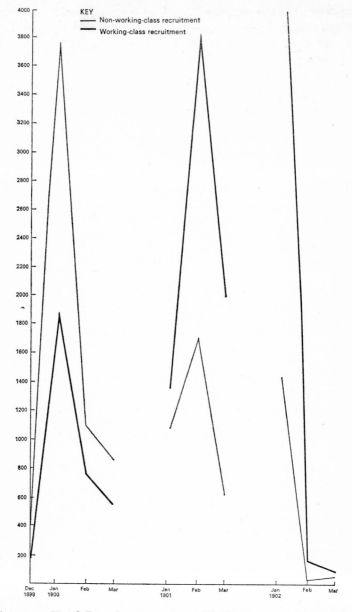

Figure 1   Total Recruitment to Imperial Yeomanry each recruiting
season, 1899–1902

illustrates this pattern over the three years of the war. Two features are immediately apparent from this graph. The first is that the greatest proportion of non-working-class recruitment took place at the end of 1899 and the beginning of 1900. This is illustrated by Table 16.

TABLE 16

NON-WORKING-CLASS RECRUITMENT DECEMBER-MARCH EACH YEAR
OF THE WAR[79]

Month	1899		1900		1901		1902	
	No.	% of total	No.	% of total	No.	% of total	No.	% of total
January			3,746	66·76	1,075	44·05	1,449	24·83
February			1,059	57·75	1,712	31·09	36	17·40
March			868	61·61	618	23·53	57	38·26
December	443	70·85						
TOTALS	443	70·85	5,673	64·08	3,405	32·09	1,542	24·90

Non-working-class recruitment peaked very early on during the war. It is notable that the month with the largest numbers of non-working-class recruits was January 1900, the aftermath of Black Week and the time of frenetic patriotism. The total of 3,746 in this month was in marked contrast to the 1,863 working-class recruits who joined during the same period. The non-working-class response was maintained to a slightly lesser degree for the rest of the 1900 recruiting season. But for the remainder of the war years the steady influx of non-working-class recruits was not maintained and they were never again to comprise as large a portion of the force as they had in 1900.

This was in part due to a general failure—noted in all the volunteer units—to sustain the high level of recruitment enthusiasm of 1900. It was especially true of those units with a large proportion of non-working-class recruits. The active-service companies often found it difficult to maintain their

[79] Table compiled from Imperial Yeomanry Attestation Forms. The months of January to March were the months when 93 per cent of recruitment was achieved —except, of course, for December 1899. The other months have, therefore, been omitted.

established strength after 1900. The *Report of the Inspector-General of Recruiting for Year 1901* reported how:[80]

it was not found possible to obtain the full number of companies nor, . . . to obtain companies at the same strength as the preceding year. The Army order . . . [was] consequently modified, and companies were allowed to proceed as such at a minimum strength of 90 all ranks. In cases where the requisite 90 were not forthcoming, Volunteers were allowed to proceed as drafts to relieve an equivalent number of men of the service company . . . provided a minimum number of 21 came forward.

Whereas in 1900 there had been over 10,000 active-service company volunteers sent to South Africa, in 1901 it was only found possible to send 5,192. The Imperial Yeomanry did not find it difficult to maintain its strength—due to the large influx of working-class volunteers in 1901 and 1902. But the same lack of enthusiasm was manifest in the failure of yeomen to re-enlist. A widespread dissatisfaction was noted, in spite of the special treatment that the yeomen received from the authorities. How well the yeomen lived compared with other units was made evident by a report in the *Volunteer Service Gazette* which noted that the Committee of the Imperial Yeomanry:[81]

being aware of the difficulty and delay in forwarding clothing, tobacco, food, and other supplies for the use and comfort of the various contingents . . . and of the pressing need there is in many cases for such things, have decided to place at the disposal of each officer commanding a battalion the sum of £500 to be distributed according to his discretion, so that the men may have the means of meeting their immediate necessities.

Despite these extra benefits, only 655 yeomen re-enlisted in 1901.

The volunteer press liked to believe that this lack of enthusiasm was a reflection of the[82]

treatment he receives at the hands of the authorities and his officers. This is the case with the regular soldier; it's the 'messing about' he gets that sickens him of the service. Just the same with the Yeomanry —only more so. In their case being in the main men of a superior class, it has been doubly galling, and most determined that their first

---

[80] *Report of the Inspector-General of Recruiting for Year 1901, op. cit.*, p. 4.
[81] *Volunteer Service Gazette*, 18 May 1900, p. 453.
[82] *Volunteer Record and Shooting News*, 4 October 1900, p. 323.

experience in 'the service' should be their last. . . . He had to wait months for his pay . . . he was sore over not receiving the furlough . . . and he was sick to death of being bullied and chivvied by officers who seemed to imagine the whole thing had been arranged for their own glorification.

There was, no doubt, some truth in this especially as so many of the 'superior class' of yeoman seemed to believe that the war would resemble a Sunday-afternoon hunting party. But there was also a simpler explanation. The fact was that most yeomen had enlisted with the expectation that they would not be required for more than one year. The Attestation Oath sworn by those who joined the Imperial Yeomanry had reflected this optimism: the recruit promised to serve for one year or until the termination of hostilities, *whichever came first*. When it was discovered that the war could drag on for many years 'men worried about their businesses at home and their jobs which in many cases were no longer kept open'.[83]

The second significant feature to emerge from Figure 1 is that the working-class response to recruitment was the reverse to that of the non-working-class group. Instead of decreasing throughout the period, the working-class group got larger. The peak month of working-class recruitment was January 1902, five months before the end of the war, and it is probable that had the war continued the 1902 total of working-class recruits would have surpassed that of 1901. As it was, the total was bound to be lower than that of 1901: there was no serious recruiting after January. But the significant fact is the large number of working-class people prepared to join the Imperial Yeomanry in this month compared with the almost insignificant numbers from the non-working-class group in that month. Thus, over 4,000 men of working-class occupations joined in that month compared with 1,449 of the non-working-class group. The figures in Table 17 illustrate the variations in the total working-class response.

In every case, as the non-working-class recruitment figures were falling, those for the working classes were increasing. It seems probable that the failure to re-enlist was essentially a non-working-class problem. The increase in the Imperial Yeomanry by 6,000 in 1901 is largely explained by this rise in

[83] C. S. Jarvis, *Half a Life* (London, 1943), p. 109.

TABLE 17

WORKING-CLASS RECRUITMENT DECEMBER-MARCH EACH YEAR OF
THE WAR[84]

Month	1899		1900		1901		1902	
	No.	% of total	No.	% of total	No.	% of total	No.	% of total
January			1,863	33·21	1,365	55·95	4,387	75·17
February			775	42·25	3,830	68·91	171	82·60
March			541	38·39	2,009	76·47	92	61·74
December	182	29·42						
TOTAL	182	29·42	3,179	35·92	7,204	67·91	4,650	75·10

working-class volunteers. Of the non-working-class group only
five of the twenty-one occupational groups showed a larger
recruitment in 1901 than 1900; they were clerks, commercial
travellers (two professions which at that time were notorious
for considering themselves a 'cut above' working-class people),
draughtsmen, hotel proprietors and retailers. The same was not
true of our working-class occupations, where of the twenty-eight
occupations into which they have been grouped at least one half
show an increase of recruits in 1901.

There are several problems that accompany the foregoing
analysis. The most serious is the arbitrary division of the
Imperial Yeomanry into two distinct sections: working class
and non-working class. Because we have been concerned
primarily with how the working-class response differed from
the non-working-class response, it was not thought necessary to
sub-divide the other section into middle- or upper-class group-
ings. Indeed, it would be very difficult to do so satisfactorily. It
is not clear from the Attestation Forms, for example, whether
the occupation 'farmer' means tenant farmer, smallholder or
large landowner, and when it means any of these three things.
And this is illustrative of the whole problem. The Attestation
Forms only reveal a minimum of information about occupation
but even if they revealed further details it is not certain that the
task would be any easier. Where, for example, should we place
shop assistants? Working class by income and origin, their
occupation, like the clerks, was probably regarded as one step

[84] Table compiled from Imperial Yeomanry Attestation Forms.

above the labourers. Whether it was high enough to rank as a lower-middle-class-status occupation we do not know. The same is true of grocers and other retailers. From the Attestation Forms we do not know whether a particular grocer or butcher owned his own shop, rented it or worked for a chain of stores. All these factors clearly have a direct bearing on class and status. But because shop-keepers, whether large or small, are traditionally petty-bourgeois they have been classed among the non-working-class group. It is not clear what is meant, for example, by 'engineer': it could apply to a mechanic who had picked up certain engineering skills, or it could apply to a fully qualified civil engineer. There are many other instances—drapers and tailors, hairdressers, even foremen. Thus, there are bound to be cases where inaccuracies have occurred due to the necessity of using intelligent guess-work as the criterion to determine which group a particular occupation falls into.

There is another feature that should be mentioned. It will be seen from the breakdown of the social composition of the force that certain trades within the working-class group have been consolidated: thus, the drink trade, food trade and textile workers. This has been done solely for convenience. Most of those in the drink-trade category are barmen or innkeepers, the majority of which can fairly safely be classified as working class. And care has been taken to ensure that, as far as possible, only those working-class members of the trade have been included.

These problems, however, do not destroy the validity of the analysis. The trends of decreasing non-working-class recruitment and increasing working-class recruitment can be shown clearly enough through an examination of individual occupational groups. We can also avoid the difficulties of classification. There can be little doubt of the middle- and upper-class status of 'gentlemen', 'professionals' or 'students' or the working-class status of 'labourer', 'carpenter' or 'smith'. Figures 2–7 illustrate the pattern of recruitment for those occupations.[85]

The problem is to find a satisfactory explanation for the apparent paradox that as the war became more unpopular, so the Volunteers from the working class increased in numbers. Contemporaries failed to notice this and have left us no plausible explanation. But, as far as the working class were concerned,

[85] See Appendix VII for totals by month and year.

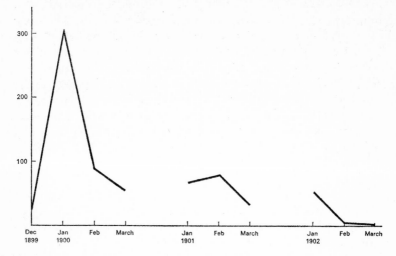

Figure 2   Recruitment pattern of 'professionals' each recruiting season, 1899–1902

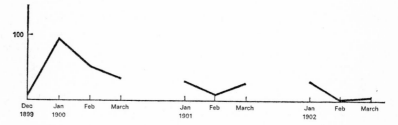

Figure 3   Recruitment pattern of students each recruiting season, 1899–1902

volunteering for the army was always related to the labour market. It is unlikely that the war in any way affected this situation. In Liverpool, during November 1899, it was noted that although recruiting was always brisk at that time of the year: [86]

the recruiting sergeants [are] doing absolutely nothing. And this is attributed to the brisk condition of employment owing to the drawing

[86] The *Labour Chronicle*, December 1899, p. 305.

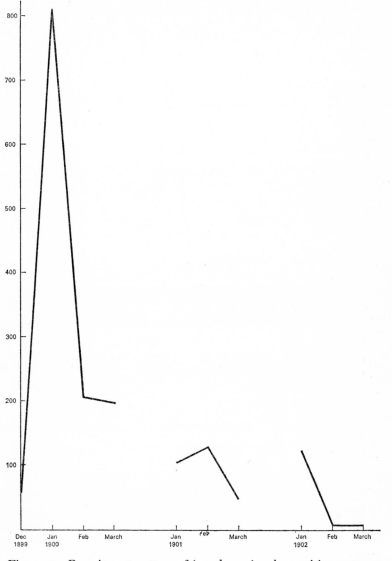

Figure 4   Recruitment pattern of 'gentlemen' each recruiting season, 1899–1902

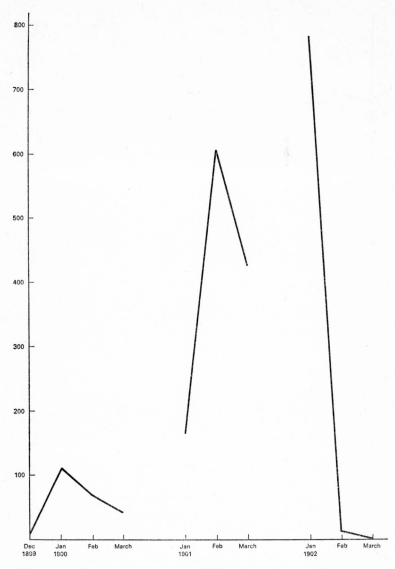

Figure 5   Recruitment pattern of labourers each recruiting season,
1899–1902

Figure 6   Recruitment pattern of carpenters each recruiting season, 1899–1902 .

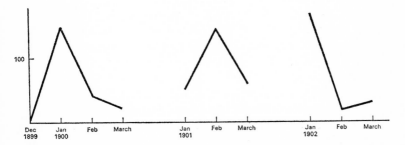

Figure 7   Recruiting pattern of smiths and saddlers each recruiting season, 1899–1902

away of the reserves. This only proves again what previous experience has taught us, that periods of depression are the times when the ranks of the army are filled; in other words the army is composed largely, if not mainly, of 'out of works'.

As Professor Cunningham pointed out before the Royal Commission on Physical Deterioration: 'When trade is good and employment plentiful it is only from the lowest stratum of the people that the Army receives it supply of men . . . when trade is bad, a better class of recruit is available.'[87] Charles Booth noted the same phenomenon when he observed that the most potent influences aiding recruitment were 'on the negative side, love troubles or difficulties, or want of civil employment. The last of these is the more evident motive, in London at any rate;

[87] *Minutes of Evidence before the Royal Commission on Physical Deterioration* (*Reports*, Vol. XXXII), Cd. 2175 (1904), p. 95, question 2188.

and we find that recruiting is briskest in the winter months.'[88] No doubt the Imperial Yeomanry benefited from the fact that drafts were called for at the beginning of each year, a time when there was most likely to be unemployment.

Thus, there is a very obvious connection between the labour market and volunteering. Unemployment, which had remained fairly low since the mid-1890s, began to rise during the war years; at the same time, real wages tended to fall, making the army a more attractive prospect.[89] In an overall sense the war did not seem to benefit the prosperity of the country. Sheffield, with its steel industry, could have been expected to have prospered as a result of the war, but wages and earnings in the town did not respond with any marked upswing during this period.[90] If the war was benefiting Sheffield the working men do not seem to have shared in the dividend. Some trades were very hard hit.

This seems to have been the case in Northampton which had been cultivating the South African market for some time. In September 1899 it was reported that 'the trouble in the Transvaal is having a very serious effect upon the trade, and many houses in this district have had orders cancelled or deliveries stopped for the present'.[91] It is interesting to note in this context that the Northampton branch of the Shoe Operatives Union was strongly opposed to the war because 'it has only had the effect of curtailing wages in this town and causing money which would have been spent in trade to be diverted'.[92] Those towns which had army contracts were better placed; Leicester was one of these and there was no suggestion there that the war was reacting adversely on employment. So, also was Finedon, a town in the East Northants constituency where Channing had reported that the working men were his strongest anti-war supporters. Thus, there would seem to be very little connection between the economic benefits of the war and working-class

[88] Charles Booth, *Life and Labour in London* (2nd ed., London, 1902–3), 2nd Series, IV, p. 59.
[89] W. T. Layton and G. Crowther, *Introduction to the Study of Prices* (London, 1938), p. 214.
[90] See Sidney Pollard, 'Wages and Earnings in the Sheffield Trades 1851–1914', *Yorkshire Bulletin of Economic and Social Research* (University of Hull), February 1954, pp. 61–3.
[91] *Boot and Shoe Trades Journal*, 30 September 1899, p. 418.
[92] National Union of Boot and Shoe Operatives, *Monthly Report* (December, 1899), p. 8.

attitudes to it.[93] Whatever the economics, the facts were that unemployment was continually on the increase throughout the period. In 1900 it averaged 2·7; in 1901, 3·4; and in the first five months of 1902, 4·0.[94] If we examine the average working-class contribution to the Imperial Yeomanry for the months of each recruiting 'season' (i.e. December of one year to the March of the following year) and compare it with the average unemployment for those months, it will be seen that as unemployment worsened so working-class recruitment increased.

TABLE 18

WORKING-CLASS RECRUITS FOR IMPERIAL YEOMANRY PER 100 OF TOTAL AND UNEMPLOYMENT PER 100 TRADE UNIONISTS, DECEMBER-MARCH OF EACH YEAR

Year	Recruits per 100	Unemployment per 100
1899/1900	32·6	2·6
1900/1901	62·6	3·8
1901/1902	76·2	4·2

The same trend is evident if one particular trade is examined. Thus, Table 19 relates the recruitment of carpenters and plumbers to the unemployment of those particular trades.

TABLE 19

CARPENTERS AND PLUMBERS RECRUITED FOR IMPERIAL YEOMANRY PER 100 OF TOTAL AND UNEMPLOYMENT PER 100 TRADE-UNION CARPENTERS AND PLUMBERS, DECEMBER-MARCH OF EACH YEAR

Year	Recruits per 100	Unemployment per 100
1899/1900	1·31	2·72
1900/1901	3·26	4·86
1901/1902	3·91	5·2

[93] The shoe trade in the small towns around Northampton was reported to be flourishing during the war. These included Rushden, Wollaston and Kettering, all of which were in Channing's constituency. See *Leather Trades Review*, 18 September 1900, p. 733.

[94] The unemployment statistics in Tables 18 and 19 were taken from the *Labour Gazette*. It is, therefore, essentially an index of skilled-labour unemployment. The recruitment figures are from the Imperial Yeomanry Attestation Forms. Graphs have not been used to illustrate the point being made in the tables because they

It is obvious that these figures must be treated circumspectly. Taken month by month, the recruitment figures do not show any exact correlation with the fluctuations of the rate of employment, neither could they be expected to do so. They do, however, show a definite trend and it should be noted that the time of highest unemployment—the winter of 1902—was also the time of greatest working-class recruitment. There are two important qualifications which must be borne in mind. In the first place, the recruiting 'season' and the time of highest unemployment, the winter months, coincided. This would be especially true of the building industry, although it might be supposed that plumbing and carpentry would be less affected than other occupations in the trade.

In the second place, and this is a general objection, there is the problem that these figures are recruitment figures and not volunteering figures. It could be argued that the increase of working-class recruits was related, not to the worsening economic situation, but to the absence of volunteers from other classes. It is impossible to know how many of the working class actually volunteered to go to South Africa in 1899–1900; we only know that relatively few were taken. And it would not be an unfair assumption that a recruiting officer would show a preference for a qualified middle- or upper-class Volunteer than for a qualified working-class Volunteer. The only consideration that might throw some light on this objection is the fact that there seems to have been only the loosest limit on numbers raised. In 1899 and 1900, Buller had asked for 8,000 mounted infantry and Wyndham had expected there to be difficulty in raising them: in fact, over 10,000 went out in the first draft. In 1901, the original target of 5,000 new recruits was exceeded by some 9,000 men. It would, therefore, seem unlikely that the smaller working-class response in 1899 and 1900 was merely a reflection of greater numbers of middle- and upper-class men coming forward.

Thus, in spite of these qualifications, the figures do suggest a possible connection which, in the light of other evidence, seems

would only show the coincidence of unemployment and recruitment peaks during the winter months, which is what would be expected. They would also show the rising trend of unemployment and recruitment but this can be seen equally well from the tables.

quite plausible. An interesting example which will illustrate this relationship can be shown by an examination of the recruitment of miners over the three years. Following the usual working-class pattern, the numbers who joined increased from a total of thirty in 1899/1900 to 239 in 1902. In the last year this increase came largely from Scotland and especially from Fife. Whereas only five Scottish miners joined the Imperial Yeomanry in 1899/1900 and thirty-nine in 1901, 111 joined in 1902. It is possible to establish a very strong connection here with the employment situation.

In the summer of 1901 an export duty was placed on coal for the first time. Much of the Fifeshire small coal was exported, especially to the Baltic, and there was some apprehension that this trade would suffer. There was a general feeling of un-certainty and insecurity about the future of the Fife coal trade. And this was reflected in the trade journals, who were rather confused about what was actually happening in Fife. On the one hand, the *Colliery Guardian* at the beginning of January noted 'it is impossible not to feel that if the tax does have as disastrous effects upon the export trades as are anticipated in many quarters, the coals of Fifeshire and Yorkshire will be the first to suffer'.[95] On the other hand, *Coal and Iron* reported at the end of the month that 'it is expected that the coming season will [be] a satisfactory one for the Fife coal trade'.[96] It does seem, how-ever, that there was unemployment. In Kirkcaldy the situation was bad enough to warrant the establishment of a relief com-mittee to alleviate distress. The position here was accentuated by a recent fire in one of the pits which, it was claimed, 'was responsible for a good many being out of work'.[97]

What seems to have happened, and this is confirmed by both trade journals, is that there was at the beginning of the year no certainty that the coal tax would not hurt the trade. It was expected that the first three months would be particularly hard because passage to the Baltic was delayed by ice during those months. And, indeed, this seems to have been the case: 'Orders are somewhat scarce in connection with the shipping trade, and at some collieries the men are not working full time. The cold

[95] *Colliery Guardian*, 10 January 1902, p. 82.
[96] *Coal and Iron*, 27 January 1902, p. 92.
[97] *Fifeshire Advertiser*, 4 January 1902.

weather keeps up the demand for household coals and the collieries which do a large home trade are found fairly busy.'[98] Thus, although the tax does not seem to have adversely affected the Fife coal industry, there was no certainty of this at the end of 1901 and beginning of 1902. Recruitment for the Imperial Yeomanry began in Fife on 7 January and ended on 22 January.[99] It was not clear until February just how the coal trade was going to be affected. Thus, although the actual amount of unemployment which resulted was small and localized, there was sufficient apprehension of it to induce men to turn to the army. Table 20 illustrates the regional origin of the miners recruited.

TABLE 20

REGION OF RECRUITMENT OF MINERS WHO JOINED THE IMPERIAL YEOMANRY[100]

Region	1899/1900		1901		1902	
	No.	% of total	No.	% of total	No.	% of total
England and Wales	25	83·3	88	69·2	128	53·5
Scotland—excluding Fife	5	16·7	32	25·3	59	24·6
Fife	—	—	7	5·5	52	21·9

Contemporaries overlooked the differing ways in which different class groups reacted to the situation. What they saw as a patriotic efflux may have been true for the middle and upper classes. It does not seem to have been true for the working class. Their response to the needs of the country seems to have been selfishly related to the necessities of living rather than to fears for the security of the Empire. It is thus probable that the working-class reaction to imperial ventures was not governed by the patriotism that was attributed to them. It is to this problem that we shall now turn, examining the relationship between the Volunteer movement and the working class and suggesting tentative conclusions as to volunteering and patriotic attitudes.

The Volunteer movement in its most recent form was essentially a result of the invasion scare of 1859. Its object was to provide a citizen's army which would act as an efficient auxiliary to the regular army and the militia. The initial impetus behind the

[98] *Colliery Guardian*, 20 February 1902, p. 403.
[99] *Fife Herald and Journal*, 1 January, 22 January 1902.
[100] Compiled from Imperial Yeomanry Attestation Forms.

movement came largely from the middle class. Thus in Edinburgh, in the first three months of the movement's inception, ten companies were formed, eight of which were companies for professional men.[101] Within a few years, however, enthusiasm amongst the leisured classes waned and[102]

they disappeared from the ranks, and if it had not been for the zeal and energy of the working classes the Volunteer force might have dwindled and possibly perished altogether. The companies that were at first recruited from the masters were driven to find recruits from the clerks and employees.

In Canterbury there were initially two companies, one for the professional men and leading tradesmen, and one for the working men. But they soon ceased to exist as separate units. That the working class was interested in the Volunteer movement is obvious from Table 21 which gives the occupations of the Ashford (Kent) company in 1860.

TABLE 21

SOCIAL OCCUPATIONS OF VOLUNTEER COMPANY OF
ASHFORD, KENT, 1860[103]

Occupation	Percentage of total	Occupation	Percentage of total
Auctioneer	2·4	Footman	2·4
Bookseller	2·4	Gas manager	2·4
Butcher	2·4	Grocer	2·4
Clerk	19·5	Innkeeper	2·4
Carpenter	9·7	Machinist	2·4
Carrier	2·4	Mechanic	7·6
Coach-trimmer	2·4	Merchant	2·4
Confectioner	2·4	Paperhanger	2·4
Draper	7·6	Shoemaker	2·4
Farmer	4·8	Tailor	12·3
Fitter	2·4	Tanner	2·4

[101] MacDonald, op. cit., p. 3.

[102] Ibid., p. 92. It was originally hoped that the Volunteer movement would 'draw men closer together . . . upset party prejudices, set at rest national grievances and strengthen the love and devotion of all for their Queen and their country. . . . The union of classes cannot fail to have an elevating tendancy.' The Rifleman, 11 April 1861, p. 324. This was another example of class conciliationist aims so common throughout nineteenth-century Britain. See also the Volunteer Journal, 4 May 1861, p. 87.

[103] Compiled from C. Igglesden, History of the East Kent Volunteers (Ashford, 1899), p. 125.

It was originally intended that the members of the movement would provide their own arms and equipment and would defray all their expenses except in the event of their being called for actual service. This was not solely a result of nineteenth-century government's usual desire to avoid any expense for itself, for the movement as a whole was opposed to any kind of government interference. The *Rifleman* in 1861 wished to reject War Office financial support: 'If funds be wanting . . . why not appeal to the public . . . the great glory of the movement lies in . . . its spontaneous origin and self-supporting power.'[104] But almost from the beginning, and coincidental with the decline of middle- and upper-class interest already noted, the movement was in financial difficulties. Once the majority of recruits came from the lower classes, financial assistance was essential. The *Volunteer Journal* of Manchester differed from most other organs of the movement when it explained the need for government aid:[105]

A great proportion of our Volunteer forces now consists of young clerks, young shopmen, small tradesmen, workmen and other persons of similar means, that is to say, men who work hard to earn . . . between £80 and £150 a year. The lowest annual expenditure of each Volunteer is £50.

Indeed, the movement looked in danger of collapse only four years after it had been founded; in 1863 the number of efficient men had fallen by 20,000. Thus, in the same year, capitation grants were provided of £63 per man, enabling working men to join the movement without being involved in large expenditure. And the capitation grant was soon recognized as an 'indispensable condition of the existence of the Volunteer force'.[106] Indeed, there was occasional pressure on the government to increase the monetary grant.[107] By the end of the century the mass of the rank and file was provided by the upper-working-class artisans and the clerks: 'The Volunteer service is recruited almost entirely (at least as far as those under the rank of commissioned officers are concerned) from the middle classes of society or the artisan world.'[108] Table 22 illustrates this.

[104] The *Rifleman*, 25 April 1861, p. 340.
[105] The *Volunteer Journal*, 29 June 1861, p. 152.
[106] The *Volunteer*, 5 February 1870, p. 41.
[107] *Ibid.*, for an example in Scotland where a unit warned the government that if the grant was not increased it would have to disband.
[108] Hale, *op. cit.*, p. 36.

TABLE 22

SOCIAL OCCUPATIONS OF VOLUNTEER INFANTRY:
RANK AND FILE, 1903[109]

Occupation	Percentage
Professional	1·8
Clerk	9·6
Shopman	5·3
Artisan	35·5
Independent businessman	3·2
Agricultural labourer	4·2
Town labourer	8·6
Miner	6·0
Factory-hand	12·9
Others	12·9

The success of the volunteer company in the Working Men's College will illustrate the attractions of the movement for the working class. One of the earliest in London, it owed its success largely to the enthusiasm of Tom Hughes and was welcomed by the college authorities until it was found to be introducing members who 'came not as students but for the purpose of belonging to the corps'.[110] Volunteering was felt to be in harmony with the Christian Socialist aims of fellowship. F. D. Maurice welcomed it because one of its results would be to make 'the members of the College more conscious of their obligations to each other and to their country'.[111] The spirit of duty was extant among its members. George Tansley, gazetted a Captain in 1869, wrote an address to the company which urged that the motive inspiring all volunteers 'should, I take it, be the wish to use some part of our leisure in doing some voluntary citizen's work . . . in the hope that it may be of some service . . . to the country'.[112] But J. F. C. Harrison was probably nearer the truth

[109] *Appendices to the Minutes of Evidence taken before the Royal Commission on Militia and Volunteers* (*Reports*, Vol. XXXI), Cd. 2064 (1904), p. 253.
[110] J. L. Davies (ed.), *The Working Men's College* (London, 1904), p. 102.
[111] J. F. C. Harrison, *A History of the Working Men's College 1854–1954* (London, 1954), p. 85.
[112] Davies, *op. cit.*, p. 139.

when he ascribed the enthusiasm with which the movement was greeted as[113]

> not solely due to patriotism; like mountaineering, and strenuous games, it provided something which was otherwise lacking in much of Victorian middle-class life. . . . There appeared . . . to be the danger of facing death with one's comrades, of sustaining bodily fatigue and physical discomfort, and of being taxed in the virtues of courage, discipline and loyalty. It seemed to offer the opportunity of proving one's manliness, and of thereby strengthening the respect of others and of oneself as well.

The vast influx of men to the college when the corps was formed would not argue any profoundly subtle reason for their interest in the Volunteers. Men probably joined for the same sort of reasons that boys join the Boy Scouts, rather than out of any conscious motive of 'duty' and 'patriotism'. It was left to the enthusiasts of the movement to rationalize it.

Whatever the popularity of the corps in the early 1860s, its attractions appear to have faded away by the end of the century. There was a suggestion in the college journal in November 1899, that 'the present war . . . might form an opportunity to revive the Volunteer corps'. And the following month it was announced:[114]

> The note about the Volunteer movement attracted the attention of Captain Payton of the 1st V.B. Royal Fusiliers, a regiment which arose from the old College corps. He very kindly came down for one evening to talk over the matter, and it is hoped that several students will join. Mr. H. F. Deane will be happy to give any information about the corps and volunteer advantages generally.

Although there was the keenest interest in those members of the college who were fighting in South Africa, nothing more was heard of the idea to re-float the volunteer corps. Exactly the same fate was to overtake the attempt to capitalize on patriotism and encourage the formation of rifle clubs in the working men's clubs.

The inadequacies of the British military machine that were so convincingly revealed by the Boer War gave a great impetus to

---

[113] Harrison, *op. cit.*, p. 82.

[114] *Working Men's College Journal*, November 1899, p. 140; December 1899, p. 150.

schemes for improving the fighting capacity of the nation. The desire to develop and extend the Rifle Club movement was one of the means by which it was thought this could be accomplished. Essentially limited to those who regarded shooting as a sport, proposals were made, early in the war, to widen their scope. The object was to encourage rifle practice amongst the general public as a means of improving national defence. Discussions between the War Office and the National Rifle Association elicited the sympathy of the Commander-in-Chief.[115] Clubs sprang up in many places in early 1900 and the idea that they should be used for training citizens in the use of firearms received the approval of Salisbury who, in a speech to the Primrose League, urged the formation of such clubs. The Volunteer movement was, in general, suspicious of rifle clubs and doubtful of their utility. This was partly because they saw them as a threat and partly because, unlike the Volunteers, they were not subject to War Office control. The movement's official magazine saw that they would be a useful way of fostering 'the patriotic spirit which the present campaign . . . has aroused', but urged that they should be incorporated in a reorganized volunteer force.[116]

The official organization of the rifle clubs, the National Rifle Association, did not evince much interest in the opportunity to exploit the patriotism of the war in this way. In 1901 they received the gift of £10,000 from William Waldorf Astor for the specific purpose of promoting rifle clubs for the country labourer.[117] The success of this project is uncertain. During the next year the number of clubs rose by eighty but which, if any, of these were country labourer clubs is not known. The absence of any mention of the project—apart from the announcement of a decision to extend the scope of the trust[118]—would suggest that it met with little response.

Thus, with a general apathy prevailing over the National Rifle Association, it was, once again, left to individual initiative to impress upon the working class the necessity of rifle clubs. The idea was to use the working men's clubs as a means to this

[115] The *Regiment*, 17 February 1900, p. 322.
[116] *Volunteer Service Gazette*, 18 May 1900, p. 456.
[117] National Rifle Association, *Proceedings*, 1902, p. 68.
[118] *Ibid.*, 1903, p. 89.

end and a meeting was held at the Mansion House, presided over by the Lord Mayor, on 23 March 1901. The meeting was presented with a scheme for the formation of a Society of Working Men's Rifle Clubs and was attended by Major Evans Gordon, MP—Conservative member for Stepney—who owed his election to the support of the local working men's club;[119] Harold Boulton, Vice-Chairman of the Federation of Working Men's Social Clubs; and Douglas Eyre of the Federation of the London Working Boy's Club and Institute Union. Lord Roberts had consented to be President and prominent members of the aristocracy, such as the Dukes of Westminster and Norfolk, had promised financial support. The object of the society was announced by Major-General Luard, the Chairman of the General Committee, whose brain-child it appears to have been:[120]

Their object in starting . . . this society was to reach the sources which had not yet been touched either by the Volunteer movement or otherwise. They were simply the vast body of working men's clubs and institutes throughout the country. Very few people had any idea of the enormous extent of these organisations. The aggregate total of membership throughout the country was over 2,000,000 and there were besides a large number of boys' clubs.

It was claimed that they would be an encouragement to recruitment rather than a threat to the Volunteers. And, like the Volunteers, the organization of the society was firmly in the hands of those who financed it. The function of the society was to provide the facilities for the nursery work of shooting—rifles and tubular galleries which could be erected in the hall of a club.[121]

Patriotism was the motive force behind the movement. Harold Boulton, who moved the resolution to found the society, asserted that the presence of such clubs would encourage volunteering and that 'working men had made great sacrifices in common with other classes during the present crisis, and they were prepared to go further'.[122] But Eyre, representing the Club and Institute Union, was more restrained. He read a letter from B. T. Hall which placed the emphasis firmly on home defence: 'However willing the people of this country might be to repel an

---

[119] *Club Life*, 27 October 1900, p. 15.
[120] *Volunteer Service Gazette*, 29 March 1901, p. 347.
[121] *Ibid.* [122] *Ibid.*

invader, they could not do so because of ignorance of the art of rifle shooting.'[123] We can be fairly certain that Hall, a Fabian Socialist, did not much like the idea of the Club and Institute Union's clubs being turned into recruiting centres. Being a non-political body, the Union was represented at the meeting as being willing to provide the clubs with facilities to form rifle clubs if they so desired. It is clear, however, that Hall wished to emphasize the aspect of national defence: an emphasis in direct contradiction to the spirit behind the formation of the clubs. Those who advocated them did so, encouraged by the patriotism of the war, in order to increase the military capacity and preparedness of the country. Unlike the promoters of the society, Hall did not wish to see them become a source of recruitment or a means of instilling patriotism and militarism in the working class. He envisaged them as agencies for training a citizen's army capable of repelling an invader. It is significant that among the clubs and organizations to make applications to the society for shooting galleries were the London Diocesan Church Lad's Brigade, the Jewish Lad's Brigade, and Oxford House, Bethnal Green, which was the headquarters of the Federation of Working Men's Social Clubs.[124]

From the working men's clubs proper the response was very different. The fear of conscription was in the air: it was being advocated widely enough for *Club Life* to devote an editorial in opposition to the idea.[125] The Mansion House meeting was reported and the first rifle club to be founded under this scheme was at Bryanston Club where a working committee and an Honorary Secretary were quickly appointed, and 'between 60 and 70 members enrolled'.[126] The Bradlaugh Club and Institute had possessed a rifle club for over a year but a report of the first year's inaugural meeting gives some idea of the general lack of success of the movement:[127]

We attended a meeting . . . to 'inaugurate the first year of the Rifle Club being formed.' Apparently soldiers can stand fire but jib water, for when we arrived through a downpour of rain we found very few members present, and as far as we could see the riflemen were conspicuous by their absence. The name of General Roberts, who was

---

[123] *Ibid.*   [124] *Ibid.*, 3 June 1901, p. 151.

[125] *Club Life*, 16 March 1901, p. 9. Lord Weymess had been advocating it in the volunteer press. See *Volunteer Service Gazette*, 25 May 1900, p. 479.

[126] *Club Life*, 13 April 1901, p. 4.   [127] *Ibid.*, 6 July 1901, p. 16.

supposed at one time to be a terror to all evil-doers, Boers included, appeared on the bills . . . but even that failed to draw an audience. Has the martial ardour faded out of the breast of our children? . . . As we have heard very little of the rifle clubs which started with much parade at the Mansion House, *the whole scheme seems to have petered out like a damp firework.* (Italics added.)

No further reports can be found of this particular rifle club, or of any other with one notable exception. The exception was a surprising one: Mildmay Club appears to have been the only one capable of supporting a thriving rifle club. A large club, numbering 200, it was founded at the beginning of 1902. By May of that year they were proficient enough to gain first prize in the 'Regiment' rifle competition which was open to all clubs, volunteer or civilian, in Great Britain.[128] It is strange that with the failure of Bryanston and the quiescence of Bradlaugh this most Radical of the clubs should have contained such a large group of rifle enthusiasts.

In general, then, there is no evidence that the patriotic promotion of rifle clubs met with any success amongst working men. In part, this may have been because the cost of $\frac{1}{4}$d. or $\frac{1}{2}$d. per round of ammunition used made an evening's shooting fairly expensive.[129] Partly, it may have been because the society was dominated by middle- and upper-class patrons and it has been noted how this was alien to the mainstream of the club movement. In this respect it is noticeable how the idea met with the greatest response from middle-class-dominated organizations such as the Federation of Working Men's Social Clubs and the Church Lad's Brigade. And partly, it may have been because this type of activity, with its blatant appeal to 'patriotism', was unattractive to working men, being essentially an attitude of the middle and upper classes. It is interesting, however, to counterpoise this failure with the attraction and success of ambulance clubs within the working men's clubs.

These were an integral part of club life; virtually every club possessed an ambulance section. T. S. Peppin described them as 'the most popular and significant type of class'.[130] In contrast to the rifle clubs, the war had the effect of encouraging the

---

[128] *Ibid.*, 10 May 1902, p. 9.
[129] *Volunteer Service Gazette*, 3 January 1902, p. 151.
[130] T. S. Peppin, *Club-Land of the Toiler* (London, 1895), p. 51.

ambulance movement. It was remarked how 'all the meetings we have attended have been crowded', and many of the ambulance men served in South Africa in that capacity.[131] The ambulance club was far more typical of working-class organizations than the rifle club. It has already been noted that the Battersea railwaymen's contribution to the Patriotic Carnival was an ambulance team.[132] Thus, during a period when the whole nation was supposed to have been anxious to serve England in her 'hour of need', here was one conspicuous example when a 'patriotic' appeal to the working class met with an impassively negative reply. What, then, was the character of working-class patriotism as it can be seen through volunteering?

The early defeats of British troops were traumatic for those who were conscious and proud of Britain's predominant position in the world. It seemed inconceivable that a band of illiterate, undisciplined farmers could take on and set to rout some of the finest regiments of the British army. Yet this was what happened during Black Week. The expeditionary force had been split into three parts. Lord Methuen was sent with 7,000 men to relieve beleaguered Kimberley and Cecil Rhodes, General Gatacre was given 4,000 men to drive back the Boers who were invading the eastern Cape Colony, and Buller with the main army of 20,000 was to defeat the Boer army which had swept into Natal and besieged Ladysmith. Between 9 and 15 December all three generals had suffered shattering defeats. Methuen had seen the virtual destruction of the Black Watch at Magersfontein where he had launched a suicidal frontal assault against an impregnable Boer position. Gatacre had been defeated at Stormberg and had retreated. And Buller made an incredibly foolish attack across the Tugela which was repulsed with heavy losses. These defeats were not merely a result of British incompetence, although Buller was made the scapegoat; for the first time since Napoleon, Britain had engaged an enemy whose Krupps and Creusot artillery was superior, whose marksmanship was better, and whose mounted infantry strategy was ideally suited for the demands of the terrain.

[131] *Club Life*, 14 July 1900, p. 1; 17 February 1900, p. 2.
[132] See Chapter IV, p. 169.

These three successive defeats shook the complacent pride of the middle class as to the strength and security of the Empire. An army chaplain wrote of those days:[133]

England passed through a time of mental agony such as we of this generation have never known before. The shock to our national pride, the fear for the honour of our race, the anxiety lest we should prove incapable of guarding the great traditions of the past, the dull weight of personal sorrow . . . shook the heart of England and awakened in us a virtue which had long lain dormant.

It was claimed that the gloom of the week was such that theatres, music halls and restaurants were emptied in London and that friends 'passed each other by in the street with a mere nod of recognition hoping that our kinfolk . . . would not stop to speak of what was uppermost in mind'.[134] For one yeoman, the fears as to Britain's strength and security were not absolved until the[135]

spectacle of the crowded transports in Table Bay [proved] to me that now . . . Brittania rules the waves more supremely than ever at Aboukir or in Trafalgar Bay; and the braying clangour of the 'massed' bands at Heidelberg has inspired me with awe and respect for the great Empire which can send a quarter of a million men across one-third of the circumference of the globe to fight her battles and do her bidding.

The same yeoman, T. F. Dewar, a doctor, wrote from his troopship during the passage to South Africa:[136]

From a passing steamer . . . we learned that Ladysmith had been relieved. What has happened since . . . we do not know and . . . I fear we don't much care; for the sea has a benumbing effect upon the mind; and all that we are now concerned with is that we are going there to do each the little that we can to uphold the honour of Britain; and that, whether it comes soon, or late, whether it costs much or little, it will come out right in the end.

This, then, was the frame of mind that motivated the middle- and upper-class men who volunteered in large numbers in 1899 and 1900. It was illustrated by another yeoman, Sydney Peel, who wrote of his feelings during Black Week: 'The thing became intolerable; it was impossible to go on doing the ordinary things of life . . . new men, new measures must be devised.'[137]

---

[133] P. B. Bull, *God and Our Soldiers* (3rd ed., London, 1914), p. 39.

[134] Maurice Fitzgibbon, *Arts under Arms: A University Man in Khaki* (London, 1901), pp. 2–3.   [135] Dewar, *op. cit.*, p. 58.   [136] *Ibid.*, p. 12.

[137] Sydney Peel, *Trooper 8008 I.Y.* (London, 1901), pp. 1–2.

Such men really believed it to be their duty to volunteer for service in the Empire. A university student of Trinity College, Dublin, explained it this way: 'When a man is 20 and when his state . . . requires his services, I do not see that either he or his connections—of course, I leave the responsibilities of the married out of consideration—have anything further to say on the subject.'[138] It was also an integral part of their response to the call for volunteers that the traditional virtues of the English gentleman would win through. The 'pluck', 'valour', 'sportsmanship' and other non-natural concepts that were evinced so clearly in the spirit of middle- and upper-class volunteering and which were institutionalized in, among others, Paget's Horse and Lovat's Scouts, were felt to be crucial to the success of British arms:

Attention was turned to the Yeomanry, men who could ride well and shoot straight. Plenty of such men were to be had for the asking: young fellows, sportsmen to the core, sons of professional men, farmers, merchants, fellows in all stations of life with the true British love of sport among them.

These men, then, were moved by considerations of patriotism and Empire, and it is very easy to see how this kind of patriotic reaction with its almost absurdly naïve emotionalism could quickly turn to jingoism. Once again, this kind of reaction and its transition into a jingo intolerance and blindness was most marked among the wealthier classes of society. Composed of crude elements of racism, nationalism and arrogance, it defies subtle analysis. Thus, the following biologically unflattering description of the Boer by Lady C. E. M. Rolleston, who ran a convalescent home in Kimberley, is typical of those who served in South Africa and who wrote about it afterwards:[139]

I can only say that honestly I much disliked their aspect . . . their countenances are singularly deficient in nobility; the eyes are generally small and dark, and very close together, the nose is short and insignificant, the drooping moustache, which usually conceals the upper lip, shows the lower one to be large and sensual . . . the face is, to my thinking, nearly always animal . . . the glance is shifty, and reminds me irresistibly of a visit to the Zoological Gardens at home.

This was the type of arrogance that manifested itself in jingoistic outbursts. It was only a short step to transfer it on to opponents

[138] Fitzgibbon, op. cit., p. 18.
[139] C. E. M. Rolleston, On Yeoman Service (London, 1901), p. 58.

at home. Thus, the opinion of a Scottish Rifle Volunteer on pro-Boers:[140]

These base culminators and traitors who still, I suppose, calling themselves patriots, try to sully the name of the British soldier by tales of rapine and excess, and by every means in their power endeavour to obstruct the settlement of the South African question, should by all moral and humane laws be court-martialled and shot. . . . What man, calling himself a true Briton, could say less on such a subject?

Jingoism, then, was a typical form of middle- and upper-class patriotism. It manifested itself, in volunteering, by the way in which the non-working-class group rushed to join the colours in the first flush of emotional patriotism which swept the country as a result of Black Week. The response to the 'country in need' was seen to be very transient. It was noted that January 1900 was the peak of middle- and upper-class volunteering and that after this the enthusiasm steadily declined. Thus, at the time of frenetic patriotism, those who rushed to join the army tended to be those of high-status groups. The large proportion of non-working-class occupations in the City Imperial Volunteers, formed entirely in 1899–1900, illustrates this. This relationship between class and eagerness to volunteer was indicative of the acceptance of patriotism as a motive for volunteering and was probably strongest amongst those groups who were working class in origin but middle class in status and pretension. The clerk was an example of this and formed a very large element of both the Imperial Yeomanry and the CIV. One of the exceptions to the rule of declining non-working-class recruitment in 1901, he was, in general, more eager to volunteer than the labourer of similar age group.

TABLE 23

CLERKS AND LABOURERS AGED BETWEEN 17 AND 25 PER 100 RECRUITED FOR THE IMPERIAL YEOMANRY[141]

	1900	1901	1902
Clerks	79	85	57
Labourers	59	73	58

[140] G. H. Smith, *With the Scottish Rifle Volunteers at the Front* (Edinburgh, 1901), p. 132. [141] Compiled from Imperial Yeomanry Attestation Forms.

Perhaps this can be partly explained by the association the clerk felt with the social system and his desire to express it in the conventionally approved way. Judged by our measurement, his patriotism followed the conventional pattern. This is not to suggest that every clerk would have given patriotism as a reason for joining the Imperial Yeomanry or CIV, but it does suggest that he was motivated by the same kind of considerations that induced men like T. F. Dewar to volunteer. In fact, it tends to suggest that his volunteering was motivated more by pure patriotism than by the sort of considerations that led the working classes to volunteer. Volunteering was, for the status-conscious, a socially acceptable activity and a mark of having risen in the world. This is illustrated by the letter of a Mrs Ormrod whose son, almost certainly a clerk, was in the City Imperial Volunteers. She wrote to the organizing committee requesting financial assistance:[142]

I have worked for the past 18 years at Office Cleaning and Devoted [*sic*] my life to bringing up my son as a Gentleman and consider I have succeeded in doing so as under the patronage of GeneralMarschell he entered the General Offices of the S.E. Rly [*sic*] at the age of 16 years and has rizen [*sic*] to a very good position in that companys [*sic*] offices up to the time of his joining the C.I.V.s, his social advancement being proved by his numerous prizes and honours at Volunteers . . . I must keep him a respectable home to come back too [*sic*].

The experience of the Working Men's College would suggest that the Volunteer movement was popular amongst the working classes for reasons that were something less than pure patriotism and desire to serve one's country. But it was certainly believed by middle-class commentators that patriotism was a universal motive. Colonel Eustace Balfour managed to awaken in a 'Foreign Officer' the realization that 'patriotism was the first motive which induced Volunteers to give up their time, and often their money, in order to learn drill, musketry, and manoeuvre'.[143] Sir J. H. A. MacDonald refuted those who claimed that[144]

the men who join the Volunteers do so without their being moved by any patriotic desire to be of use to their country, but only because drill

[142] CIV Collection, MS. 10207/1.
[143] *London Scottish Regimental Gazette*, May 1901.
[144] MacDonald, *op. cit.*, p. 159.

and shooting are congenial exercises, to which they betake themselves just as others take up cricket or football or golf . . . [these men] constitute a very small percentage. . . . And it is quite reasonable to suppose that while patriotic sentiment may be more sluggish in some than in others, it is not absent, but only in a degree dormant, and at the first alarm of the nation's need would be wakened into lively action.

But such attempts to disguise the true meaning of volunteering for most people were futile. The working-class mind just did not work in that way. Patriotism as a concept was probably the last thing that would motivate him to volunteer for the army. It was noted during the Crimean War that:[145]

the soldiers who had their homes in the hamlet were not looked upon as fighting men, but as young adventurers who had enlisted as the only way of seeing the world before they settled down to marriage and the plough tail. Judging from their letters the only enemies that they had to face were sand storms, mosquitoes, heat stroke, or ague.

The Volunteer movement had been called into existence by the hysterical reaction of the respectable classes to a non-existent threat of invasion. Until the Boer War it never made any noticeable contribution to Britain's strength or greatness. It continually had to suffer the ridicule of 'playing at being soldiers'. Obviously, those involved in running the movement could not allow its *raison d'être*—the patriotic desire of its members to prepare for the defence of their country—to be shattered by the ugly truth that men joined for status or pleasure reasons. The confusion this resulted in is aptly illustrated by an editorial in the *Volunteer Service Magazine* replying to an article in the *Daily Chronicle* which had attacked the patriotic motives of volunteers:[146]

We must not shut our eyes to the fact that patriotism does undoubtedly play a very important part in this laudable work. If pleasure is the

[145] Flora Thompson, *Lark Rise to Candleford* (Oxford, 1954), p. 283. Such a pre-occupation with personal ills is not surprising. From the various working-class people I have talked to whose husbands or friends fought in the Boer War, the most striking characteristic to emerge is how they all remember whether their informant came down with enteric or not, and how many days he had to walk without boots. None of their acquaintances, it would seem, expressed any opinion about the enemy or the Boer way of life. This is borne out by the small amount of soldiers' letters we do possess where there are references to the political issues of the war.

[146] *Volunteer Service Magazine*, May 1898, pp. 580–2. That this was not a new theme, see the *Rifleman*, 9 May 1861, p. 354, for a letter from Lord Enfield claim-

principal aim and motive of the volunteer—and we think there is a lot of truth in this assertion—then it must be confessed that the movement has degenerated considerably . . . taken collectively it must be admitted that, to a large extent, the volunteer force has degenerated into a band of pleasure.

Whatever the motives that led working men to join the Volunteers in peace time, during the war it might have been expected that patriotism would have been blatantly and shamelessly used as a reason as it was among men of higher social orders. In fact, patriotism in the sense that the middle class meant and reacted to it would not seem to be applicable to the working classes. The statistics revealed that the working-class reaction to Black Week, the time when patriotic pressures to volunteer were greatest, was very muted. They revealed that volunteering followed the reverse pattern to that of other classes and that there was a very strong relationship with economic security. Reminiscences such as those quoted above do not exist for a study of working-class motives in volunteering.[147] There is some evidence, however, to support the distinction between non-working-class and working-class volunteering. An article in *Club Life* written by a clubman, whose occupation seems to have been that of warehouseman, detailed his reasons for volunteering. It is worth quoting in full:[148]

Since I have been back in England I have been asked a number of times why I left my native land. . . . I know it is the rule to expect all soldiers, volunteers, or servicemen to exclaim, 'Why I went to fight for dear old England, my Motherland, against the foreign foe.' Well, to tell you the truth those who go say nothing of the kind. What they are supposed to say is all a fake of the newspapers . . . I can safely say among all the men I met . . . hardly half-a-dozen said anything about 'Dear Old England or Motherland.' What they did talk about was where the next bit of 'bacca was to come from, or the desire for beer,

---

ing that 'pride, not patriotism, actuates a large number of those who join. We see it exemplified in the shifting from corps to corps in the childish pursuit of a pretty uniform.'

[147] Some letters of rank-and-file soldiers were collected and printed, e.g. *Mick Gallagher at the Front* (Liverpool, 1900), but these follow the typical working-class practice of descriptive narrative rather than the expression of any opinion.

Mr Kenneth Griffith, the actor, is reputed to possess a collection of soldiers' letters, but these have not been made available to the author.

[148] 'A South African Trip', *Club Life*, 4 May 1901, p. 1.

or when the war would be over, and a word or two about dear old Dad and the Ma at home. These bursts of heroic aspirations are all 'guiver,' and I expect the best part of the men who went out at the time I did left England for the same reason i.e. the monotony of their surroundings. Here was I cooped up in a city warehouse a strong active fellow full of high spirits and a desire to see the world. What more to the taste could there be than a few months in a different land . . . I seized the opportunity at once, and . . . I did not care tuppence about the merits of the dispute, and the rubbish about 'fighting for the dear old flag,' and our desire to kill Boers or anyone else, for the glory of old England . . . the best part of the men went away from the same cause, a desire to see life and to escape the continual sameness insepar-able from trade in the City . . . it was to escape for a time the monotony of existence, and if other volunteers were only to speak the truth they would tell you the same thing.

This, then, would tend to support the implications of our statistical evidence: that working-class volunteering was far more a response to environmental pressures and needs and day-to-day living than to the pretentious patriotism characteristic of the period.

VI

Conclusion

There has always been the assumption—often unspoken—among intellectuals that the working class as a social group is easily aroused to irrational actions, is easily influenced by unprincipled demagogues and can be manipulated for any bad purposes. It is very commonly held that the ignorance of the masses makes them untrustworthy, that they can usually be found supporting tyranny of one kind or another and are seldom to be found on the side of the enlightened. It has been very easy, therefore, for us to accept the idea that imperialism received fervent support from the working class; we have, after all, the word of that eminently rational Liberal, J. A. Hobson, that this was so. In fact, it was clearly not as simple as that. As with any period of history and especially with any problem that involved the inarticulate the myths and misconceptions are numerous. The age of the new imperialism is no exception, and the existence of a jingoistic working class has been so uncritically accepted that it has achieved the status of historical truth without being seriously examined. In essence this myth is very clearly derived from the failure of the anti-war agitation and from Radicals and Socialists who felt that they had been betrayed. The leaders of the cause of righteousness had been deserted by their army. Thus Robert Spence Watson, pro-Boer and President of the National Liberal Federation, believed that the absence of a 'new Midlothian' had been due, not to any inherent weakness of the anti-war agitation, but to the failure of the working class to respond:[1]

> The working men greatly disappointed those of us who believed when we were fighting for an extension of the franchise to the Boroughs and Counties we were taking a step which would go a considerable way towards a more peaceful method of dealing with international disputes than that which was usually adopted.

This facile attitude has lingered to distort our appreciation of the period. The evidence discussed in this study indicates that, contrary to what is often assumed, there existed a considerable, if insufficiently organized, body of working-class dissent to the war. This dissent represented an opposition far exceeding the handful of doctrinally committed Socialists who often acted as the hard-core of local anti-war committees. It has been shown how, for instance, anti-war meetings were the rule and not the exception within the working men's clubs which appear to have provided a willing and numerous audience to any discussions of the war. In working-class Battersea anti-war sentiment had an unchallenged field illustrating the importance of leadership and organization: imperialist meetings could be captured without any difficulty and even Cronwright-Schreiner could address a crowd without interruption.

Yet, if the working class failed to emerge as a decisive and powerful force in opposition to the war, it was not necessarily because they were not in agreement with what Radicals had to say. It was, in fact, because British Radicalism, as a whole, failed to provide either the leadership or the programme that could bring the anti-war sentiment that did exist among working men into focus. The pro-Boer and anti-war agitation was conspicuous by the absence of a dominating, charismatic figure, who, by his

---

[1] P. Corder, *Robert Spence Watson* (London, 1914), pp. 280–1. The ILP and SDF were never quite sure whom to blame for the failure of the anti-war agitation. At times they blamed the peace movement's lack of leadership, but at other times they accepted the Radical interpretation of working-class antagonism. Thus, Keir Hardie offered both as an explanation at different times. See *Labour Leader*, 6 January 1900, p. 3; 13 March 1900, p. 4. But towards the end of the war *Labour Leader* seemed to settle on the working class as the culprits, see 7 December 1901, p. 4; 25 January 1902, p. 1. The SDF represented the same confusion. At first it tended to play up the anti-war sections of the working class, but by the spring of 1901 they had become the main cause of anti-war failure. See *Justice*, 26 May 1900, p. 2; 2 March 1901, p. 1.

personal appeal and political expertise, could transform the agitation from a sectionalist phenomenon into a mass opposition. More significantly, however, was the absence of an anti-war programme that would appeal to working men. The Stop-the-War Committee could only be supported by extreme Evangelicals, its Fundamentalist rhetoric could have no attraction for working men. The South African Conciliation Committee self-consciously resembled a ladies' tea circle; it made no attempt to talk to a mass audience because the passion implied in such an undertaking was antithetical to its very principles. The pro-Boers, failing to capture the Liberal Party and leaderless, were an atomized group of individuals of secondary importance who had no national base from which to operate and could only be effective in their home locales.

What was it, then, that could be defined as the essential ingredients of the working-class attitude to imperialism during this period? It was, in the first place, orientated towards social reform. Their objections were the doctrinal objections of political Radicalism. This was seen, not only in the resolutions of Trades Council and meetings within the clubs, but also in working-class support for pro-Boer members of parliament. It was at this point that Radicalism and working-class political attitudes fused most closely. The pro-Boer MPs were all on the left wing of the Liberal Party, they had all earned their political reputations as being advocates of domestic reform. The identification of Radicalism as a political creed with working-class interests was very strong in all 'thinking' working men. The success of the National Democratic League and the anti-war meetings within the clubs can be explained by the existence, in many clubs, of a small core of working men inspired by political Radicalism.

This can be illustrated in many ways. W. C. Wade, a club-man and Secretary of the Metropolitan Radical Federation, was an exponent of extensive ownership of the land as a measure of social reform, the object being to make everyone more independent—'masters of their own labour power'. He believed that the great danger of Foreign and Colonial entanglements was that they sidetracked the nation from the necessity of social reform.[2] Similarly, the working-class attitude to Rhodes and the

2 'Labour Letter', *Club Life*, 8 April 1899, p. 16.

mine owners had a distinctly Radical dislike of 'speculators' and 'millionaires':[3]

The discreditable gang of South African millionaires and their sub-sidised press and politicians are at their old game of stirring up strife between the Boers and the English nation. At the bottom of all this . . . is the failure of Rhodesia as a money-making speculation . . . he [Rhodes] is prepared to use every means, honest or otherwise, to obtain the gold fields of the Transvaal, so that joined to Rhodesia, the whole thing may be made a paying concern.

It should be noted that there was no very great difference between the Radical peace movement's objections to the war and those of the Socialist press. The close relationship between local peace committees and Socialist organizations, and the sublima-tion of anti-war agitation into a broad Radical-Socialist coalition has already been noted. The same kind of phrases and argu-ments that one could hear from a Radical MP also occur in *Labour Leader* and *Justice*. Thus, the conspiracy theory with Rhodes and Chamberlain as the prime *bêtes noires* recurs. The war is being fought for 'gold-greedy ghouls' who rejoice in the 'thought that every drop of [blood] . . . will be turned into gold for themselves'.[4] Or, more moderately, it was claimed, echoing Wade's sentiments, that 'the Stock Exchange gang . . . have engineered the war . . . [so that] Britain shall destroy the independence of the Boer Republics and pool the riches of the Transvaal to save the bankruptcy of Rhodesia'.[5] Chamberlain was the man primarily responsible for dragging Britain into war. *Justice* claimed that it was his 'nice little war' and the *Labour Leader* that he 'must be held . . . responsible for all that has happened. Millionaires might have worked the press in vain had there not been at hand an unprincipled Minister . . . only too willing to serve his own ends by obeying their behests.'[6]

What is very noticeable is the lack of any Socialist analysis of the war and capitalism. The frame of reference of both papers is that the war was both immoral and criminal—common themes of Radicalism. When the war was termed a 'capitalist war', it

[3] 'Jottings from the Mildmay', *Club Life*, 6 May 1899, p. 14.

[4] *Justice*, 14 October 1899, p. 1. I am grateful for the help of Mr Alan Babler for his analysis of the attitudes of *Justice* and *Labour Leader* during these years.

[5] *Labour Leader*, 18 November 1899, p. 1.

[6] *Justice*, 14 October 1899, p. 1; 24 August 1901, p. 1; *Labour Leader*, 27 April 1901, p. 5.

meant that a few capitalists had 'conspired' to bring it about not that such wars were an integral part of late-nineteenth-century mature capitalism. On only three occasions did either *Justice* or *Labour Leader* take their analysis of the war to any deeper level than that of Liberal-Radicalism.[7] Radical objections to the war, therefore, provided the only comprehensive anti-war attitude. And these, as we have seen were not suited to appeal to working men.

The greatest difference between working-class objections and those of the middle-class pro-Boers was in the emphasis on morality and social reform. These were prime themes in both working-class and middle-class objections to the war, but for the latter the war was wrong because it contravened certain precepts of behaviour which they believed should be observed. To the typical pro-Boer MP the war was diplomatically unnecessary and therefore immoral. Thomas Shaw, MP for Hawick, observed in his autobiography how an analysis of the negotiations preceding the war had led him to the conclusion that it had been avoidable and was therefore unjust.[8] Henry Wilson MP, saw 'no reason for supporting any government in doing wrong'.[9] But it is noticeable that in the appeals to their working-class electorates they either linked the war with the 'selfish intrigues of the Capitalists'[10] and/or emphasized the fact that it detracted from social reform.

This emphasis on morality, seen especially in the Stop-the-War Committee, again helps to explain the failure of the anti-war agitation to make any real impact on the working classes. In general, working-class objections to imperialism were based upon what was a typical working-class characteristic: a concern for the immediate and the material. Translated into political terms this meant social reform which, thus, provided the core of the 'thinking' working man's opposition to the war. The individual reputations of the pro-Boer members of parliament rested, in the main, not on their anti-imperialism but on their advocacy of measures for improving the condition of the people. The

[7] *Justice*, 2 June 1900, p. 4; *Labour Leader*, 6 January 1900, p. 5; 10 August 1901, p. 1.
[8] Thomas Shaw, *Letters to Isabel* (London, 1921), p. 194.
[9] Wilson to Joe Hadfield, Chairman of Holme Liberal Association, 12 October 1900, Wilson Papers, MD. 2500, f. 1.
[10] This was one of the themes of Wilson's election address.

willingness of clubmen to work for the London left-wing Liberals was due to the fact that they were 'sound' on social issues. This explains why the essentially moral appeal of the Radicals was unsuccessful until it was linked with the practical demands of social reform. It provides a key to a generalized formulation of working-class attitudes to the war.

Lacking as we do any adequate direct evidence it is, in the final analysis, fruitless to try to establish that the working classes were either for or against imperialism. Even the evidence of Chapter II has been derived from what was left behind by only a very small proportion of clubmen who not only attended meetings but bothered to write reports of them. The situations examined in Chapters III to V, however, can take us further than the pursuit of the spectre of working-class anti-imperialism. They revealed that the typical working-class reaction was not imperialistic, patriotic or jingoistic. This was illustrated in the imperialism versus social reform contests of the Khaki Election where the latter usually emerged the winner. The study of the jingo crowd illustrated how the instigators of rowdyism were drawn entirely from the respectable classes of society. Indeed, it would appear that the stewards of these meetings were almost solely from working-class organizations. The Socialists were old hands at this work, but the clubs played their part too. Thus, an anti-war meeting at Highbury Corner was threatened with destruction by the local Tories so 'the Radicals took the precaution of mobilising the gymnasium class of the Mildmay Radical Club to act as stewards'.[11] The study of recruitment suggested that motives more basic than patriotism determined the working-class reaction to the 'country in need'. And the clubs, colleges and working-class society of Battersea illustrated the absence of jingoism and the failure of appeals to patriotic activities in the reaction to the rifle-club proposals.

The lack of jingoism in the working-class institutions, the lack of a working-class jingoistic reaction to the Khaki Election, peace meetings and volunteering, should be explained not in terms of opposition to the war, but in terms of indifference. This was noted by H. F. Wyatt, an Imperial South African Association lecturer, who addressed many gatherings in working men's clubs. He recounted that the most common objections to the

[11] T. A. Jackson, *Solo Trumpet* (London, 1953), p. 47.

Empire, 'past, present and prospective', were arguments of 'a violent selfishness'. It was asked: 'What use is the British Empire to me? What does it matter to me what's being done out in Australia, or amongst the blacks anywhere? *All I want is victuals.*'[12] (Italics added.) Similarly, a meeting at Holborn Gladstonian Working Men's Club which discussed 'The Empire, The War, and The Working Man' found that speakers from the audience followed the theme of 'how much stake in the Empire has the working man got?'[13] A Radical, frustrated by the 'contradictory emotions' which moved the average English workman, claimed: 'You can get up a demonstration one Sunday in favour of universal peace, and on the next Sunday you can get up another, which would be attended by the same people in favour of war'.[14] Another observer, writing as if he were one of the 'people from the abyss', emphasized that:[15]

Over our heads pass the forces that make and unmake Emperors. International combats wage in South Africa . . . great problems agitate the minds of nations. . . . To us these are nothing . . . echoes faint . . . as if coming from another world.

In actual terms the political apathy within the clubs was a reflection of this essential indifference. Whilst it was, in part, an inherent consequence of the functions of the working men's clubs, it is significant that an issue which stimulated so much excitement throughout all other sectors of society should have been received so calmly in the clubs and colleges.

Only when some event brought the war within the range of their everyday life and experience did an 'attitude' emerge. The author's grandmother remembers only one example of the war really mattering in the small village society in which she lived: that was when a well-liked local man returned home mentally and physically disabled. It was only then that her father—an employed baker—expressed strong feelings in strong language against the war. It is this which explains the defensively class-conscious reaction, noted especially in Aberdeen, when attacks were made on the conduct of the British soldier; it also explains the combination of anti-war meetings and the reception given to

[12] H. F. Wyatt, 'The Ethics of Empire', *Nineteenth Century*, CCXLII (April 1897), p. 520.　　[13] *Club Life*, 23 March 1901, p. 7.
[14] 'Labour Letter', *ibid.*, 14 January 1899, p. 3.
[15] [C. F. G. Masterman], *From the Abyss* (London, 1902), p. 24.

returning volunteers in the clubs and colleges. These were situations which could be understood and experienced in terms which were almost personal. It further explains the reason why anti-war meetings could be held so successfully in the pre-dominantly 'social' clubs. And it explains, too, the cynicism (another strong working-class characteristic)[16] which was exhibited in the following verses, printed in *Club Life*, satirizing the attempts to catch De Wet:[17]

> When he's on St. Helena stuck,
> We'll shout and scream of British pluck,
> We'll treat our wives for once for luck,
> When we catch De Wet
> ....
>
> Ev'ry Britisher, it's said,
> Will have to stand upon his head,
> The girls will stand a drink instead,
> When we catch De Wet.
>
> We will gather at the Bar,
> When we catch De Wet,
> And kid ourselves we heroes are,
> When we catch De Wet,
> We catch him nearly ev'ry day,
> Oh, have we no trump card to play?
> Why, we shall all be old and grey
> When we catch De Wet.
>
> After many, many tries
> We may catch De Wet;
> Should his soul to Heaven rise,
> We shall catch De Wet;
> He may be caught within a year,
> When we catch De Wet;
> But that's too much to wish, I fear;
> When the Millennium is here,
> Then we'll catch De Wet.

[16] *Ibid.*, p. 22, 'Our first inquiry of any would-be reformer is not What does he want? But What does he get?'

See also, Stephen Reynolds and Bob and Tom Woolley, *Seems So, A Working Class View of Politics* (London, 1913), pp. 6 and 12, where a canvasser urging a working-class family to vote received the reply: 'What's the use? What have 'em ever done for me? . . . Is it any easier to keep out of debt?' And: 'Neither one of the sides is worth voting for, an' if you do vote then that don't make nothing no better.'

[17] *Club Life*, 9 March 1901, p. 14.

It was this essential irrelevance of imperialism which explains the working-class reaction to volunteering; a reaction based generally more upon economic and social circumstances than upon the ethos of patriotism and desire to serve the mother-country. It also explains the rejection of good imperialists at the 1900 election. The imperialism embodied in a candidate like Sir Alfred Newton had little or no meaning to working-class life and society.

Thus, it is evident that the ethos of imperialism which surrounded the Boer War had little impact on the working class. The factors which motivated their attitudes and reactions were completely different from those which we have come to associate with the age of imperialism. One of the most important themes of this study, which illustrates this point, is the marked difference between the working-class and the non-working-class reaction. Those who associated themselves with higher social orders really did volunteer because of the 'needs of the country'. The attraction, to certain social groups, of such concepts as patriotism, was seen by the fact that young clerks were more eager to volunteer than young labourers.[18] This does not mean that the young labourer was opposed to the war, it rather means that he did not respond in the conventionally patriotic manner; the young clerk, with his middle-class pretensions and status, did. Peace meetings were disturbed by those who really identified with the imperialism of the war in South Africa. The contrast between the violent middle-class and the negative working-class reaction to such meetings leads to the conclusion that imperialism as a concept was too tenuous for working-class society to react to in any clearly identifiable manner. Only when it was linked and directly related to their own experience or to their everyday life did it really become an issue. This is perhaps the most important point to emerge from this study. It is not to be assumed, however, that this implies a confirmation of the idea of an 'unthinking' working class. For it cannot be suggested that the irrelevance of imperialism was characteristic of working-class attitudes to other issues that were more immediately related to their experience. Indeed, some American scholarship has illustrated a very high degree of social and political awareness by working-class groups which does suggest the existence

[18] See Table 23.

of a coherent conceptual world view.[19] But what constantly needs to be remembered and what desperately needs scholarly attention, is the difference—hinted at in this book—that exists in the values, thought processes and frames of reference between the 'articulate' and the 'inarticulate'. When trained intellectuals —be they present-day historians or J. A. Hobson—view the Mafeking crowds or the patriotic volunteering, they draw a series of logical conclusions about what it means which are frequently based on a series of false premises born of their own intellectualized conceptions of the issue and what is involved. To the participants it may—and did—mean something entirely different. Thus, we could catalogue very easily the enormities of Mafeking Night and weekend, we could list the opinions of contemporary observers about working-class attitudes to the war, we could look at pictures of the cheering crowds sending off the City Imperial Volunteers. All of this we could do but in reality we still would not have added to our knowledge or appreciation of the Victorian working class.

[19] Jesse Lemisch, 'The Radicalism of the Inarticulate: Merchant Seamen in the Politics of Revolutionary America', in Alfred Young (ed.), *Dissent: Explorations in the History of American Radicalism* (DeKalb, 1968).

Appendix I

The Social Institutes Union and Federation of Working Men's Social Clubs

The Club and Institute Union was not the only organization devoted to the propagation of working men's clubs. Political organizations which ran clubs such as the Conservative Association of Working Men's Clubs have been purposely ignored. The distinction between these and the Liberal and Radical working men's clubs is that the latter were not the result of a party organization. They tended to grow up spontaneously, like the Hatcham Liberal Club, which was the result of a group of Radical railwaymen who used to meet in a public house to discuss politics and who in the late 1870s decided to form their own working men's club.[1] The only other oganizations concerned with clubs were the Social Institutes Union (SIU) and the Federation of Working Men's Social Clubs. Compared with the 1,000-strong Club Union they were minute. The SIU in 1908 claimed eighty branches and in 1910, 100; the Federation of Working Men's Social Clubs in 1900 claimed to have seventy clubs, mostly in London.[2]

The Social Institutes Union was founded by J. B. Paton, a Congregationalist teacher interested in the education and physical well-being of the working class. At Nottingham in 1876 he founded some Elementary Trade and Scientific Schools whose objects were similar to Solly's Trades Guilds of Learning,[3] except that they were directed towards fitting youth for the

---

[1] Information from a letter from the Secretary of Hatcham Liberal Club, 2 February 1967.
[2] *Social Institutes Magazine*, May 1908, p. 4; February 1910, p. 5.
[3] See Henry Solly, *Trades Guilds of Learning* (London, 1873).

trades they were apprenticed to. He realized that evening education, to be attractive, had either to have a direct bearing on daily
occupations or had to include such recreational activities as
musical drill and choral singing.

But Paton, like Solly, was concerned with the way working
people utilized their leisure time. He saw this as the root of the
evil and he realized that the popularity of the public house was
due to the fact that it catered for the need of social fellowship and
recreation.[4] Thus his organization, the Recreative Evening
Schools Association, which had grown out of the earlier body,
proposed to the Charity Commissioners that they should set up
Social Institutes in Board School buildings and group them in
each district round a Polytechnic. They would provide for clubs,
social meetings, recreation, and being attached to a Polytechnic
they would 'thus form a complete and organized system for promoting the higher education, the physical training and social
well-being of the people'.[5] The Charity Commissioners gave
£2,300 to the project and the first one was opened in Islington
in 1894.

The Federation of Working Men's Social Clubs was founded
in 1886, originating from the Anglican mission at Oxford House
in Bethnal Green where its headquarters lay until 1900 when
they moved to the Rose and Shamrock Club in Red Lion Square.
It was never financially very healthy and in 1907 it amalgamated
with the SIU until the latter organization went into dissolution
during the First World War.

Although these two organizations had basically the same ends
as the Club and Institute Union, there were important differences. In the first place they were more strongly educational.
Paton wrote in a letter to the Rev. Thomas Towers of Birmingham in May 1905, pinpointing this difference:[6]

Working Men's Clubs have, by the hundred, succumbed to the peril
which besets them, and even Temperance Clubs have often become
merely pot-houses without the beer, with no uplifting influences in
them. We have always wished to discriminate Social Institutes from
ordinary Working Men's Clubs. . . . The idea of mere 'club' life is not
elevating in England today, but rather the opposite. The phrase

[4] J. L. Paton, *John Brown Paton* (London, 1914), p. 214; *Social Institutes
Magazine*, January 1909, p. 3.
[5] Paton, *op. cit.*, p. 215.   [6] *Ibid.*, p. 220.

'Social Institute' means that there is something higher intended, some educational influence and interest that is to pervade the whole place.

And in the same year he had written to a Mrs Bush giving four factors which should distinguish an Institute from an ordinary club. In the first place, there were to be rules against gambling and bad language enforced by a strong executive composed of members and others interested in the social well-being of the neighbourhood. Secondly, the institute was to be of the nature of a neighbourhood guild where all classes could mix on the basis of brotherhood and fellowship. Thirdly, that there should be some educational interest and desire to promote the higher interests of life. And fourthly, it should 'evoke and organize a spirit of service on the part of all its members' by the formation of such organizations as the Young Men's Brigade of Service.[7]

The second great point of difference was that they do not seem to have gone through the process of 'democratization' that occurred in the Club Union in the 1880s. Paton was still Secretary of the SIU in 1908 and the middle-class influence in the form of churchmen was very strong. They were not working-class organizations, but were still firmly under the control of middle-class patronage and superintendence. Thus, a large number of SIU clubs were associated with the University Settlements of Mansfield House, Oxford House, Browning House. The Presidents of the clubs tended to be local vicars.[8]

This middle-class control is illustrated when, in 1910, it was decided to expand the movement into a field untapped by the Club and Institute Union; the Village Institute. In order to do this it was felt necessary to relax the non-alcoholic rule in relation to these institutes because of their dependence upon the founders of the clubs 'who were very often the owners of the estates in the neighbourhood and best know the requirements of the local people'.[9]

[7] *Ibid.*, p. 223.
[8] *Social Institutes Union Magazine*, November 1908, pp. 5–6.
[9] *Ibid.*, September 1910, pp. 3–4.

Appendix II

The National
Democratic League

There seems to be some slight confusion over the nature of the NDL. G. D. H. Cole, in *British Working Class Politics*, claims that it was in effect an off-shoot of the anti-war movement which temporarily allied the left-wing Liberals with the socialists.[1] In fact the war played no part in its programme. It is true that co-operation between progressives as a result of the war facilitated such an alliance as was found in the NDL, but it was not a result of the anti-war campaign.

For several years *Reynolds News* had been urging that the old party divisions were no longer relevant and that the time had come for electoral and parliamentary reform. This was the purpose of the NDL, which was launched at a convention on 27 October 1900. The declared programme consisted of five points: automatic registration with a three months' residence qualification, one man one vote, election expenses paid by the state, a second ballot, and the abolition of the hereditary principle in the House of Lords. These demands were in the Radical tradition of electoral reform and Thompson consciously appealed to the traditions of the past when he likened the League to the Chartists: 'They were, in a sense, the successors of the Chartists.'[2] It is also significant that the provisional committee had 'proposed that the colours of the new National Democratic Party should be Red, White and Green, *the emblem under which the Reform League marched to victory*'.[3] (Italics added.)

This programme of reform was to be the means of securing labour representation. It was to be the means of getting '400 representatives of the people into Parliament', who would then

[1] G. D. H. Cole, *British Working Class Politics* (London, 1941), p. 166.
[2] *Reynolds News*, 28 October 1900.   [3] *Ibid.*, 14 October 1900.

be able to use their power in the interests of the masses. The traditional radicalism of Thompson's approach can be illustrated by his use of the words 'classes', 'masses' and 'the people'. The 'classes' meant the plutocrats and aristocrats who controlled parliament and governed the country but who had failed: 'They have brought about disaster and humiliation in South Africa. They have obliged us to become the serf of Germany. . . . In China where we had a monopoly of trade, we are now regarded as a fourth class power.' The NDL sought to 'substitute the government of the People for that of the Aristocrats and Pluto-crats. . . . The classes having now miserably failed, let the masses have a chance.'[4] It was an appeal to the traditions and methods of the past.

Its Radicalism was also evident in its precarious left-wing unity. Thompson, no doubt, hoped that the results of this reform would see the creation of a 'Parliamentary group . . . which shall . . . *represent the working classes and the Radical Democracy generally.*'[5] (Italics added.) But it was clear that unity could only be maintained by this sort of electoral reform programme. There was no attempt to pronounce on other political issues, or to draw up a programme of detailed social reform. It was realized that this would immediately cause divisions. Thompson explained this at the convention:[6]

They did not at the moment put before them a detailed programme, because. . . . They would be torn to pieces by difference of opinion on every possible subject. Therefore, they said, simplicity, for simplicity would bring about unity.

This explained the co-operation of the Socialists. At the convention twenty ILP and twelve SDF branches sent delegates and among the labour leaders in attendance were Ben Tillett, Tom Mann and John Ward. Tom Mann, Secretary of the League, explained the strictly limited nature of its purpose in a letter he wrote to *Reynolds News* in reply to complaints that the programme did not include collectivist measures such as the nationalization of the railways:[7]

The real and avowed object of the League is to Democratise the machinery of Parliament that it may be used by the people in the

---

[4] *Ibid.*, 2 December 1900. [5] *Ibid.*, 16 September 1900.
[6] *Ibid.*, 28 October 1900. [7] *Ibid.*

247

people's interest. The National Democratic League does not seek to supersede other organizations which have already well-formulated programmes covering the whole field of economic and social reform, but it does aim at stimulating the lethargic to healthy activity, and to focus attention on essential preliminary measures, which, when secured, will render the other and far-reaching measures comparatively easy of attainment.

The point was that, as Mann's own experience illustrated, parliamentary reform was essential to secure labour representation—or it was one way, no one foresaw the Macdonald-Gladstone pact. Mann, whilst standing 'firmly by his socialism . . . was prepared to work with anyone . . . for the common cause'.[8] What was to happen when this was secured was ignored as it had to be. The sole function of the NDL was to democratize parliament. To this end Thompson urged 'unity in this great effort, for they were all sacrificing something of their principles in order to have a common platform, a platform upon which Socialist and Tory workmen and every other section or complexion could unite'.[9] And it declared itself ready to co-operate with any political organization to secure the aims of the League.

From the outset the clubs were well represented. The General Council of the League included J. Maddy of North Lambeth Liberal and Radical Club, Charles Dean of Willesden Radical, and W. Dellon of North Camberwell Radical Club. And the following clubs were amongst those represented at the convention: Heigham Radical, North Camberwell Progressive, North Camberwell Radical, North Lambeth Radical, South Hackney Reform Club, Plumstead Radical, North Brixton Gladstone Club, Paddington Radical and Willesden Radical.[10]

Thus the League was an attempt to secure parliamentary reform through the medium of the unity of the left, along the lines of the old Reform League. In the strict sense it was not a rival to the Labour Representation Committee; its objects were the same but its methods were the methods of traditional Radicalism. This, of course, was why it failed. There was no demand for this kind of parliamentary reform; enthusiasm could no longer be generated along these lines. And the NDL became just another Radical organization which soon lost its way. The local branches found it impossible to sustain an agitation for

[8] *Ibid.*   [9] *Ibid.*   [10] *Ibid.*, 21 October 1900.

electoral and parliamentary reform and began almost immediately to broaden the scope of their activities far beyond the range envisaged by the Executive Committee and General Council: NDL branches at Peckham Rye and Birmingham organized anti-war meetings.[11] Its short-term success, however, especially in the clubs, showed that the appeal of traditionally Radical methods of political organization were not completely dead amongst the working class. Its long-term failure showed that the traditional objects and aims of the League were without any attraction.

[11] *The Times*, 4 November 1901, p. 6; 18 April 1901, p. 11.

Appendix III

The Pro-Boer Members and
Constituencies in 1900

Member	Constituency	Held seat since	Liberal seat since[1]
W. Abraham	Rhondda	1885	1885
T. Ashton	S. Bedfordshire	1895	1885
J. Barlow	Frome	1892/6	1885–6
			1892–5
			1896
T. Bayley	Chesterfield	1892	1885–6
			1892–
Sir J. T. Brunner	Northwich	1885	1885–6
			1887–
J. Bryce	Aberdeen South	1885	1885
T. Burt	Morpeth	1874	1885
J. Burns	Battersea	1892	1885
W. Caine	Camborne	1900	1885–95
			1900–
R. Cameron	Houghton-le-Spring	1895	1885–6
			1892
F. Cawley	Prestwich	1895	1885
F. Channing	East Northants	1885	1885
R. Cremer	Haggerston	1885	1885–95
			1900
J. Dalziel	Kirkcaldy Districts	1892	1885
J. Ellis	Rushcliffe	1885	1885
S. Evans	Mid-Glamorgan	1890	1885
C. Fenwick	Wansbeck	1885	1885
W. Gurdon	N. Norfolk	1899	1885
Lloyd George	Carnarvon	1890	1885–6
			1890–

[1] The farthest right-hand column denotes the history of the seat, e.g. Frome held by J. Barlow was Liberal from 1885–6 and again from 1892–5 when it was lost, only to be recaptured again in 1896.

Member	Constituency	Held seat since	Liberal seat since
Sir W. Harcourt	West Monmouth	1895	1885
Keir Hardie	Merthyr	1900	1885
C. Seale-Hayne	Mid-Devon	1885	1885
J. Hope	West Fife	1900	1885
J. Jacoby	Mid-Derbyshire	1885	1885
L. Atherley-Jones	N.W. Durham	1885	1885
W. Jones	N. Carnarvon	1895	1885
J. Lewis	Flint	1892	1885
M. Levy	Loughborough	1900	1885–6 1892
H. Labouchere	Northampton	1880	1885
J. Logan	S. Leicestershire	1891	1885–6 1891
T. Lough	W. Islington	1892	1885–6 1892
C. Morley	Brecknockshire	1895	1885
J. Morley	Montrose	1896	1885
A. E. Pease	Cleveland	1897	1885
B. Pickard	Normanton	1885	1885
D. Pirie	Aberdeen North	1896	1885
R. Price	Norfolk East	1892	1892
A. Priestley	Grantham	1900	1885–6 1900–
R. Reid	Dumfries	1880	1885
B. Roberts	Eifion	1885	1885
J. H. Roberts	Denbighshire	1892	1885
C. Schwann	North Manchester	1886	1885
C. P. Scott	Leigh	1895	1885
T. Shaw	Hawick	1892	1885
J. Sinclair	Forfarshire	1897	1885–6 1892–4 1895–
S. Smith	Flintshire	1886	1885
D. A. Thomas	Merthyr	1888	1885
C. H. Wilson	Hull West	1885	1885
H. J. Wilson	Holmfirth	1885	1885
J. H. Wilson	Mid-Durham	1890	1885
J. Weir	Ross and Cromarty	1892	1885
J. H. Yoxall	Nottingham West	1895	1885–92 1895

Appendix IV

Social Composition
of Battersea

This table is compiled from the *Census of the County of London* (*Accounts and Papers*, Vol. CXIX), Cd. 875 (1902), Table 35, pp. 98–9. It includes only males over the age of ten who were at work. In the Census the occupation of Females was also listed but in a separate column. These have been ignored.

Non-working class		Working class	
Occupation	*Number*	*Trade/occupation*	*Number*
Professional	3,391	Domestic service	1,518
Commercial, e.g. agent, clerk	4,994	Conveyance of men and goods, e.g. railwayman	5,701
Retired, pensioner	1,282	Metal worker	4,172
Dealer	4,945	Building trade	8,418
Chemist	141	Wood trade	1,292
Wine merchant	55	Leather, skin trade	314
Government worker	2,202	Paper trade, e.g. printing	1,947
		Textiles	90
		Dress trade, e.g. tailor, boot and shoe	1,686
		Precious-metal craftsman, watchmaker, jeweller, etc.	1,184
		Mine and quarry worker	102
		Agricultural, gardener etc.	187
		Explosives, oil, soap worker	413
		Food worker	889
		Tobacco manufacture	24

Non-working class		Working class	
Occupation	*Number*	*Trade/occupation*	*Number*
		Barman and others in inn and hotel service	556
		Undefined labourer	4,293
TOTALS	17,010		32,786

Certain categories have been condensed from the Census, for example, all those listed as Dealer under various categories in the Census have been brought together under one heading.

Appendix V

Social Composition
of CIV

Non-working class		Working class	
Occupation	*Number*	*Occupation*	*Number*
Accountant	3	Baker	5
Actuary	1	Blacksmith	8
Agent	11	Bookbinder	16
Architect	15	Boot maker	18
Artist	5	Box maker	9
Auctioneer	1	Brass worker	15
Banker	4	Bricklayer	13
Barrister	43	Builder	32
Broker	3	Candle maker	1
Civil service	31	Carpenter	86
Clerk	606	Carrier and carman	5
College principal	1	Cloth maker	1
Customs officer	3	Collar maker	3
Dentist	5	Colourmaker	1
Farmer	7	Compositor	29
Independent	28	Confectioner	1
Journalist	1	Cook	9
Librarian	2	Cooper	3
Medical	12	Cutter	2
Merchant	21	Cycle maker	1
Metallurgist	1	Draper	49
Pianist	9	Dyer	2
Publisher	3	Electrician, engineer	74
Retailer	82	Engraver	4
Salesman	10	Fitter	17
Schoolmaster	5	Folder	1
Solicitor	23	Fretworker	4
Stationer	21	Gamekeeper	1

Non-working class		Working class	
Occupation	*Number*	*Occupation*	*Number*
Stockbroker	4	Gardener	13
Stock Exchange	7	Gas fitter	6
Student	12	Gas worker	4
Surveyor	7	Groom	10
Traveller	29	Gun maker	3
		Harness plater	2
		Hatter	1
		Horse keeper	1
		Jeweller	10
		Joiner	9
		Labourer	87
		Lamp maker	1
		Leather cutter	5
		Liftman	2
		Locksmith	1
		Machinist	10
		Mechanic	5
		Messenger	12
		Metal spinner	1
		Milkman	1
		Miscellaneous	45
		Mosaic worker	1
		Packer	12
		Painter	39
		Pebble cutter	1
		Pen maker	2
		Photographer	5
		Plasterer	6
		Plate worker	3
		Plumber	26
		Polisher	3
		Postman	24
		Printer	37
		Saddler	4
		Shoeing smith	3
		Shop assistant	4
		Silk cutter	1
		Silk mercer	1
		Silversmith	10
		Slater	2

Non-working class		Working class	
Occupation	Number	Occupation	Number
		Soap worker	1
		Stick mounter	2
		Stonemason	6
		Storekeeper	2
		Tailor	23
		Tea blender	1
		Tinman	2
		Umbrella maker	1
		Upholsterer	7
		Varnish tester	1
		Warehouseman	75
TOTALS	1,006		943

From *Reports of C.I.V.*, *op. cit.*, pp. 39–41.

Appendix VI

Social Composition of the Imperial Yeomanry

| Non-working class | | Working class | |
Occupation	Number	Occupation	Number
Agent	233	Bricklayer	221
Artist, actor	115	Brick worker	8
Auctioneer	61	Builder	194
Butcher	861	Carman, cab driver	439
Cab proprietor	21	Carpenter	392
Chemist	99	Carter, carrier	242
Commerce	3,117	Civil engineer	68
Commercial traveller	590	Decorator	139
Contractor	26	Dock worker	18
Dealer and merchant	461	Draper, tailor	578
Draughtsman	71	Drink trade	504
Farmer	2,179	Driver	102
Gentleman	1,724	Electrical engineer	73
Grocer	423	Electrician	145
Hotel proprietor	21	Engineer	882
Ironmonger	124	Engine keeper	29
Journalist	46	Farm labourer	269
Manufacturer	79	Farrier	241
Professional	742	Food trade	454
Stockbroker	69	Foreman	76
Student	286	Furnishing trade	7
		Groom and servant	2,325
		Hairdresser	85
		Horse keeper	110
		Hosiery, cloth trade	103
		Iron worker	89
		Jeweller	60
		Labourer	1,944

Non-working class		Working class	
Occupation	*Number*	*Occupation*	*Number*
		Machine hand	79
		Machinist	55
		Mechanic	76
		Mechanical engineer	37
		Miller	48
		Miner	391
		Packer	72
		Painter	305
		Plumber	305
		Policeman	187
		Porter	226
		Printer	196
		Railwayman	193
		Scaffolder	14
		Shop assistant	432
		Skilled craftsman	2,440
		Smith	743
		Soldier	210
		Steel worker	20
		Telegraphist	43
		Textile worker	106
TOTALS	11,348		15,956

Compiled from Imperial Yeomanry Attestation Forms. The discrepancy between the total Imperial Yeomanry figures given in the *Annual Report of the Inspector-General of Recruiting for 1902* and the total given here is due essentially to four factors:

1 There is missing from this table a Miscellaneous category totalling almost 1,300 consisting of occupational entries too diverse and numerically insignificant to form clusters of any importance.
2 Many actual Attestation Forms are missing; they were returned to the War Office when the men claimed pensions in the 1930s and thereafter disappeared.
3 The Returns themselves are sometimes inaccurate, thus, the 1902 figure given by the Inspector-General of Recruiting is at marked variance with the number of Attestation Forms found.
4 The difference between this total and that in the distribution table is a result of scattered recruitment during the nine months of each year not accounted for in the tables. It amounted to about 700 over the three years.

Appendix VII

Recruits of Selected Occupations
December – March each Year of the War

Professionals	1899	1900	1901	1902
January		303	68	54
February		89	80	4
March		55	34	2
December	22			
TOTALS	22	474	186	70

Students	1899	1900	1901	1902
January		94	28	29
February		51	9	
March		33	25	4
December	5			
TOTALS	5	183	66	34

Gentlemen	1899	1900	1901	1902
January		805	104	125
February		206	129	8
March		197	43	8
December	64			
TOTALS	64	1,208	276	141

Labourers	1899	1900	1901	1902
January		110	161	783
February		67	604	14
March		42	426	
December	12			
TOTALS	12	219	1,191	797

Carpenters	1899	1900	1901	1902
January		14	37	104
February		18	99	3
March		13	67	1
December	4			
TOTALS	4	45	203	108

Smiths and saddlers	1899	1900	1901	1902
January		146	50	168
February		42	143	18
March		22	57	30
December	4			
TOTALS	4	210	250	226

Bibliography

A. UNPUBLISHED MATERIAL

1 *British Library of Political and Economic Science*
   Broadhurst Collection
   Courtney Collection
   L.R.C. Minutes and Letters
   Solly Collection
2 *British Museum*
   John Burns Papers
   Campbell-Bannerman Papers
   Herbert Gladstone Papers
   Letters of Captain C. Lafone
   J. A. Spender Papers
3 *Guildhall Library*
   CIV Collection
4 *Islington Public Library*
   North London Socialist Club Minutes, 1896–1902
5 *By courtesy of Mr Julius Jacobs*
   London Trades Council Minutes, 1896–1902
6 *Leeds City Library*
   Leeds Liberal Federation Annual Reports, 1896-1902 Type-script MSS.
7 *Leeds University, Brotherton Library*
   Mattison Collection
8 *Public Records Office*
   Buller Papers, W.O. 132
   Colonial Office Files, 427 and 428. 'Resolution on the State of Affairs between South African Republic and Great Britain'
   Home Office Files, 45
   Metropolitan Police Papers, Mepol. 5
   War Office Papers: 32, Miscellaneous
                    128, Imperial Yeomanry Attestation Forms
9 *Sheffield Central Library*
   H. J. Wilson Papers

261

10 *By courtesy of Viscount Harcourt*
Harcourt Papers

B. PUBLISHED MATERIAL

1 *Official Publications*

(a) Accounts and Papers
Annual Returns of the Volunteer Corps of Great Britain:
1899, Vol. XLIX (1900)
1900, Vol. XL (1901)
1901, Vol. LVIII (1902)
1902, Vol. LI (1904)
Census Reports of England and Wales, Vols CVIII–CXX (1902)
General Annual Report of the British Army for Year 1902, Vol. XXXVIII (1903)
Report of the Committee on the Organization, Arms, and Equipment of the Yeomanry Force, Vol. XL (1901)
(b) Reports
Annual Reports of the Inspector-General of Recruiting:
1899, Vol. X (1900)
1900, Vol. IX (1901)
1901, Vol. X (1902)
1902, Vol. XI (1903)
Royal Commission on Militia and Volunteers, Vols XXX–XXXI (1904)
Royal Commission on Physical Deterioration, Vol. XXXII (1904)
(c) Hansard, *Parliamentary Debates*, 4th Series, 1900
(d) Board of Trade, *Labour Gazette*, 1899–1902

2 *Newspapers and Periodicals*

(a) Newspapers

Ashton-under-Lyme Herald
Birmingham Daily Mail
Bradford Daily Argus
Bradford Labour Echo
Brighton Herald
Caithness Courier
Camden and Kentish Towns, Hampstead, Highgate,
Holloway, and St Pancras Gazette
City Press
Clapham Observer
Cornish Post and Mining News
Crewe Guardian
Daily Free Press (Aberdeen)

Darlington and
    Stockton Times
Derby Daily
    Telegraph
Derby Express
Dover Express
Dover Observer
Dundee Advertiser
East End News
East London Advertiser
Eastern Post and City
    Chronicle
Edinburgh Evening
    Despatch
Edinburgh Evening News
Evening Express
    (Edinburgh)
Fifeshire Advertiser
Financial News
Gateshead Daily
    Chronicle
Glasgow Evening News
Grantham Times
Hackney Express and
    Shoreditch Observer
Hastings and St Leonards
    Observer
Keble's Margate and
    Ramsgate Gazette
Hull Daily News
Labour Leader
Leicester Daily
    Post
Leigh Chronicle
Liskeard Weekly
    Mercury
Liverpool Daily Post
Manchester Guardian
Mercury (Hackney)
Mid-Surrey Gazette
Middleton Guardian
Midland Free Press
Morning Leader

Morpeth Herald
North Briton Daily
    Mail
Nottingham Daily
    Chronicle
Nottingham Daily
    Express
Northampton Daily
    Chronicle
Northampton Daily
    Reporter
Northampton Mercury
Penistone Express
Peoples Journal
    (Aberdeen)
Reynolds News
Rochdale Labour News
Scarborough Evening
    News
Scarborough Mercury
Scarborough Post
The Scotsman
Sheffield and Rotherham
    Independent
Sheffield Daily Telegraph
Southwark and Bermondsey
    Reporter
South London Chronicle
South-Western Star
Star
Stockport Borough
    Express
Sunderland Herald
    and Daily Post
The Times
Tottenham and Stamford Hill
    and Stoke Newington Gazette
Tunbridge Wells Gazette
Walsall Free Press
Walthamstow Reporter
West Ham Citizen
Western Morning News
Yorkshire Post

(b) Periodicals

Bermondsey Record
Cheltenham Working Men's
  College Magazine
Club and Institute
  Journal
Club Life
Club World
Concord
Daylight
Herald of Peace
House and Home
I.L.P. News
Iron and Coal Trades
  Review
London Scottish
  Regimental Gazette
London Trades and
  Labour Gazette
Morley College
  Magazine
New Age

Our Magazine
Quarterly Newssheet of the
  Federation of Working
  Men's Social Clubs
Regiment
Social Institutes
  Magazine
Toynbee Record
Vagrant
Volunteer Record
  and Shooting News
Volunteer Service
  Gazette
War Against War
War Against War
  in South Africa
The Working Man
Working Men's College
  Calendars
Working Men's College
  Journal

3 Non-official Publications

(a) Pamphlets

Battersea Stop-the-War Committee. *The Capitalist's War. Battersea's Plea for Peace.* London: Battersea Stop-the-War Committee, 1902.

Clark, Dr G. B. *Speech on the Transvaal Crisis.* London: the Transvaal Committee, July 1899.

Courtney, Leonard. *The Competition Among Nations.* Edinburgh: Young Scot's Publication Department, 1902.

— *Present Difficulties in Political Thinking and Acting.* Edinburgh: Young Scot's Publication Department, 1902.

— *The War in South Africa.* Birmingham: Joseph Sturge, 1900.

Ellis, J. E. *Speeches on South African Affairs.* J. E. Ellis, May 1900.

Gooch, G. P., *The War and Its Causes.* London: Transvaal Committee, 1899.

Harrison, Frederic. *The State of Siege.* London: SACC Pamphlet No. 92, n.d.

Imperial South African Association, *Speech by Geoffrey Drage at Derby 7 December 1899*. London: Imperial South African Association, Pamphlet No. 21, 1899.

Liberal Party. *Great Britain and the Transvaal*. London: Liberal Publication Department, 1899.

— *A Misunderstood Despatch*. London: Liberal Publication Department, 1899.

— *The Transvaal Question, Imperialism, and Social Reform*. London: Liberal Publication Department, 1899.

— *The Transvaal War, Temperance, and Housing*. London: Liberal Publication Department, 1899.

Manchester Transvaal Committee, *Pamphlets 1–16*. Manchester: Manchester Transvaal Committee, 1899.

Marks, Alfred. *The Churches and The War in South Africa*. London: New Age Press, 1905.

Maude, Aylmer. *War and Patriotism*. London: Grant Richards, 1900.

Metropolitan Radical Federation. *Programme*. London: Metropolitan Radical Federation, 1897.

Pease, Alfred E. *Imperial Justice*. London: National Press Agency, March 1900.

Shaw, Thomas. *Gladstone: A Living Teacher*. Edinburgh: Young Scot's Publication Department, 1902.

South African Conciliation Committee. *List of Names and Addresses*. London: SACC, March 1900.

— *Pamphlets Nos. 1–62*. London: SACC, 1900–2.

Stead, W. T. *The Candidates of Cain: A Catechism for the Constituencies*. London: Stop-the-War Committee, 1900.

— *Are We In The Right? An Appeal to Honest Men*. London: Review of Reviews Office, 1899.

— *Hell Let Loose*. London: Stop-the-War Committee, 1899.

— *Shall I Slay My Brother Boer?* London: Review of Reviews Office, 1899.

— *The Truth About the War in Plain Answers to Straight Questions*. London: Stop-the-War Committee, 1900.

Stop-the-War Committee. *Manifesto*. London: Stop-the-War Committee, 1900.

Transvaal Committee. *List of Preliminary Committee*. London: Transvaal Committee, 1899.

(b) Reports and Proceedings

Battersea Borough Council. *Annual Reports*. 1900–2.

Battersea Trades and Labour Council. *Annual Report 1902*.

Imperial South African Association. *Annual Reports.* 1897–8, 1899–1903.

Independent Labour Party. *Conference Reports.* 1899–1902.

London Trades Council. *Annual Reports.* 1896, 1898–1900.

Morley College. *Annual Reports.* 1891–1902.

National Rifle Association. *Proceedings.* 1899–1902.

National Union of Boot and Shoe Operatives. *Monthly Reports.* 1899–1902.

Newton, Alfred. *Reports on Raising, Organizing etc. of C.I.V. to South Africa.* London: Alfred Newton, 1903.

Northampton Trades Council. *Annual Report and Balance Sheet.* 1899–1902.

Sheffield Federated Trades Council. *Annual Reports.* 1892, 1894–5, 1898.

Stop-the-War Committee. *Report and Statement of Accounts.* London: Stop-the-War Committee, January 1901.

Transvaal Committee. *Report of Six Months' Work.* London: Transvaal Committee, 1900.

Working Men's Club and Institute Union. *Annual Reports.* 1898–1902.

4 *Memoirs and Biographies*

Anderson, Mosa. *H. J. Wilson. Fighter for Freedom.* London: James Clarke, 1953.

Anon. *Reminiscences of a Stonemason.* London: John Murray, 1908.

Armstrong, G. *Richard Acland Armstrong.* London: Philip Green, 1906.

Ashby, M. K. *Joseph Ashby of Tysoe 1854–1919.* Cambridge: Cambridge University Press, 1961.

Atherley-Jones, L. *Looking Back: Reminiscences of a Political Career.* London: Witherly, 1925.

Barclay, Tom. *Memoirs and Medleys.* Leicester: Edgar Backus, 1934.

Barnett, H. *Canon Barnett: His Life, Work, and Friends,* 2 vols. London: John Murray, 1918.

Bassett, Arthur Tilney. *Life of J. E. Ellis.* London: Macmillan, 1914.

Bourne, G. *Memoirs of a Surrey Labourer.* London: Duckworth, 1907.

Broadhurst, Henry. *From a Stonemason's Bench to the Treasury Bench.* London: Hutchinson, 1901.

Bryant, H. *Autobiography of a Military Great Coat Being the Story of the 1st Norfolk Active Service Company.* London: Jarrold, 1907.

Burt, Thomas. *Thomas Burt, Pitman and Privy Councillor: An Autobiography.* London: T. Fisher Unwin, 1914.

Channing, Francis Allison. *Memories of Midland Politics 1885–1918.* London: Constable, 1918.

Clarke, Sir Edward. *The Story of My Life.* London: John Murray, 1918.

Corder, P. *Robert Spence Watson.* London: Headley, 1914.

Crane, Denis. *Sir Robert W. Perks.* London: Culley, 1909.

Dent, J. J. *Hodgson Pratt, Reformer.* Manchester: Cooperative Union, 1932.

Dewar, Thomas F. *With the Scottish Yeomanry.* Arbroath: T. Buncle, 1901.

Evans, H. *Sir Randal Cremer. His Life and Work.* London: T. Fisher Unwin, 1909.

Fisher, H. A. L. *James Bryce,* 2 vols. London: Macmillan, 1922.

FitzGibbon, Maurice. *Arts Under Arms. A University Man in Khaki.* London: Longmans, 1901.

Gallagher, Michael. *Mick Gallagher at the Front.* Liverpool: Mac's Sugar House Press, 1900.

Gardiner, A. G. *The Life of Sir William Harcourt,* 2 vols. London: Constable, 1923.

Gooch, G. P. *Frederic Mackarness. A Brief Memoir.* London: Methuen, 1922.

— *Life of Lord Courtney.* London: Macmillan, 1920.

— *Under Six Reigns.* London: Longmans, 1958.

Gould, F. J. *Life Story of a Humanist.* London: Watts, 1923.

Hammond, J. L. *C. P. Scott.* London: Bell, 1934.

Hart, Heber L. *Reminiscences and Reflections.* London: John Lane, the Bodley Head Press, 1939.

Hirst, F. W. *In the Golden Days.* London: Muller, 1947.

Hobson, S. G. *Pilgrim to the Left. The Memoirs of a Modern Revolutionist.* London: Edward Arnold, 1938.

[Hughes, D. P.] *Life of Hugh Price Hughes.* London: Hodder and Stoughton, 1904.

Hyndman, H. M. *Further Reminiscences.* London: Macmillan, 1912.

Jackson, T. A. *Solo Trumpet.* London: Lawrence and Wishart, 1953.

James, Robert Rhodes. *Rosebery.* London: Weidenfeld & Nicolson, 1963.

Jarvis, C. S. *Half a Life.* London: John Murray, 1943.

Jeyes, Samuel Henry and How, F. D. *Life of Sir Howard Vincent.* London: George Allen, 1912.

Kent, William. *John Burns: Labour's Lost Leader.* London: Williams & Norgate, 1950.

MacDonald, Sir J. H. A. *Fifty Years of It. The Experiences and Struggles of a Volunteer of 1859.* London: J. R. Blackwood, 1909.

Masterman, N. C. *John Malcolm Ludlow. The Builder of Christian Socialism.* Cambridge: Cambridge University Press, 1962.

Mills, J. Saxon. *Sir Edward Cook K.B.E.* London: Constable, 1921.

Morgan, J. H. *John Viscount Morley.* London: John Murray, 1924.

Nevinson, Henry W. *Changes and Chances.* London: Nesbit, 1923.

Newton, John. *W. S. Caine. A Biography.* London: Nesbit, 1907.

Paton, John Lewis. *John Brown Paton. A Biography.* London: Hodder & Stoughton, 1914.

Pease, Sir Alfred E. *Elections and Recollections.* London: John Murray, 1932.

Peel, Sydney. *Trooper 8008 I.Y.* London: Longmans, 1903.

Perks, Sir Robert W. *Notes for an Autobiography.* London: the Epworth Press, 1936.

[Rankin, Reginald.] *A Subaltern's Letters to His Wife.* London: Longmans, 1901.

Rathbone, Eleanor. *William Rathbone: A Memoir.* London: Macmillan, 1904.

Reitz, Denis. *Commando.* London: Faber & Faber, 1929.

Robson, S. E. *Joshua Rowntree.* London: George Allen & Unwin, 1916.

Rogers, Frederick. *Life, Labour and Literature.* London: Smith, Elder, 1917.

Rolleston, Lady C. E. M. *Yeoman Service.* London: Smith, Elder, 1901.

Rose-Innes, C. *With Paget's Horse to the Front.* London: John Macqueen, 1901.

Ross, P. T. *A Yeoman's Letters.* London: Simpkin, Marshall, 1901.

Russell, G. W. E. (ed.) *Sir Wilfred Lawson: A Memoir.* London: Smith, Elder, 1909.

Sanders, W. S. *Early Socialist Days.* London: L. & V. Woolf, 1927.

Shaw, Thomas. *Letters to Isabel.* London: Cassell, 1921.

Smith, G. H. *With the Scottish Rifle Volunteers to the Front.* Edinburgh: William Hodge, 1901.

Smith, Samuel. *My Life Work.* London: Hodder & Stoughton, 1902.

Solly, Reverend Henry. *These Eighty Years, or, The Story of An Unfinished Life,* 2 vols. London: Simpkin & Marshall, 1893.

Soutter, Francis William. *Fights for Freedom.* London: T. Fisher Unwin, 1925.

Spender, J. A. *Life of Sir Henry Campbell-Bannerman,* 2 vols. London: Hodder & Stoughton, 1923.

— *Sir Robert Hudson: A Memoir.* London: Cassell, 1920.

— and Asquith, C. *Life of Lord Oxford and Asquith*. London: Hutchinson, 1932.

Spurgin, Karl B. *On Active Service with Northumberland and Durham Yeomanry*. London and Newcastle: Walter Scott Publishing Co., 1902.

Stewart, W. *J. Keir Hardie*. London: ILP Publishing Department, 1925.

Thompson, L. *Robert Blatchford. Portrait of an Englishman*. London: Gollancz, 1951.

Thorold, Algar. *The Life of Henry Labouchere*. London: Constable, 1913.

Tsuzuki, Chushichi. *H. M. Hyndman and British Socialism*. London: Oxford University Press, 1961.

Turner, Ben. *About Myself*. London: Toulmin, 1929.

Walker Smith, Derek and Clarke, E. *Life of Sir Edward Clarke*. London: Thornton Butterworth, 1939.

Watson, Aaron. *A Great Labour Leader. The Life of Thomas Burt*. London: Brown, Langham, 1908.

Watson, Robert Spence. *Joseph Skipsey: A Memoir*. London: T. Fisher Unwin, 1909.

Webb, Beatrice. *Our Partnership*. London: Longmans, 1948.

Wetton, T. C. *Reminiscences of the 34th Battalion I.Y.* London: Sidey & Bartlett, 1908.

Whyte, Frederic. *Life of W. T. Stead*, 2 vols. London: Jonathan Cape, 1925.

Wyndham, Guy. *Letters of George Wyndham*, 2 vols. Edinburgh: privately published, 1915.

5 Other Works

Adderley, J. *In Slums and Society*. London: T. Fisher Unwin, 1916.

Anon. *Working Men and Women*. London: Tinsley Bros, 1879.

Altick, Richard Daniel. *The English Common Reader. A Social History of the Mass Reading Public. 1800–1900*. Chicago: Chicago University Press, 1957.

Appleton, F. *The Volunteer Service Company (1st S. Lancashire Regt.) In South Africa during the Boer War*. Warrington: Mackie, 1901.

Barker, A. G. *1862–1932, Seventy Years a Club*. London: Walthamstow Working Men's Club and Institute, 1933.

Barnett, Canon Saul A. *Religion and Politics*. London: Wells Gardner, Darton, 1911.

Baylen, J. O. 'W. T. Stead and the Boer War: The Irony of Idealism', *Canadian Historical Review*, Vol. 40 (1959), pp. 304–14.

Beales, A. C. *The History of Peace*. London: Bell, 1931.

Bealey, F. 'Les Travaillistes et la Guerre des Boers', *Le Mouvement Social*. October-December 1963.

Bell, Lady F. Moberley. *At the Works*. London: Edward Arnold, 1907.

Besant, Sir Walter. *East London*. London: Chatto & Windus, 1901.

Birkin, Lt. Col., H. L. *History of 3rd Regiment Imperial Yeomanry*. Nottingham: J. J. Vice, 1905.

Blackwood, J. R. *The Soul of F. R. Robertson*. New York: Harper Bros., 1947.

Blunt, W. S. *My Diaries*, 2 vols. London: Martin Becker, 1919–20.

Booth, Charles. *Life and Labour of the People in London*, 15 vols, 2nd ed. revised. London: Macmillan, 1902–3.

Bourne, George. *The Bettesworth Book. Talks with a Surrey Peasant*. London: Lamley, 1901.

Briggs, Asa. *Victorian Cities*. London: Odhams, 1963.

Buckley, K. D. *Trades Unionism in Aberdeen*. Aberdeen University Series, No. 135. Aberdeen: Aberdeen University Press, 1955.

Bull, P. B. *God and Our Soldiers*, 3rd ed. London: Mowbray, 1914.

Canetti, Elias. *Crowds and Power*. London: Gollancz, 1962.

Clarke, Sir Edward. *Selected Speeches*. London: Smith, Elder, 1908.

Cole, G. D. H. *British Working Class Politics*. London: George Routledge & Sons, 1941.

Cole, G. D. H. and Postgate, Raymond. *The Common People 1746–1946*. London: Methuen, 1960.

Comer, W. *The Story of the 34th Company (Middlesex) Imperial Yeomanry*. London: T. Fisher Unwin, 1902.

Cooke, J. H. *5000 Miles with the Cheshire Yeomanry*. Warrington: Mackie, 1913–14.

Cornford, John. 'The Transformation of Late Nineteenth Century Conservatism', *Victorian Studies*, Vol. VII (May 1963).

Courtney, Leonard. *Cornish Granite: Selections from Courtney's Writings*. London: Leonard Parsons, 1925.

Cronwright-Schreiner, S. C. *The Land of Free Speech*. London: New Age Press, 1906.

Curtis, Lionel and Lloyd, Bertram. *One Thousand Miles with C.I.V.* London: Methuen, 1901.

Davies, John Llewelyn (ed.) *The Working Men's College*. London: Macmillan, 1904.

Edwards, Joseph (ed.) *The Reformer's Yearbook for 1901*. Wallasey: Joseph Edwards, 1901.

Frazer, Peter. *Joseph Chamberlain: Empire and Radicalism 1868–1914*. London: Cassell, 1966.

Freeman, Benson. *The Yeomanry of Devon*. London: St Catherine's Press, 1927.

Galbraith, John S. 'The Pamphlet Campaign of the Boer War', *Journal of Modern History*, Vol. XXIV (June, 1952), pp. 111–26.

Gardiner, F. J. *The Fiftieth Birthday of a Model Institute 1864–1914*. Wisbech: Gardiner, 1914.

Gray, F. *The Confessions of a Candidate*. London: M. Hopkinson, 1925.

Grossmith, George and W. *The Diary of a Nobody*. Penguin Modern Classics, No. 510. London: Penguin Books, 1965.

Hale, M. *Volunteer Soldiers*. London: Kegan Paul, Trench, Trubner, 1900.

Haley, Elie. *Imperialism and the Rise of Labour (1895–1905)*, 2nd ed. London: Ernest Benn, 1961.

Hall, B. T. *Our Fifty Years: The Story of the Working Men's Club and Institute Union*. London: Working Men's Club and Institute Union, 1912.

— *Working Men's Club. Why and How to Establish and Manage Them*. London: Working Men's Club and Institute Union, 1912.

— (ed.) *Working Men's Social Clubs and Educational Institutes*, 2nd ed. London: Simpkin & Marshall, 1904.

Harrison, J. F. C. *A History of the Working Men's College 1854–1954*. London: Routledge & Kegan Paul, 1954.

Hirst, F. W., Hammond, J. L. and Murray, Gilbert. *Liberalism and the Empire: Three Essays*. London: R. Brimley Johnson, 1900.

Hobsbawm, E. J. *Labouring Men. Studies in the History of Labour*. London: Weidenfeld & Nicolson, 1964.

Hobson, J. A. *The Psychology of Jingoism*. London: Grant Richards, 1901.

— *The War in South Africa*. London: James Nesbit, 1900.

— *Imperialism. A Study*, 3rd ed. London: George Allen & Unwin, 1961.

Hodson, A. L. *Letters from a Settlement*. London: Edward Arnold, 1909.

Hope, James F. *A History of the 1900 Parliament*, 2 vols. London: J. R. Blackwood, 1907.

Hurst, M. E. *The Quakers in War and Peace*. London: the Swarthmore Press, 1923.

Igglesden, C. *History of the East Kent Volunteers*. Ashford: Kentish Express, 1899.

Jenkin, A. K. *The Cornish Miner*. London: George Allen & Unwin, 1947.

Kent, C. R. *The English Radicals*. London: Longmans, 1899.

Layton, W. T., and Crowther, G. *Introduction to the Study of Prices.* London: Macmillan, 1938.

Levi, Leone. *Wages and Earnings of the Working Classes.* London: John Murray, 1867.

Lockwood, D. *The Black Coated Worker.* London: George Allen & Unwin, 1958.

MacCalmont, F. H. *Parliamentary Poll-Book of All Elections,* 7th ed. Nottingham: Thomas Forman & Sons, 1910.

Maccoby, S. *English Radicalism 1886–1914.* George Allen & Unwin, 1953.

Maclean, A. H. *Public Schools and the War in South Africa.* London: Edward Stanford, 1903.

Markino, Yoshio. *A Japanese Artist in London.* London: Chatto & Windus, 1911.

Marriott, William Thackeray. *Some Real Wants and Some Legitimate Claims of The Working Classes.* London: Mainwaring, 1860.

[Masterman, C. F. G.] *From the Abyss.* London: R. Brimley Johnson, 1902.

— (ed.) *The Heart of the Empire.* London: T. Fisher Unwin, 1901.

Mayhew, Henry. *A Report Concerning the Trade and Hours of Closing among Unlicensed Victualling Establishments open for the Unrestricted Sale of Beer, Wine and Spirits at certain so-called 'Working Men's Clubs'.* London: H. Mayhew, 1872.

O'Leary, Cornelius. *The Elimination of Corrupt Practices at British Elections 1868–1911.* Oxford: Clarendon Press, 1962.

Orr, A. S. *Scottish Yeomanry in South Africa. A Record of the Work and Experiences of the Glasgow and Ayrshire Companies.* Glasgow: James Hedderwick & Sons, 1901.

Pearse, Henry H. S. *The History of Lumsden's Horse.* London: Longmans, 1903.

Pelling, Henry. *A Social Geography of British Elections 1885–1910.* London: Macmillan, 1967.

Peppin, T. S. *Club-Land of the Toiler.* London: J. M. Dent, 1895.

Poirier, Philip. *The Advent of the Labour Party.* London: George Allen & Unwin, 1958.

Pollard, Sydney. *A History of Labour in Sheffield.* Liverpool: Liverpool University Press, 1959.

— 'Wages and Earnings in the Sheffield Trades 1851–1914', *Yorkshire Bulletin of Economic and Social Research,* Vol. VI (1954).

— Owen, J., Mendelson, J., and Thornes, V. M. *Sheffield Trades and Labour Council 1858–1958.* Sheffield Trades and Labour Council, n.d.

Pratt, Hodgson. *Notes of a Tour Among the Clubs: Warnings and*

Examples. London: Working Men's Club and Institute Union, 1872.

Pyrah, G. B. *Imperial Policy and South Africa 1902–1910*. Oxford: Clarendon Press, 1955.

Reynolds, Stephen and Bob and Tom Woolley. *Seems So. A Working Class View of Politics*. London: Macmillan, 1911.

Richards, Denis. *Offspring of the Vic*. London: Routledge & Kegan Paul, 1958.

Robertson, J. M. *The Meaning of Liberalism*. London: Grant Richards, 1912.

Robertson-Scott, J. M. *Life and Death of a Newspaper*. London: Methuen, 1952.

Rowntree, B. Seebohm. *Poverty. A Study of Town Life*. London: Macmillan, 1902.

[Russell, G. W. E.] *A Londoner's Log-Book 1901–1902*. London: Smith, Elder, 1902.

Sadler, M. E. [ed.] *Continuation Schools in England and Elsewhere*. Manchester: Victoria University Publications, 1907.

Salmond, J. B. *The Muster Role of Angus 1899–1900*. Arbroath: Brodie & Salmond, 1900.

Samuel, Herbert. *Liberalism: Its Principles and Proposals*. London: Grant Richards, 1902.

Sellars, I. 'The Pro-Boer Movement in Liverpool', *Transactions of the Unitarian Historical Society*, October 1960.

Seton-Karr, B. *The Call to Arms*. London: Spon, 1902.

Sinclair, D. *History of the Aberdeen Volunteers*. Aberdeen: Journal Office, 1907.

Solly, Reverend Henry. *James Woodford. Carpenter and Chartist*, 2 vols. London: Simpkin & Marshall, 1887.

— *Party Politics and Political Education*. London: Workmen's Social Education League, 1879.

— *Trades Guilds of Learning*. London: William Kent, 1873.

— *Working Men: A Glance at some of their Wants*. London: Working Men's Club and Institute Union, 1863.

— *Working Men's Social Clubs and Educational Institutes*. London: Working Men's Club and Institute Union, 1867.

Stansky, Peter. *Ambitions and Strategies*. London: Oxford University Press, 1964.

Stead, W. T. *The Last Will and Testament of Cecil Rhodes*. London: Review of Reviews Office, 1902.

Stevens, Robert. *The National Liberal Club*. London: R. Holden, 1925.

Symons, Julian. *Buller's Campaign*. London: Cresset Press, 1963.

Tate, G. K. *The London Trades Council*. London: Lawrence & Wishart, 1950.

— *London's Struggle for Socialism 1848–1948*. London: Thames Publications, 1948.

Thompson, Paul. 'Liberals, Radicals, and Labour in London 1880–1900,' *Past and Present*, No. 27 (1964).

— *Socialists, Liberals, and Labour*. London: Routledge & Kegan Paul, 1967.

Tremlett, George. *The First Century*. London: Working Men's Club and Institute Union, 1962.

Tressell, R. *The Ragged Trousered Philanthropists*. London: Lawrence & Wishart, 1951.

Tsiang, T. F. *Labor and Empire*. New York: Columbia University Press, 1923.

Turton, R. B. *The North Yorks Militia*. Leeds: J. Whitehead & Sons, 1907.

Vincent, John. *The Formation of the Liberal Party 1858–1867*. London: Constable, 1966.

Watson, Robert Spence. *The National Liberal Federation*. London: T. Fisher Unwin, 1907.

Webb, Sydney and Beatrice. *The History of Trade Unionism*, 2nd ed. London: Longmans Green, 1950.

Wilde, E. T. *Tower Hamlets Rifle Volunteer Brigade*, 2nd ed. London: Coningham Bros., 1903.

Wood, A. C. 'Nottingham's Parliamentary Elections 1869–1900', *Transactions of the Thoroton Society* (1956).

Working Men's Club and Institute Union. *A History*. London: Working Men's Club and Institute Union, 1902.

— *Occasional Papers*. London: Working Men's Club and Institute Union, 1863–7.

Wright, T. *Our New Masters*. London: Strahan, 1873.

Wyatt, H. F. 'The Ethics of Empire', *Nineteenth Century*, Vol. CCXLII (April 1897), pp. 516–30.

Index